Multi-Platform Graphics Programming with Kivy

Basic Analytical Programming for 2D, 3D, and Stereoscopic Design

Moisés Cywiak
David Cywiak

Multi-Platform Graphics Programming with Kivy: Basic Analytical Programming for 2D, 3D, and Stereoscopic Design

Moisés Cywiak
Leon, Guanajuato, Mexico

David Cywiak
Queretaro, Mexico

ISBN-13 (pbk): 978-1-4842-7112-4
https://doi.org/10.1007/978-1-4842-7113-1

ISBN-13 (electronic): 978-1-4842-7113-1

Managing Director, Apress Media LLC: Welmoed Spahr
Acquisitions Editor: Susan McDermott
Development Editor: James Markham
Coordinating Editor: Jessica Vakili

Distributed to the book trade worldwide by Springer Science+Business Media New York, 1 NY Plaza, New York, NY 10004. Phone 1-800-SPRINGER, fax (201) 348-4505, e-mail orders-ny@ springer-sbm.com, or visit www.springeronline.com. Apress Media, LLC is a California LLC and the sole member (owner) is Springer Science + Business Media Finance Inc (SSBM Finance Inc). SSBM Finance Inc is a **Delaware** corporation.

For information on translations, please e-mail booktranslations@springernature.com; for reprint, paperback, or audio rights, please e-mail bookpermissions@springernature.com.

Apress titles may be purchased in bulk for academic, corporate, or promotional use. eBook versions and licenses are also available for most titles. For more information, reference our Print and eBook Bulk Sales web page at http://www.apress.com/bulk-sales.

Any source code or other supplementary material referenced by the author in this book is available to readers on GitHub via the book's product page, located at www.apress.com/978-1-4842-7112-4. For more detailed information, please visit http://www.apress.com/source-code.

Printed on acid-free paper

Table of Contents

About the Authors

Moisés Cywiak is a researcher in physical optical sciences. He has over 20 years of teaching experience in physics, mathematics, electronic engineering, and programming in C, C++, and Python at the Centro de Investigaciones en Óptica A.C.

David Cywiak received his PhD in Physics in 2014 from the Universidad de Guanajuato. From 2012 to 2013, he collaborated as a guest researcher at the Dalton Cardiovascular Research Center, University of Missouri-Columbia, in the development of an optical-photoacoustic system intended for the detection of photoacoustic signals generated by cancerous cells. Since 2014, he has been working as a metrologist in the Thermometry Department at the Centro Nacional de Metrologia, México. His research includes photoacoustics, optical engineering, and radiation thermometry. He has over seven years of experience teaching physics, mathematics, and programming in C to undergraduate students. He also has over five years of experience teaching temperature measurement techniques and calibration of instruments in the thermometry area to industry professionals.

About the Technical Reviewer

Ahmed Gad is a machine learning engineer pursuing his Phd in computer engineering at the University of Ottawa. He works with companies like Paperspace and NeptuneAI on machine learning projects and their documentation. Ahmed created PyGAD, a Python open-source library for building the genetic algorithm and has a history of four books in the field.

Acknowledgments

We would like to thank Natalie Pao, Jessica Vakili, Ahmed Gad, and James Markhan for providing valuable comments and suggestions during the review of this book.

CHAPTER 1

Getting Started: Software installation

The code presented in this book can be executed on any platform running Python. However, to translate the programs into applications that can be installed and executed on Android, the developing operating system must be Ubuntu. We briefly describe the preliminary steps to run Python along with the required applications in Ubuntu. In this case, we are using Ubuntu 20.04.1 LTS.

Although Python3 is already installed in Ubuntu, we need to install pip3 and IDLE. We cover how to use pip3 later, which is necessary to install the additional packages and libraries that the programs will require. IDLE is the shell that allows you to write and execute the code.

1.1 Installing pip3 and IDLE

To install pip3, open a Terminal window by using Ctrl+Alt+T. It will be convenient to add the Terminal to the favorites bar. From this point on, your computer will require Internet access.

© Moisés Cywiak, David Cywiak 2021
M. Cywiak and D. Cywiak, *Multi-Platform Graphics Programming with Kivy*,
https://doi.org/10.1007/978-1-4842-7113-1_1

To install pip3 and IDLE, you have to type the following three commands, in the order indicated.

1. `sudo apt update`. At this step, you need an administrator password.

2. `sudo apt install python3-pip`. This command installs pip3.

3. `sudo apt install idle3`. This command installs Python-Shell.

pip3 and IDLE 3 should now be installed on your computer. To verify that IDLE 3 has been installed properly, click Ubuntu's Show Applications icon and look for the IDLE icon. Now is also a good time to right-click the icon and select the Add to Favorites option.

To check for the pip3 installation, you can type `pip3 list` in the Terminal window. In response, you will obtain a list of packages installed for the Python3 environment.

For the programs in this book, you need mathematical and graphical capabilities. For this, we will use two powerful Python libraries: *NumPy* and *Kivy*.

To install NumPy, type `pip3 install numpy` in the Terminal window. After the installation completes, you can verify that NumPy has been added to the installed packages by typing `pip3 list`.

The installation of Kivy is described in the following subsection.

1.2 Installing Kivy

In our experience, it is advisable to install Kivy by carefully executing the step-by-step commands listed in Listing 1-1.

Listing 1-1. Step-by-Step Commands for Installing Kivy

```
1.   sudo apt update
2.   sudo apt install libsdl2-dev
3.   sudo apt install libsdl2-ttf-dev
4.   sudo apt install libsdl2-image-dev
5.   sudo apt install libsdl2-mixer-dev
6.   sudo apt install python3-kivy
```

You can verify that Kivy has been installed by typing pip3 list. In our case, we obtained Kivy version 1.10.1. As you will see, it is important to make a note of the version number.

1.3 Installing Buildozer

At this point, we have the entire engine is ready to carry out programming in Ubuntu. However, since you are interested in translating the programs into Android APKs, you need an additional tool, called Buildozer.

We suggest following the installation according to the step-by-step commands presented in Listing 1-2. By following this recipe, you can successfully install Buildozer.

Listing 1-2. Commands for Installing Buildozer

```
1.   sudo apt update
2.   sudo apt install lld
3.   sudo apt install libtool
4.   sudo apt install pkg-config
5.   sudo apt install zlib1g-dev
6.   sudo apt install libncurses5-dev
7.   sudo apt install libncursesw5-dev
8.   sudo apt install libtinfo5
9.   sudo apt install cmake
```

```
10.   sudo apt install libffi-dev
11.   sudo apt install git
12.   sudo apt install libssl-dev
13.   pip3 install autoconfig
14.   pip3 install cython==0.28.2 (see table 1-1)
15.   sudo pip3 install buildozer
```

You'll notice in Step 14 that we installed a specific version of Cython. The version number of Cython depends on the version number of Kivy installed on your computer. Required versions are listed in Table 1-1. This table is available at `https://kivy.org/doc/stable-1.10.1/installation/deps-cython.html`.

Table 1-1. *Required Cython Version for Installed Kivy Version*

Installed Kivy Version	Required Cython Version
1.9.0	0.21.2
1.9.1	0.23.1
1.10.0	0.25.2
1.10.1	0.28.2
1.11.0	0.29.9
1.11.1	0.29.9
2.0.0	0.29.10

Finally, Buildozer requires Java to be installed on your computer. To install a compatible Java version, the following command is required:

```
sudo apt install openjdk-8-jdk
```

Once it's installed, you can verify the installed version of Java by typing `javac -version`. In this case, we obtained Javac 1.8.0_265. This is the required version for Buildozer 1.2.0. To obtain the installed Buildozer version, type `pip3 list`.

Now that you have installed all the requirements needed for developing the programs, you are ready to start programming. In the following chapter, you begin with analytical equations for rotating two-dimensional polygons.

1.4 Summary

In this chapter, we covered the installation of the software requirements to start programming. We provided step-by-step listings to install pip3, IDLE, Kivy, and Buildozer, as well as the corresponding Java and Cython versions.

CHAPTER 2

Two-Dimensional Mapping and Rotation Equations of a Point

In this chapter, we cover basic equations for rotating two-dimensional points and mapping them on the computer's screen.

2.1 Rotation Equations

In this section, you learn the basic transformation equations to rotate points on a two-dimensional plane. You'll begin by finding the equations that relate the coordinates of a point in a two-dimensional static coordinate system to a rotated one. The static coordinate system (x, y) has two-unit direction vectors, i and j. Analogously, in the rotated system with coordinates (x', y') the direction vectors are i' and j'. The angle of rotation between both coordinate systems is θ, as depicted in Figure 2-1.

© Moisés Cywiak, David Cywiak 2021
M. Cywiak and D. Cywiak, *Multi-Platform Graphics Programming with Kivy*,
https://doi.org/10.1007/978-1-4842-7113-1_2

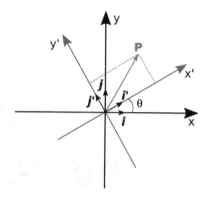

Figure 2-1. *Two-dimensional static coordinate system and a rotated one to calculate coordinates of a point given by a constant position vector P*

As shown in Figure 2-1, the direction vectors in the rotated system can be expressed in terms of the unit vectors of the static system and of the angle of rotation as:

$$i' = cos(\theta)i + sin(\theta)j \qquad (2.1)$$

$$j' = -sin(\theta)i + cos(\theta)j \qquad (2.2)$$

We now express the constant vector P in both systems as:

$$P = xi + yj = x'i' + y'j' \qquad (2.3)$$

Substituting Equations (2.1) and (2.2) in Equation (2.3) gives:

$$P = xi + yj = x'\left[cos(\theta)i + sin(\theta)j\right] + y'\left[-sin(\theta)i + cos(\theta)j\right] \qquad (2.4)$$

Equating vector components in Equation (2.4) gives:

$$x = x'cos(\theta) - y'sin(\theta) \qquad (2.5)$$

$$y = x'sin(\theta) + y'cos(\theta) \qquad (2.6)$$

For programming purposes, the static coordinate system (x, y) corresponds to the screen and the coordinate system (x', y') corresponds to a reference system that rotates around the origin. Thus, from Equations (2.5) and (2.6), we express the (x', y') coordinates as:

$$x' = x cos(\theta) + y sin(\theta) \tag{2.7}$$

$$y' = -x sin(\theta) + y cos(\theta) \tag{2.8}$$

Equations (2.7) and (2.8) are used in our programs to rotate the polygons.

2.2 Mapping Spatial Two-Dimensional Points to the Screen

To correctly map points from a two-dimensional Cartesian coordinate plane to the computer's screen, it is necessary to consider inherent differences between them. On the Cartesian, two-dimensional plane, a pair of real numbers *(x, y)* determines the position of a determined point. In contrast, in a computer display, pixels are arranged in a two-dimensional grid in which a pair of integer numbers, which we will denote as *(n, m)*, determines the position of a pixel. The integer *n* corresponds to the column index of the pixel and *m* to its row index. Thus, mapping points from a two-dimensional coordinate system to the computer's screen requires mapping pairs of floating numbers *(x, y)* to pairs of integer numbers *(n, m)*. Strictly speaking, the function in charge of this task is not bijective.

To obtain analytical relations between the Cartesian coordinate plane and the screen, we first assume that the coordinates of the points on the screen are real numbers rather than integers. This assumption will not alter the results because, in the end, we will take the integer part of the calculated values.

For our calculations, let's draw two coordinate planes, one below the other, as depicted in Figure 2-2. The upper drawing is a region of a Cartesian coordinate plane around the origin. The lower one consists of a rectangle region on the Cartesian plane resembling the computer's screen with its center shifted from (0, 0). We want to obtain analytical expressions to map points, from the upper coordinate plane to the ones on the screen on the lower Cartesian plane. The procedure is as follows.

Let's consider a point on the upper Cartesian (x, y) plane, pointed by vector P and a point with coordinates (x_p, y_p) pointed by vector Q on the screen, on the lower plane, as shown in Figure 2-2.

We want to find an analytical correspondence between the coordinates of both points. We will impose the vector Q on the computer's screen to be a scaled version of P. We have to fulfill this requirement with each vertex of the polygons, built in the Cartesian plane, to display a scaled version of them on the screen.

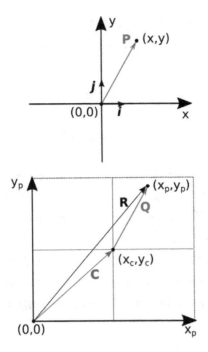

Figure 2-2. *Mapping a point with coordinates (x, y) to a point (x_p, y_p) on the computer's screen. Vector C points toward the center of the screen*

Based on this description, we will write $Q = ScaleP$. Here, the scale factor is represented by the parameter *Scale*.

From Figure 2-2, we can see that $R = C + Q$; $R = X_p i + Y_p j$, and $C = X_C i + Y_C j$. The coordinates (X_c, Y_C) represent the center of the screen. It then results that:

$$X_p i + Y_p j = \left(X_C + Scalex\right)i + \left(Y_C + Scaley\right)j \qquad (2.9)$$

From Equation (2.9), dividing the vector equation into its components gives the pair of required mapping equations, which can be written in a more general form as:

$$X_P = X_C + (Scale\_X)x + X_0 \qquad (2.10)$$

$$Y_P = Y_C + (Scale\_Y)y + Y_0 \qquad (2.11)$$

In Equations (2.10) and (2.11), we have increased the scaling options by introducing two independent scaling terms in the x and y directions, $Scale\_X$ and $Scale\_Y$. Since we need to shift the points to other regions of the screen, we have introduced additional shifting parameters, (X_0, Y_0).

Equations (2.7)-(2.8) and (2.10)-(2.11) can be used for constructing and rotating polygons in a two-dimensional space and displaying them on the computer's screen. In the following chapter, we illustrate the use of these equations.

2.3 Summary

In this chapter, we obtained analytical equations for rotating points in a two-dimensional Cartesian plane. Additionally, we derived analytical equations for mapping them on the computer's screen. These equations are used in the following chapter to construct two-dimensional polygons in a two-dimensional coordinate system to be displayed and rotated on the computer's screen.

## CHAPTER 3

Two-Dimensional Polygon Programming

In this chapter, we introduce programming elements for placing and rotating polygons on the screen. The concepts presented are based on the analytical equations derived in Chapter 2.

Although there is no limit to the number of vertices and edges that the polygons can take, for simplicity for this working example, we selected three simple shapes—a square, a triangle, and a skewed-arrow—placed at different positions on the screen. Figure 3-1 shows a screenshot of the program running on an Android cell phone with a screen resolution of 480x680. The polygons are closed figures.

© Moisés Cywiak, David Cywiak 2021
M. Cywiak and D. Cywiak, *Multi-Platform Graphics Programming with Kivy*,
https://doi.org/10.1007/978-1-4842-7113-1_3

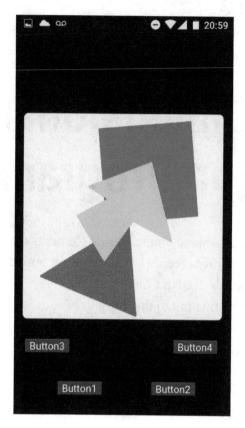

Figure 3-1. *Screenshot of the program running on an Android cell phone*

The functionality of the buttons is as follows: by holding Button3 or Button4 pressed, the polygons keep rotating counterclockwise or clockwise, respectively, until the button is released. For illustrative purposes, we included Button1. This button draws the edges, but it does not fill the polygons. Button2 is used to clear the scene.

Each polygon has a dedicated structure containing data of its properties, such as the coordinates of the vertices, among others, to allow you to keep track of each polygon as the program evolves. This is described in the following sections.

3.1 Polygon Structure

The structures for the three polygons used in the example are shown in Listings 3-1 through 3-3.

Listing 3-1. Rectangle Structure

```
Rectangle=[
    5,          #Number of vertices +1
    [1, 1],     #Vertex 1
    [1, -1],    #Vertex 2
    [-1,-1],    #Vertex 3
    [-1, 1],    #Vertex 4
    [1,1],      #Vertex 1 repeated to allow closing #the polygon
    [60,120],   # Position of the polygon and  center #of
                rotation measured in screen units
    [1,0,0]     #Red, green, blue color. Entries must #be
                between 0 and 1
    ]
```

Listing 3-2. Triangle Structure

```
Triangle=[
    4,          ##Number of vertices +1
    [1, -1],    #Vertex 1
    [-1, -1],   #Vertex 2
    [0, 1],     #Vertex 3
    [1, -1],    #Vertex 1 repeated
    [-80,-90],  #Position and center of rotation
    [1,0,1]     #Color (r,g,b)
    ]
```

Listing 3-3. TwistedArrow Structure

```
TwistedArrow=[
    8,                 #Number of vertices +1
    [0.6, 0.7],  #Vertex 1
    [1.0, -0.7], #Vertex 2
    [-0.7,-1.0], #Vertex 3
    [-0.2,-0.2], #Vertex 4
    [-1.0, 0.5], #Vertex 5
    [0.0, 1.0],  #Vertex 6
    [0.3, 0.3],  #Vertex 7
    [0.6, 0.7],  #Vertex 1 repeated
    [0,0],         #Position and center of rotation
    [0,1,0.6]    #Color (r,g,b)
    ]
```

In Listings 3-1 through 3-3, comments are preceded by the # symbol and last until the end of the line.

As you can observe, the first entry in each structure corresponds to the number of vertices +1. As you will see later, to simplify the code that draws the polygon, it will be helpful to repeat the coordinates of the first vertex at the end of the list.

After the first entry of the structure, the list of the polygon vertices follows. The listing should be written in a clockwise or counterclockwise direction. In this example, we are listing the vertices in a clockwise direction.

The penultimate entry in the list corresponds to the coordinates of the center of rotation of the polygon. These coordinates also correspond to the position of the polygon on the screen and are measured in pixels.

The last entry in the list corresponds to the color of the polygon expressed in the format RGB (red, green, blue). These values must be between zero and one, corresponding to minimum and maximum intensities, respectively.

To exemplify how to access the elements of the structures, we now focus on the rectangle structure.

Rectangle[0] is the first entry of the table. It corresponds to the number of vertices, +1. For this example, the directive Num=Rectangle[0] assigns to the variable Num a value equal to 5.

Rectangle[1] gives the (x,y) coordinates of the first vertex. In this example, the directive x,y =Rectangle[1] will assign to (x,y) the value (1,1). The directive x,y=Rectangle[2] will assign to (x,y) the coordinates of the second vertex, in this case, (1,-1).

It is also possible to individually access the x or y-coordinate. For example, the directive x=Rectangle[2][0] will give the value x=1. The directive y=Rectangle[2][1] gives y=-1. Although accessing individual parameters requires more instructions, the results are the same.

To access the position of the polygon, or equivalently, its center of rotation, you must proceed as follows. First, with the directive Num=Rectangle[0], assign to the variable Num the number of vertices, +1. Now use the directive X0,Y0=Rectangle[Num+1]. This directive will assign to (X0,Y0) the position of the polygon. You can separately obtain the individual values with the X0=Rectangle[Num+1][0] and Y0=Rectangle[Num+1][1] directives.

Finally, the r,g,b=Rectangle[Num+2] directive assigns the RGB color of the polygon stored in the structure, in the variables r,g,b, respectively. You can use the r=Rectangle[Num+2][0], g=Rectangle[Num+2][1], and b=Rectangle[Num+2][2] directives as well. These methods are equivalent and will be used indistinctly in the code.

At this point, we want to mention that semicolons used as ending statements are optional in Python. Furthermore, in Python, semicolons are used to separate directives in a single row. In our code, we end each statement with a semicolon, except for import statements. This usage may be appealing to C programmers.

3.2 Drawing the Edges of the Polygon

Now that we have established the methodology to get access to the elements stored in the polygon structures, as the program evolves, we need to create functions with the capacity of accessing them on demand. To access one of the polygon structures, we use one of the following directives: P=Rectangle, P=Triangle, or P=TwistedArrow. As a result, the variable P will point to a requested polygon, giving us access to the parameters defined in its structure.

To draw the polygon's sides, we need to note the number of vertices. We also need the coordinates of its center. We read these values in the next two steps, as follows:

1. The value that holds the number of vertices +1 is assigned to the variable Num, by using the directive Num=P[0].

2. The coordinates that correspond to the center of the polygon are assigned to X0 and Y0 using the directive X0,Y0=P[1] or equivalently, by using X0=P[1][0]; Y0=P[1][1].

Finally, to draw the edges, we use a for loop using a variable n ranging from the first vertex to the last vertex. See the pseudocode in Listing 3-4.

Listing 3-4. Pseudocode for Drawing the Edges of a Polygon Pointed by P

```
for n in range(1,Num):
    x1=XC+ScaleX*P[n][0]+X0; y1=YC+ScaleY*P[n][1]+Y0;
    x2=XC+ScaleX*P[n+1][0]+X0; y2=YC+ScaleY*P[n+1][1]+Y0;
```

```
r=P[Num+2][0]; g=P[Num+2][1]; b=P[Num+2][2];
Draw a line from (x1,y1) to (x2,y2) using color(r,g,b).
```

The precise code for drawing lines on-screen is described in Section 3.5.

In the algorithm of Listing 3-4, the variables XC *and* YC correspond to the center of the screen measured in pixels units.

The variable n in the for loop initiates with a value equal to 1 and finishes with the value Num-1, increasing in steps of one unit.

In Python, indentation serves to enclose statements that belong to functions, for loops, conditionals, if, else, and others. You can compare indentation with the pair of braces used in the C language. Therefore, care has to be taken accordingly.

3.3 Filling the Polygon with Lines

Once the edges of the polygon have been drawn, we will fill the polygon with horizontal lines beginning with the polygon minimum y-coordinate up to its maximum. We refer to these values as YMin *and* YMax, respectively. Each horizontal line is referred to as a raster scan line or simply a scan line.

The filling process consists of drawing lines within the polygon. You have to calculate the x-coordinates that correspond to all the intersections between each scan line and the polygon edges. These intersections are stored in an array and sorted in ascending x-order. In this manner, we proceed to draw the corresponding horizontal segments between pairs of intersecting points.

To determine if a scan line intersects a polygon edge limited between vertices (x1, y1) and (x2, y2), we must first order the vertices such that y1<y2, swapping them if necessary. Then, an intersection will take place if the scanning line lies between y1 and y2. The intersection x-value is calculated as follows.

First, we write the equation of the straight line that passes through the vertices as:

$$y = mx + b \qquad (3.1)$$

In Equation (3.1), m and b represent the slope and the y-intercept of the straight line, respectively. In Equation (3.1), using vertices (x_1, y_1) and (x_2, y_2) gives:

$$m = \frac{(y_2 - y_1)}{(x_2 - x_1)} \qquad (3.2)$$

and

$$b = y_1 - mx_1 \qquad (3.3)$$

Using Equations (3.1) and (3.3) gives:

$$x = \frac{y - y_1}{m} + x_1 \qquad (3.4)$$

In Equation (3.4), the y value corresponds to the scan line, then the x-value will correspond to the intersection of the edge with the scan line, provided that $y_1 < y < y_2$. By defining, $M = \dfrac{1}{m}$, we can rewrite Equation (3.4) as:

$$x = M(y - y_1) + x_1 \qquad (3.5)$$

Equation (3.5) will be used to calculate the intersection of the edges with the scan line.

The function in charge of filling the polygons is FillPolygon(P, B). The parameter P, as described, gives access to a specific polygon. The parameter B is a handle that permits accessing the screen, as described in Section 3.5.

At this point, we need NumPy. To get access to this library, use the following directive:

```
import numpy as np
```

From now on, NumPy is called *np* and you can access its functions by means of the *dot operator*. For example, you can use the directive `Pi= np.pi`. With NumPy, you can use the operations on arrays and mathematical functions.

In this program, we create an array named `Intersect` to store up to 30 intersection points. For the working example, we do not expect to store more than 30 intersection points. For more elaborate polygons, this number can be increased. The allocated memory region is obtained by means of this directive:

```
Intersect=np.zeros(30).
```

We will use a parameter named `Counter`. *This* parameter will store the count of intersections that may occur between a determined polygon and a scan line. Because the polygon represents a closed figure, these intersections should occur in pairs. Therefore, filling the polygon requires drawing horizontal line segments between pairs of consecutive points.

The filling algorithm, for each scan line, begins by initializing `Counter` *to* zero. Each time an intersection occurs, we store the corresponding x-coordinate in `Intersect`, and we increment `Counter` in one. At the end, for each scan line, if the condition `Counter>1` holds, the intersections have occurred and we proceed to draw the corresponding line segments.

Finally, to simplify filling the polygon, a new array called `Intersect1` receives and sorts all the intersection values collected in `Intersect` in ascending order. It does so by utilizing this directive:

```
Intersect1=np.sort(Intersect[0:Counter])
```

This directive creates the array called Intersect1. Its size corresponds to the number of intersections between the scan line and the polygon. The array stores the x-coordinates of the intersecting points in ascending order. This way, we can draw the corresponding segments between pairs of intersecting points by utilizing a for loop. It is worth mentioning that Intersect is maintained unaltered.

The pseudocode for filling the polygon pointed by the parameter P is shown in Listing 3-5.

Listing 3-5. Function for Filling, Line by Line, the Polygon Pointed by P

```
Intrsect=np.zeros(30); #Array to store up to 30
    #intersection points
def FillPolygon(P, B):
    Num=P[0]; XO=P[Num+1][0]; YO=P[Num+1][1]; #Reading number
    of vertices and polygon center
    r,g,b=P[Num+2]; #Reading filling color
    #Calculating polygon YMin, Ymax
    YMin=P[1][1]; YMax=P[1][1]
    for n in range(1,Num):
        if YMin>P[n][1]:
            YMin=P[n][1];
        if YMax<P[n][1]:
            YMax=P[n][1];
    #We have now (YMin, YMax)
    #We now proceed filling lines between Ymin and #Ymax
    for y in np.arange (YMin, YMax, 0.03): # numpy #allows to
    increment the for loop in decimal steps
        Counter=0;
        for n in range(1, Num): #We will search #intersections
        edge by edge
```

```
#We first order the two vertices of each #edge such
that Y1<Y2
if ( P[n][1] <P[n+1][1] ):
    Y1=P[n][1];   X1=P[n][0];
    Y2=P[n+1][1]; X2=P[n+1][0];
else:
    Y1=P[n+1][1]; X1=P[n+1][0];
    Y2=P[n][1];   X2=P[n][0];
if (Y1<y and y<Y2):
    if (Y2-Y1)!=0:
        M=(X2-X1)/(Y2-Y1);
    else:
        M=1.0e8;  # if Y1=Y2, the edge #slope is
        infinite. We assign to it a large value
    Intersect[Counter]=(y-Y1)*M+X1; #We #store the
    x value
    Counter=Counter+1; # And we #increment Counter
    as a new value has being stored
if(Counter>1):
    Intersect1=np.sort(Intersect[0:Counter]);#Interse
    ct1 #contains ordered pair of x values
    for n in range(0,Counter,2): # We now #trace lines
    between pairs of intersections
        XIntersect1=XC+ScaleX*Intersect1[n] +  XO
        XIntersect2=XC+ScaleX*Intersect1[n+1] + XO
        Y=YC+ScaleY*y+YO;
        Draw_Line(XIntersect1,Y, XIntersect2,Y) using
        r,g,b colors.
```

The code for drawing the straight segment from (Xintersect1,Y) to (Xintersect2,Y) using colors r,g,b is explained in Section 3.5.

3.4 Rotating the Polygon

The function in charge of rotating the polygons is Rotate(P, Sense). The P parameter receives the structure of the polygon to be rotated. If the Sense parameter is equal to 1, the polygon is rotated clockwise. If it is equal to -1, it is rotated counterclockwise. It is worth mentioning that Rotate(P, Sense) only interacts with the vertices listed in the polygon structure and does not draw on the screen. The vertices of the polygon structure are rotated in steps of five degrees. We will use NumPy to access trigonometric functions.

The algorithm is shown in Listing 3-6.

Listing 3-6. Algorithm for Rotating a Polygon Pointed by Parameter P

```
def Rotate(P, Sense):
    if Sense==-1:
        Teta=np.pi/180*(-5);
    else:
        Teta=np.pi/180*(5);
    Cos_Teta=np.cos(Teta)
    Sin_Teta=np.sin(Teta);
    Num=P[0];
    for n in range(1,Num+1):
        XP=P[n][0]*Cos_Teta  +  P[n][1]*Sin_Teta;
        YP=-P[n][0]*Sin_Teta +  P[n][1]*Cos_Teta;
        P[n][0]=XP
        P[n][1]=YP
```

Once a polygon structure has been rotated, to show the polygon in its new state, the old scene is cleared and the new structure is drawn and filled on the screen. Performing this action gives the visual impression of rotating the polygons in real time. The following section describes the basic elements of the Kivy platform needed to draw the polygons on the screen.

3.5 Using the Kivy Platform

Kivy gives you the option of writing your program in two separate files. One of the files, which has a py extension, is where you write most of the program code, whereas in the second file, with a kv extension, is where you declare visual components and controls, also referred to as *widgets*. As described in the following chapter, we will use Buildozer to construct the Android application, which requires naming the py file main.py. Therefore, we will keep this name from now on.

There is no restriction on the name that the kv file can take; we will name it File.kv. Optionally, it is possible to designate this file equal to the main class in the py file. In this case, the kv file will be loaded automatically.

Our graphics container will be named Form1, and it will correspond to a Kivy FloatLayout type. From a programming point of view, this container is a class in Kivy, as can be seen in the main.py file shown Listing 3-7.

We now analyze the File.kv file, shown in Listing 3-8. Note that Form1 heads the listing and has an ID, assigned by means of the id: Form1 directive.

Our graphics container Form1 is a FloatLayout type and it contains, in turn, a StencilView type region where we will draw the polygons. A StencilView type is convenient here, as nothing will be drawn outside its region. We will name Screen1 our StencilView region by using the directive id: Screen1. Note that in the File.kv listing, similar directives are used for the buttons and the functions that will be in charge of responding to the corresponding events.

In main.py, we need to import two additional libraries, the os and Builder libraries. As we are planning to export this program to Android, we need to provide the absolute location of File.kv. Otherwise, the program will work properly in Ubuntu but it will crash on Android devices.

In the main.py file, we declare two functions that respond to the computer clock ticks. One of them is as follows:

Clock.schedule_once(Handle,Initialize)

The second one is as follows:

Clock.schedule_interval(Handle.Temporal,0.03)

The first function is executed only once, when the program starts. We take advantage of this characteristic to initialize some variables. The second function executes at every tick of the computer's clock. This way, at each tick, the program verifies if Button3 or Button4 are pressed by checking the global variable Flag. If this variable is true, the scene is cleared and the polygons are rotated and drawn in their new positions on Screen1. The process is repeated until the button is released.

Finally, each event button provides us with a handle for accessing the Kivy components (widgets). The handles correspond to the B variable in the functions. To access Screen1, we use the following:

B.ids.Screen1

Now we describe the directives required for drawing a line from (x1, y1) to (x2, y2) on Screen1. First, we have to select a line color, and then we draw the line. The corresponding directives are:

B.ids.Screen1.canvas.add(Color(r,g,b)).
B.ids.Screen1.canvas.add(Line(points=(int(x1),int(y1),int(x2), int(y2)), width=2)).

Note that the int(variable) directive takes the integer part of a variable. In the previous code, we chose a line width equal to 2.

The complete code for main.py and File.kv is shown in Listings 3-7 and 3-8, respectively.

Listing 3-7. main.py Listing

```
#Import required libraries
from kivy.app import App
from kivy.uix.floatlayout import FloatLayout
from kivy.graphics import Line, Color
from kivy.clock import Clock
import os
import numpy as np

from kivy.lang import Builder #Android requires the absolute path
Builder.load_file(
    os.path.join(os.path.dirname(os.path.abspath(__file__)),
    'File.kv')
    )

from kivy.config import Config
Config.set("graphics","resizable", False)  # Avoid #Form1 of
being re-sizable
#Our cell-#phone is 480 by 680 pixels
Config.set('graphics', 'width',  '480');
Config.set('graphics', 'height', '680');
#XC,YC,W and H will be set by the function #Initialize()
#after Clock.schedule_once has been executed.
XC=0; YC=0; W=0; H=0;
Flag=False; #If False not drawing allow
#=======Polygon structures   =============
#The first entry corresponds to the number of #vertexes+1.
#Following pair of entries correspond to the list of #vertices
ordered in clockwise direction.
#The first vertex is repeated at end of the list of #vertices.
```

#Following pair of entries correspond to the center #of rotation in pixels or screen coordinates.
#The triplet at the end of the structure corresponds #to the polygon color: red, green, blue.

```
Rectangle=[
    5,           #Four vertices +1
    [1, 1],      #Vertex 1
    [1, -1],     #Vertex 2
    [-1,-1],     #Vertex 3
    [-1, 1],     #Vertex 4
    [1,1],       #Vertex 1 repeated to allow drawing #the last
                 edge of the polygon
    [60,120],    #Center of rotation
    [1,0,0]      #Red, green, blue color. Entries must #be
                 between 0 and 1
    ]

Triangle=[
    4,           # Three vertices+1
    [1, -1],     #Vertex 1
    [-1, -1],    #Vertex 2
    [0, 1],      #Vertex 3
    [1, -1],     #Vertex 1 repeated
    [-80,-90],   #Center of rotation
    [1,0,1]      #Color (r,g,b)
    ]

TwistedArrow=[
    8,           #Seven vertices +1
    [0.6, 0.7],  #Vertex 1
    [1.0, -0.7], #Vertex 2
    [-0.7,-1.0], #Vertex 3
```

```
        [-0.2,-0.2], #Vertex 4
        [-1.0, 0.5], #Vertex 5
        [0.0, 1.0],  #Vertex 6
        [0.3, 0.3],  #Vertex 7
        [0.6, 0.7],  #Vertex 1 repeated
        [0,0],       #Center of rotation
        [0,1,0.6]    #Color (r,g,b)
         ]
#Here, we choose some scaling terms
ScaleX=110; ScaleY=110;

def DrawEdges(P, B):
    Num=P[0]; X0=P[Num+1][0]; Y0=P[Num+1][1];
    for n in range(1,Num):
        x1=XC+ScaleX*P[n][0]+X0;    y1=YC+ScaleY*P[n][1]+Y0;
        x2=XC+ScaleX*P[n+1][0]+X0;  y2=YC+ScaleY*P[n+1][1]+Y0;
        r=P[Num+2][0]; g=P[Num+2][1]; b=P[Num+2][2];
        B.ids.Screen1.canvas.add( Color(r,g,b) );
        B.ids.Screen1.canvas.add( Line(points=(int(x1),int(y1),
        int(x2),int(y2)), width=2) );
def Rotate(P, Sense):
    if Sense==-1:
        Teta=np.pi/180*(-5);
    else:
        Teta=np.pi/180*(5);
    Cos_Teta=np.cos(Teta)
    Sin_Teta=np.sin(Teta);
    Num=P[0];
    for n in range(1,Num+1):
        XP=P[n][0]*Cos_Teta  +  P[n][1]*Sin_Teta;
        YP=-P[n][0]*Sin_Teta +  P[n][1]*Cos_Teta;
```

```python
    P[n][0]=XP
    P[n][1]=YP
#Function for filling the polygon line by line
Intersect=np.zeros(30); #Array to store up to 30 #intersection
points
def FillPolygon(P, B):
    Num=P[0]; X0=P[Num+1][0]; Y0=P[Num+1][1]; #Reading number
    of vertices and polygon center
    r,g,b=P[Num+2]; # reading polygon color
    #Calculating polygon YMin, Ymax for limiting #number of
    line scans
    YMin=P[1][1]; YMax=P[1][1]
    for n in range(1,Num):
        if YMin>P[n][1]:
            YMin=P[n][1];
        if YMax<P[n][1]:
            YMax=P[n][1];
    #We have now (YMin, YMax)
    #We now proceed filling lines between Ymin and #Ymax
    for y in np.arange (YMin, YMax, 0.03): # numpy #allows
    increasing y in steps of 0.03 in the for loop
        Counter=0;
        for n in range(1, Num): #We will search line #cuts
        segment by segment
            #We first order the two vertices of each #segment
            such that Y1<Y2
            if ( P[n][1] <P[n+1][1] ):
                Y1=P[n][1];    X1=P[n][0];
                Y2=P[n+1][1]; X2=P[n+1][0];
            else:
                Y1=P[n+1][1]; X1=P[n+1][0];
                Y2=P[n][1];    X2=P[n][0];
```

```
if (Y1<y and y<Y2):
    if (Y2-Y1)!=0:
        M=(X2-X1)/(Y2-Y1);
    else:
        # if Y1=Y2, the slope is infinite. We
        #assign to it a large value. This avoids an
        #additional if
        M=1.0e8; #
    Intersect[Counter]=(y-Y1)*M+X1; #We #store the
    x value
    Counter=Counter+1; # And we #increment Counter
    as a new value has being stored
if(Counter>1 and Counter <30): # Geometrical #closed
figure.
    Intersect1=np.sort(Intersect[0:Counter]);#Interse
    ct1 #holds ordered pair of x values
    for n in range(0,Counter,2): # We now #trace lines
    between pairs of intersections
        XIntersect1=XC+ScaleX*Intersect1[n] + X0
        XIntersect2=XC+ScaleX*Intersect1[n+1] + X0
        Y=YC+ScaleY*y+Y0;
        #Picking the color and drawing the #horizontal
        line between x pairs
        B.ids.Screen1.canvas.add(  Color(r,g,b) );
        B.ids.Screen1.canvas.add( Line(points=(int
        (XIntersect1),int(Y), int(XIntersect2),int(Y)),
        width=2) ) ;

class Form1(FloatLayout):
    def __init__(Handle, **kwargs):
        super(Form1, Handle).__init__(**kwargs);
        Event1=Clock.schedule_once(Handle.Initialize);
        Event2=Clock.schedule_interval(Handle.Temporal,0.03);
```

```
def Initialize(B, *args):
    global W,H, XC,YC;
    W,H=B.ids.Screen1.size;
    XI,YI=B.ids.Screen1.pos
    XC=XI+int (W/2);
    YC=YI+int(H/2);

def Temporal(B, *args):
    global Flag;
    if (Flag==True):
        if (B.ids.Button3.state=="down"):
            Sense=-1;
        if (B.ids.Button4.state=="down"):
            Sense=1;
        B.ids.Screen1.canvas.clear(); # Clear the #scene
        Rotate(Rectangle, Sense);
        DrawEdges(Rectangle,B);
        FillPolygon(Rectangle,B);

        Rotate(Triangle,Sense);
        DrawEdges(Triangle,B);
        FillPolygon(Triangle,B);

        Rotate(TwistedArrow,Sense);
        DrawEdges(TwistedArrow,B);
        FillPolygon(TwistedArrow,B);

def Button1_Click(B):
    DrawEdges(Rectangle, B);
    DrawEdges(Triangle, B);
    DrawEdges(TwistedArrow,B);

def Button2_Click(B):
    B.ids.Screen1.canvas.clear();
```

```python
    def Button3_Click(B):
        global Flag;
        Flag=True;

    def Button3_Release(B):
        global Flag;
        Flag=False;

    def Button4_Click(B):
        global Flag;
        Flag=True;

    def Button4_Release(B):
        global Flag;
        Flag=False;

# This is the Start Up code.
class StartUp (App):
    def build (BU):
        BU.title="Form1"
        return Form1();
if __name__ =="__main__":
    StartUp().run();
```

Listing 3-8. File.kv Listing

```
#:set W 440
#:set H 440
<Form1>:
    id : Form1
    StencilView:
        id: Screen1
        size_hint: None,None
        pos_hint: {"x":0.04, "y":0.25}
```

```
        size: W,H
        canvas.before:
            Color:
                rgba: 0.9, 0.9, 0, 1
            RoundedRectangle:
                pos:  self.pos
                size: self.size
    Button:
        id: Button1
        on_press: Form1.Button1_Click()
        text: "Button1"
        size_hint: None,None
        pos_hint: {"x": 0.2, "y":0.05}
        size: 100,30

    Button:
        id: Button2
        on_press: Form1.Button2_Click()
        text: "Button2"
        size_hint: None,None
        pos_hint: {"x": 0.63, "y":0.05}
        size: 100,30
    Button:
        id: Button3
        on_press: Form1.Button3_Click()
        on_release: Form1.Button3_Release()
        text: "Button3"
        size_hint: None,None
        pos_hint: {"x": 0.05, "y":0.16}
        size: 100,30
```

```
Button:
    id: Button4
    on_press: Form1.Button4_Click()
    on_release:  Form1.Button4_Release()
    text: "Button4"
    size_hint: None,None
    pos_hint: {"x": 0.73, "y":0.16}
    size: 100,30
```

3.6 Using Buildozer

Once the program runs properly on Ubuntu, and once you feel satisfied with the results, you can proceed to build your *APK,* which will be installed and run on an Android device. To accomplish this task, you need Buildozer.

For the conversion process from Ubuntu to Android, you need to create a folder on your computer to be used exclusively for this process. Place the main.py and File.kv files in this folder. Both files must be located in the same folder. Additionally, no other files with py or kv extensions should be in this folder.

Now open a Terminal window by pressing Ctrl+Alt+T and navigate to this folder using the cd command. It is advisable to verify that you are in the correct folder and that your two files are there by using the ls command, which will list the files in the current folder.

The first step of converting the application to Android consists of typing the following:

```
buildozer init
```

Buildozer will create a file with the name buildozer.spec in the folder. Open this file using a text editor or IDLE. This file contains some characteristics for building your APK, and you are expected to change some parameters. However, if you take into account that the minimum Android version supported by Buildozer is 6, our advice is to change the following lines only. The row that reads:

```
title = My Application
```

can be replaced with a different application name without any problem.

The row that reads:

```
requirements = python3,kivy
```

should be changed to the following:

```
requirements = python3,kivy,numpy,pillow
```

We added numpy and pillow because, in the following chapters, we will need these libraries for image processing.

The row that reads:

```
source.include_exts = py,png,jpg,kv,atlas
```

should read as follows:

```
source.include_exts = py,png,jpg,kv,atlas,ttf
```

This will allow you to add text of true-type fonts with extensions .ttf.

We have tested our programs on Android 6, 8, and 10, with no apparent problems.

You should now save the changes made in the buildozer.spec file.

To construct the APK, you need Internet access. To begin the conversion process, type the following:

```
buildozer -v android debug
```

Buildozer will start the conversion process and you will see a lot of reports displayed in the Terminal window. The conversion time depends on the characteristics of your computer. The processing time in a dual-core computer running at 3.2GHz took about 25 minutes. In addition, the first time you run Buildozer, it will download the required platforms as SDK and NDK. You'll be prompted to accept the corresponding agreements in order for the program to continue.

Once Buildozer finishes with the conversion process, provided no errors are encountered, you will find a new folder called bin in your working folder. Inside this folder, you will find your APK file. Copy this file to the Android device and install it. Alternatively, Buildozer can install the APK on your device by connecting it through USB to your computer. First, you need to enable the debug options on your Android device and type the following on the Terminal window of Ubuntu:

```
buildozer android deploy run logcat
```

With this command, Buildozer will install and run the program on the Android device. Detailed documentation about Buildozer is available at https://buildozer.readthedocs.io/en/latest/quickstart.html.

As a final note, it is worth mentioning that once the first *APK* has been built, you can make changes to the program code. The time required to build the new APK will then decrease drastically, as Buildozer will use all of the resources previously created. The processing time can be as little as one minute, provided that the libraries imported in the program are unaltered. Therefore, you should include all the required libraries the first time you use Buildozer.

3.7 Summary

In this chapter, we presented a screenshot of the program running on an Android cell phone in which we show the placement of the buttons. We described polygon structures containing the necessary data of their properties. We established the methodology to access the data stored in the polygon structures and the methodology to display, fill, and rotate them on the screen. We also described the Kivy platform and the corresponding graphics container in which we constructed the polygons. Finally, we introduced Buildozer and described the conversion process from Ubuntu to Android.

CHAPTER 4

Three-Dimensional Projections and Rotations

In this chapter, we present two basic concepts required for constructing and rotating three-dimensional polygons. The first concept refers to the analytical equations to project points from a three-dimensional space onto a two-dimensional screen. The second concept refers to the equations to calculate the rotation of points in a three-dimensional space.

4.1 Projecting a Three-Dimensional Point Onto a Plane

Figure 4-1 depicts two three-dimensional points, P and P', with coordinates (x, y, z) and (x', y', z'), respectively. Point P', the *projected point*, is obtained by projecting P on the computer's screen by drawing a straight line from a fixed point V with coordinates (V_X, V_Y, V_Z) up to P' and passing through P. Point V is referred to as the *point of projection*. Vectors P and P' correspond to the vectors that go from the origin with coordinates $(0, 0, 0)$ to (x, y, z) and to (x', y', z'), respectively.

© Moisés Cywiak, David Cywiak 2021
M. Cywiak and D. Cywiak, *Multi-Platform Graphics Programming with Kivy*,
https://doi.org/10.1007/978-1-4842-7113-1_4

The unit direction vectors of the three-dimensional space are given by $i, j,$ and k, as depicted in Figure 4-1. For simplicity, the screen is placed parallel to the $x - y$ plane and the normal distance between planes is D.

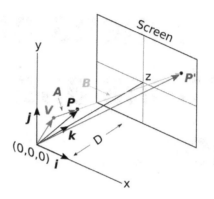

Figure 4-1. *Projection on a screen of a point P with coordinates (x, y, z) to a point P' with coordinates (x', y', z'). The point of projection has coordinates (V_X, V_Y, V_Z). Their corresponding vectors are P, P', and V, respectively*

Let A denote the vector from point V to P and let B denote the vector from point V to P'. As both vectors are parallel to each other, we can write:

$$B = tA \tag{4.1}$$

In Equation (4.1), t is a scalar.

It can be seen from Figure 4-1 that:

$$P = V + A \tag{4.2}$$

and:

$$P' = V + B \tag{4.3}$$

Using Equations (4.1)-(4.3) gives the following:

$$P' - V = t(P - V) \tag{4.4}$$

On the two-dimensional screen, as depicted in Figure 4-2, the bottom-left corner has coordinates $(0, 0)$, while its center has coordinates (X_C, Y_C). Vector Q corresponds to the vector that goes from $(0, 0)$ to (X_C, Y_C). Vector T goes from (X_C, Y_C) to P', while vector R goes from $(0, 0)$ to P'. As these three vectors are on the screen, each one of them is normal to k.

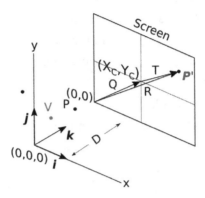

Figure 4-2. *Vectors Q, T, and R on the screen*

From Figure 4-2, we can write:

$$R = Q + T \tag{4.5}$$

Noticing in Figure 4-1 that the vector Dk goes from $(0, 0, 0)$ to the center of the screen, we can write:

$$P' = Dk + T \tag{4.6}$$

Using Equations (4.6) and (4.4) gives the following:

$$Dk + T = t(P - V) + V \tag{4.7}$$

Now, as vector T is normal to k, the dot product vanishes. Therefore, the dot product of Equation (4.7) with k gives the following:

$$Dk \cdot k = t(P - V) \cdot k + V \cdot k \tag{4.8}$$

Performing the dot products in Equation (4.8) allows us to obtain the following:

$$t = \frac{D - V_Z}{z - V_Z} \qquad (4.9)$$

To obtain Equation (4.9), we used $P = Dk$.

Note from Figure 4-1 that z in Equation (4.9) is the distance from the origin $(0, 0, 0)$ to point P, along the unitary k vector. For programming purposes, it is more convenient to measure this distance starting from the screen. This distance is denoted as Z_P. Therefore, $z = D - Z_P$. This value will be substituted in Equation (4.9).

Now, we use the value of t given by Equation (4.9) and the value of T obtained from Equation (4.5) to rewrite Equation (4.7) as follows:

$$R = Q + \frac{D - V_Z}{D - Z_P - V_Z}(P - V) + V - Dk \qquad (4.10)$$

In Equation (4.10), we substituted z with $D - Z_P$.

Equation (4.10) allows us to calculate the coordinates of point P' on the screen. For this, according to Figure 4-2, we will express vectors R and Q on the screen as $R = X_P i + Y_P j$ and $Q = X_C i + Y_C j$. Therefore, Equation (4.10) gives the position of point P' in terms of the vector pointing to the center of the screen (Q), the normal distance to the screen (D), the vector of projection (V), and the position of the three-dimensional point (P).

By expressing $R = X_P i + Y_P j$ and $Q = X_C i + Y_C j$ in Equation (4.10), the vector components give the following three equations:

$$X_p = X_C + \frac{D - V_Z}{D - Z_P - V_Z}(x - V_X) + V_X \qquad (4.11)$$

$$Y_p = Y_C + \frac{D - V_Z}{D - Z_P - V_Z}(y - V_Y) + V_Y \qquad (4.12)$$

$$0 = \frac{D - V_Z}{D - Z_P - V_Z}(D - Z_P - V_Z) + V_Z - D \qquad (4.13)$$

Equations (4.11) and (4.12) represent the main tool for determining the projection of the three-dimensional point on the screen. Equation (4.13), although algebraically correct, will not be used, as it does not provide further information.

In addition to Equations (4.11) and (4.12), we will also need equations to rotate the polygons. In the following section, we obtain these equations.

4.2 Rotating a Point on a Plane

Rotation equations for a three-dimensional point projected on a screen can be calculated by successive rotations performed in two-dimensional planes. Therefore, our description here is presented in a two-dimensional space.

In Figure 4-3, the center of the screen, with coordinates (x', y'), is given by the position vector C on a coordinate plane (x, y).

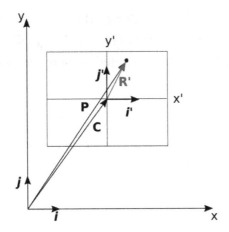

Figure 4-3. *Screen with coordinates (x', y') on a coordinate plane (x, y)*

In Figure 4-3, the black dot represents an arbitrary point on the two-dimensional (x, y) space. As depicted, P and C represent vectors going from the origin of the (x, y) system to the point and to the center of the screen, respectively. Vector R' goes from the center of the screen to the point. It can be observed that:

$$P = C + R' \tag{4.14}$$

In terms of their components, vectors in Equation (4.14) will be written as follows:

$$P = xi + yj \tag{4.15}$$

$$C = X_c i + Y_c j \tag{4.16}$$

$$R' = x'i' + y'j' \tag{4.17}$$

It will also be noticed that:

$$i = i' \text{ and } j = j' \tag{4.18}$$

We assume that the black dot depicted in Figure 4-3 is fixed on the screen. Therefore, if the screen rotates an angle θ, as illustrated in Figure 4-4, the coordinates of the rotated point remain fixed on the screen.

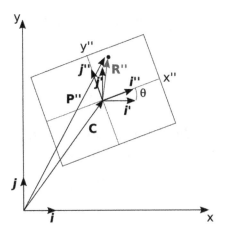

Figure 4-4. *Rotated screen with coordinates (x'', y''). The coordinate system (x, y) remains static. The point on the screen represented by the black dot rotates with the screen, remaining fixed on it*

From Figure 4-4, we obtain the following:

$$P'' = C + R'' \tag{4.19}$$

$$i'' = cos(\theta)i + sin(\theta)j \tag{4.20}$$

$$j'' = -sin(\theta)i + cos(\theta)j \tag{4.21}$$

In Equations (4.20) and (4.21), we substituted i' and j' with their corresponding values given in Equation (4.18).

As mentioned, the rotated point maintains fixed coordinates on the screen; therefore, we can write:

$$R'' = x''i'' + y''j'' = x'i'' + y'j'' \tag{4.22}$$

Substituting Equations (4.20) and (4.21) in Equation (4.22) gives the following:

$$R'' = x'\left[cos(\theta)i + sin(\theta)j\right] + y'\left[-sin(\theta)i + cos(\theta)j\right] \tag{4.23}$$

Now, x' and y' can be calculated using the component vectors of Equation (4.14) as:

$$x' = x - X_C \tag{4.24}$$

$$y' = y - Y_C \tag{4.25}$$

By explicitly writing the components of R'' in Equation (4.23) and using Equations (4.24) and (4.25), we obtain the following:

$$x'' = X_C + (x - X_C)\cos(\theta) - (y - Y_C)\sin(\theta) \tag{4.26}$$

$$y'' = Y_C + (x - X_C)\sin(\theta) + (y - Y_C)\cos(\theta) \tag{4.27}$$

Equations (4.26) and (4.27) give the coordinates of the rotated point. These equations are used in Chapter 5 to program the rotation of the polygons.

4.3 Summary

In this chapter, we derived analytical equations for projecting three-dimensional points onto a two-dimensional screen. Additionally, we obtained equations to calculate the rotation of points in a three-dimensional space. These equations are used in Chapter 5 to position and rotate polygons on the screen.

CHAPTER 5

Programming Three-Dimensional Polygons

In this chapter, we describe how to construct and rotate polygons by using the equations obtained in Chapter 4.

As an example, Figure 5-1 shows a screenshot of the program running on an Android cell phone.

© Moisés Cywiak, David Cywiak 2021

M. Cywiak and D. Cywiak, *Multi-Platform Graphics Programming with Kivy*,

https://doi.org/10.1007/978-1-4842-7113-1_5

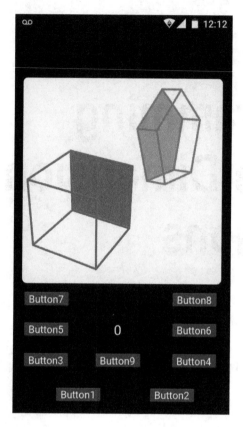

Figure 5-1. *Cell phone screenshot with two polygons on the screen*

Figure 5-1 shows the program running on an Android cell phone. Two polygons are placed on the screen. Button1 draws the polygons and Button2 clears the screen. The three buttons at the left—Button3, Button5, and Button7—rotate one of the two polygons in the counterclockwise direction, in the $x - y$, $x - z$, or $y - z$ planes, respectively. Accordingly, Button4, Button6, and Button8 rotate the polygon in the clockwise direction. One of the polygons is selected each time that Button9 is pressed. The selected polygon number is indicated by a label.

5.1 Polygon Structure

Similar to the two-dimensional case, these three-dimensional polygons require a structure with the properties of the polygon. To describe the contents and use of the structures, we focus on the structure that corresponds to the cube polygon shown in Listing 5-1.

The first entry in the structure corresponds to the number of vertices +1, as in the two-dimensional case. Next, we list the vertices that correspond to the front face of the cube, referring to their corresponding offsets. Then we list the vertices of the back face. The last entries of the structure correspond to the color of the polygon and its center of rotation.

In this example, the center of rotation coincides with the (x,y,z) offsets of the polygon. The polygon structure is given in Listing 5-1. First, let's define the dimensions of the cube as LX=60, LY=60, and LZ=60. Offsets from the origin for the (x,y,z) directions are defined as OffX=-70, OffY=-40, and OffZ=200, respectively.

Listing 5-1. Three-Dimensional Polygon Structure

```
#Offsets from the origin. OffZ is measured
#starting from the screen
OffX=-70; OffY=-40; OffZ=200;
#Dimensions of the cube
LX=60; LY=60; LZ=60;
Cube=[
    5,                      #Number of vertexes +1
    #Front face
    [ LX+OffX,  LY+OffY,  LZ+OffZ],    #Vertex 1
    [ LX+OffX, -LY+OffY,  LZ+OffZ],    #Vertex 2
    [-LX+OffX, -LY+OffY,  LZ+OffZ],    #Vertex 3
    [-LX+OffX,  LY+OffY,  LZ+OffZ],    #Vertex 4
    [ LX+OffX,  LY+OffY,  LZ+OffZ],    #Vertex 1
```

```
#Back face
[ LX+OffX,   LY+OffY,   -LZ+OffZ],      #Vertex 1
[ LX+OffX,  -LY+OffY,   -LZ+OffZ],      #Vertex 2
[-LX+OffX,  -LY+OffY,   -LZ+OffZ],      #Vertex 3
[-LX+OffX,   LY+OffY,   -LZ+OffZ],      #Vertex 4
[ LX+OffX,   LY+OffY,   -LZ+OffZ],      #Vertex 1

#Red, green, blue color.
#Entries must be between 0 and 1. Place= 2*Num+1
[0,0,1],

#Center of rotation. Entry=2*Num+2
[OffX,OffY,OffZ]
];
```

5.2 Basic Functions

Now that the structure of the polygon has been constructed, we need a function to draw the polygon on the screen. This function is DrawEdges(P,B), as shown in Listing 5-2.

DrawEdges(P,B) receives two parameters. The first parameter points to the structure. The second parameter is a handle to the widgets defined in the kv file.

The edges of the polygon are drawn by calculating the position of each vertex on the screen using Equations (4.11) and (4.12) from Chapter 4. For convenience, they are repeated here:

$$X_p = X_C + \frac{D - V_Z}{D - Z_P - V_Z}(x - V_X) + V_X \tag{5.1}$$

$$Y_p = Y_C + \frac{D - V_Z}{D - Z_P - V_Z}(y - V_Y) + V_Y \tag{5.2}$$

The pseudocode for DrawEdges(P,B) is shown in Listing 5-2.

Listing 5-2. The Function to Draw Polygon Edges

```
def DrawEdges(P, B):
    Num=P[0]; # Reading number of face edges +1
    r,g,b=P[2*Num+1]; # Reading colors
    for n in range(1,Num): # Drawing front edges
        Factor=(D-VZ)/(D-P[n][2]-VZ);
        x1=XC+Factor*(P[n][0]-VX)+VX;
        y1=YC+Factor*(P[n][1]-VY)+VY;
        Factor=(D-VZ)/(D-P[n+1][2]-VZ);
        x2=XC+Factor*(P[n+1][0]-VX)+VX;
        y2=YC+Factor*(P[n+1][1]-VY)+VY;
        Draw_line_from (x1,y1) to (x2,y2)
        using (r,g,b) color.

    for n in range(Num+1,2*Num): #Drawing back edges
        Factor=(D-VZ)/(D-P[n][2]-VZ);
        x1=XC+Factor*(P[n][0]-VX)+VX;
        y1=YC+Factor*(P[n][1]-VY)+VY;
        Factor=(D-VZ)/(D-P[n+1][2]-VZ);
        x2=XC+Factor*(P[n+1][0]-VX)+VX;
        y2=YC+Factor*(P[n+1][1]-VY)+VY;
        Draw_line_from (x1,y1) to (x2,y2)
        using (r,g,b) color.

    #Drawing edges between back and front faces
    for n in range(1,Num):
        Factor=(D-VZ)/(D-P[n][2]-VZ);
        x1=XC+Factor*(P[n][0]-VX)+VX;
        y1=YC+Factor*(P[n][1]-VY)+VY;
        Factor=(D-VZ)/(D-P[Num+n][2]-VZ);
```

```
x2=XC+Factor*(P[Num+n][0]-VX)+VX;
y2=YC+Factor*(P[Num+n][1]-VY)+VY;
Draw_line_from (x1,y1) to (x2,y2)
using (r,g,b) color.
```

As you can see in Listing 5-2, the edges are drawn by calculating the coordinates of each vertex in the screen using Equations (5.1) and (5.2). In the first for loop, the edges of the front face are drawn. In the second for loop, the edges of the back face are drawn. Finally, in the last for loop, the edges going from the front to the back face vertices are drawn.

For illustrative purposes, we will only fill one face of the polygons. The FillPolygon(B,P) function, shown in Listing 5-3, receives two parameters. The P parameter gives access to the polygon structure, while the B parameter gives access to the screen widgets. Before we declare the function, we allocate a region of memory of 30 points of intersection with the scan line, as described in Chapter 3 for the two-dimensional case. We do this by using:

```
Intersect=np.zeros(30);
```

The corresponding pseudocode for FillPolygon(B,P) is shown in Listing 5-3.

Listing 5-3. Pseudocode for the FillPolygon(B,P) Function

```
def FillPolygon(P, B):
    Num=P[0]; #Reading number of face edges +1
    r,g,b=P[2*Num+1]; #Reading colors
    #Calculating polygon YMin, Ymax
    #for limiting number of line scans
    Factor=(D-VZ)/(D-P[Num+1][2]-VZ);
    YMin=YC+Factor*(P[Num+1][1]-VY)+VY;
    YMax=YMin;
```

```
for n in range(Num+1,2*Num):
    Factor=(D-VZ)/(D-P[n+1][2]-VZ);
    if YMin>YC+Factor*(P[n+1][1]-VY)+VY:
        YMin=YC+Factor*(P[n+1][1]-VY)+VY;
    if YMax<YC+Factor*(P[n+1][1]-VY)+VY:
        YMax=YC+Factor*(P[n+1][1]-VY)+VY;
#We have now (YMin, YMax). We now proceed
#filling lines between Ymin and Ymax
for y in np.arange (YMin, YMax, 2):
    Counter=0;
    #We search line cuts, segment by segment
    for n in range(Num+1, 2*Num):
        #We first order the two vertices of each
        #segment such that Y1<Y2
        Factor1=(D-VZ)/(D-P[n][2]-VZ);
        YA=YC+Factor1*(P[n][1]-VY)+VY;

        Factor2=(D-VZ)/(D-P[n+1][2]-VZ);
        YB=YC+Factor2*(P[n+1][1]-VY)+VY;

        if ( YA<YB ):
            Y1=YA;
            X1=XC+Factor1*(P[n][0]-VX)+VX;
            Y2=YB;
            X2=XC+Factor2*(P[n+1][0]-VX)+VX;
        else:
            Y1=YB;
            X1=XC+Factor2*(P[n+1][0]-VX)+VX;
            Y2=YA;
            X2=XC+Factor1*(P[n][0]-VX)+VX;
```

```
if (Y1<=y and y<Y2):
    if (Y2-Y1)!=0:
        M=(X2-X1)/(Y2-Y1);
    else:
            #if Y1=Y2, the slope becomes
            #infinite. Therefore,
            #we assign to M a large value
            M=1.0e8;
    #We store the x value
    Intersect[Counter]=(y-Y1)*M+X1;
    #And we increment Counter as a
    #new value has being stored
    Counter=Counter+1;
#Our polygon is a closed figure. We ask If
#an even number of cuts have occurred
if(Counter>1 and Counter %2==0):
    #Intersect1 stores ordered pairs of
    #x values
    Intersect1=np.sort(Intersect[0:Counter]);
    #We proceed tracing horizontal lines
    #between pairs of intersections
    for n in range(0,Counter,2):
        XIntersect1=int(Intersect1[n]);
        XIntersect2=int(Intersect1[n+1]);
        Y=int(y);
        Draw line from (XIntersect1,Y) to
        (Xintersect2,Y)
        using (r,g,b) color.
```

Note that FillPolygon(P,B) is analogous to the two-dimensional case described in Chapter 3. Here, one face of the polygon is filled with horizontal lines beginning from its minimum y-coordinate up to its maximum. The only difference here is that we need to calculate the x and y coordinates according to Equations (5.1) and (5.2) because we have depth dependence.

The rotation of the polygon consists of updating the vertices' values stored in the structure. For this, we use Equations (4.26) and (4.27) obtained in Chapter 4, replacing θ with $-\theta$. Then, these equations read as follows:

$$x'' = X_C + (x - X_C)\cos(\theta) + (y - Y_C)\sin(\theta) \tag{5.3}$$

$$y'' = Y_C - (x - X_C)\sin(\theta) + (y - Y_C)\cos(\theta) \tag{5.4}$$

In Equations (5.3) and (5.4), the plane of rotation is x-y. Analogous equations are used for rotations in the x-z and y-z planes.

To simplify the code for the three planes of rotation, each component in the x, y, and z directions will be referred to as X_1, X_2, and X_3, respectively. Then, for a given plane of rotation, we use a pair of global variables called p and q. They correspond to coordinates Xp and Xq. The appropriate code is given in Listing 5-4.

Listing 5-4. Function to Rotate Polygon Points

```
def Rotate(P, Sense):
    global p,q;
    if Sense==-1:
        Teta=np.pi/180*(-5);
    else:
        Teta=np.pi/180*(5);
    Cos_Teta=np.cos(Teta)
    Sin_Teta=np.sin(Teta);
    Num=P[0];
    #Reading center of rotation
    RCp=P[2*Num+2][p]; RCq=P[2*Num+2][q];
```

```
for n in range(1,Num+1): #Rotating front face
    Xp=(P[n][p]-RCp)*Cos_Teta \
        + (P[n][q]-RCq)*Sin_Teta +RCp;
    Xq=-(P[n][p]-RCp)*Sin_Teta \
        + (P[n][q]-RCq)*Cos_Teta +RCq;
    P[n][p]=Xp;
    P[n][q]=Xq;
#Rotating Back face
for n in range(Num+1,2*Num+1):
    Xp=(P[n][p]-RCp)*Cos_Teta \
        + (P[n][q]-RCq)*Sin_Teta +RCp;
    Xq=-(P[n][p]-RCp)*Sin_Teta \
        + (P[n][q]-RCq)*Cos_Teta +RCq;
    P[n][p]=Xp;
    P[n][q]=Xq;
```

As indicated in Listing 5-4, RCp and RCq refer to the center of rotation.

The complete code for main.py and File.kv are shown in Listings 5-5 and 5-6, respectively.

Listing 5-5. The main.py Code Listing

```
from kivy.app import App
from kivy.uix.floatlayout import FloatLayout
from kivy.graphics import Line, Color
from kivy.clock import Clock
import os
import numpy as np
from kivy.lang import Builder
Builder.load_file(
    os.path.join(os.path.dirname(os.path.abspath(
        __file__)), 'File.kv')
                );
```

```
#Avoid Form1 of being resizable
from kivy.config import Config
Config.set("graphics","resizable", True)
Config.set('graphics', 'width',  '480');
Config.set('graphics', 'height', '680');
#These values are adjusted by the
#function Initialize()
#after Clock.schedule_once has been executed.
#These values are canvas center (XC,YC)
#and width and height (W,H);
XC=0; YC=0; W=0; H=0;
Flag=False;
NUMBER=0;
#=============== Polygon structures ===============
#The first entry corresponds to the
#number of vertexes +1.
#Following pair of entries correspond to the list
#of vertexes ordered in clockwise direction.
#The first vertex is repeated in the
#list as the last vertex.
#Following pair of entries correspond to the center
#of rotation in screen coordinates
#The triplet before the end of the structure
#corresponds to polygon colors, red, green, blue.
D=800;
VX=-20; VY=0; VZ=0;

LX=60; LY=60; LZ=60; # Cube dimensions
#Offsets from the origin. OffZ is measured
#starting from the screen
OffX=-70; OffY=-40; OffZ=200;
```

```
Cube=[
    5,                      #Number of vertexes +1
    #Front face
    [ LX+OffX,  LY+OffY,  LZ+OffZ],     #Vertex 1
    [ LX+OffX, -LY+OffY,  LZ+OffZ],     #Vertex 2
    [-LX+OffX, -LY+OffY,  LZ+OffZ],     #Vertex 3
    [-LX+OffX,  LY+OffY,  LZ+OffZ],     #Vertex 4
    [ LX+OffX,  LY+OffY,  LZ+OffZ],     #Vertex 1

    #Back face
    [ LX+OffX,  LY+OffY,  -LZ+OffZ],    #Vertex 1
    [ LX+OffX, -LY+OffY,  -LZ+OffZ],    #Vertex 2
    [-LX+OffX, -LY+OffY,   -LZ+OffZ],   #Vertex 3
    [-LX+OffX,  LY+OffY,   -LZ+OffZ],   #Vertex 4
    [ LX+OffX,  LY+OffY,   -LZ+OffZ],   #Vertex 1

    #Red, green, blue color.
    #Entries must be between 0 and 1. Place= 2*Num+1
    [0,0,1],

    #Center of rotation. Entry=2*Num+2
    [OffX,OffY,OffZ]
    ];

L=90; LZ=20;   # Pentagon dimensions
#Offsets from the origin. OffZ is measured
#starting from the screen
OffX=90; OffY=80; OffZ=100;
Pentagon=[
        6,    #Number of vertexes +1
        #Front face
        #Vertex 1
        [ 1*L+OffX,        0*L+OffY,      LZ+OffZ],
```

```
#Vertex 2
[ 0.309*L+OffX,   .95*L+OffY,    LZ+OffZ],
#Vertex 3
[ -0.809*L+OffX,  0.58*L+OffY,   LZ+OffZ],
#Vertex 4
[ -0.809*L+OffX,  -0.58*L+OffY,  LZ+OffZ],
#Vertex 5
[ 0.309*L+OffX,   -0.95*L+OffY,  LZ+OffZ],
#Vertex 1 repeated
[ 1*L+OffX,       0*L+OffY,      LZ+OffZ],

#Back face
#Vertex 1
[ 1*L+OffX,       0*L+OffY,      -LZ+OffZ],
#Vertex 2
[ 0.309*L+OffX,   .95*L+OffY,    -LZ+OffZ],
#Vertex 3
[ -0.809*L+OffX,  0.58*L+OffY,   -LZ+OffZ],
#Vertex 4
[ -0.809*L+OffX,  -0.58*L+OffY,  -LZ+OffZ],
#Vertex 5
[ 0.309*L+OffX,   -0.95*L+OffY,  -LZ+OffZ],
#Vertex 1 repeated
[ 1*L+OffX,       0*L+OffY,      -LZ+OffZ],

[1,0,0],  #red, green, blue color.
#Center of rotation. Entry=2*Num+2
[OffX,OffY,OffZ]

];
```

#--

```python
def DrawEdges(P, B):
    Num=P[0]; #Reading number of face edges +1
    r,g,b=P[2*Num+1]; #Reading colors
    for n in range(1,Num): #Drawing front edges
        Factor=(D-VZ)/(D-P[n][2]-VZ);
        x1=XC+Factor*(P[n][0]-VX)+VX;
        y1=YC+Factor*(P[n][1]-VY)+VY;
        Factor=(D-VZ)/(D-P[n+1][2]-VZ);
        x2=XC+Factor*(P[n+1][0]-VX)+VX;
        y2=YC+Factor*(P[n+1][1]-VY)+VY;
        B.ids.Screen1.canvas.add( Color(r,g,b) );
        B.ids.Screen1.canvas.add( Line(points=
            (int(x1),int(y1),int(x2),int(y2)),
                                    width=2) );

    for n in range(Num+1,2*Num): #Drawing back edges
        Factor=(D-VZ)/(D-P[n][2]-VZ);
        x1=XC+Factor*(P[n][0]-VX)+VX;
        y1=YC+Factor*(P[n][1]-VY)+VY;
        Factor=(D-VZ)/(D-P[n+1][2]-VZ);
        x2=XC+Factor*(P[n+1][0]-VX)+VX;
        y2=YC+Factor*(P[n+1][1]-VY)+VY;
        B.ids.Screen1.canvas.add( Color(r,g,b) );
        B.ids.Screen1.canvas.add( Line(points=
            (int(x1),int(y1),int(x2),int(y2)),
                                    width=2) );
    #Drawing edges between back and front faces
    for n in range(1,Num):
        Factor=(D-VZ)/(D-P[n][2]-VZ);
        x1=XC+Factor*(P[n][0]-VX)+VX;
        y1=YC+Factor*(P[n][1]-VY)+VY;
        Factor=(D-VZ)/(D-P[Num+n][2]-VZ);
```

```python
        x2=XC+Factor*(P[Num+n][0]-VX)+VX;
        y2=YC+Factor*(P[Num+n][1]-VY)+VY;
        B.ids.Screen1.canvas.add( Color(r,g,b) );
        B.ids.Screen1.canvas.add( Line(points=
            (int(x1),int(y1),int(x2),int(y2)),
                                    width=2) );

#------------------------------------------------------
def Rotate(P, Sense):
    global p,q;
    if Sense==-1:
        Teta=np.pi/180*(-5);
    else:
        Teta=np.pi/180*(5);
    Cos_Teta=np.cos(Teta)
    Sin_Teta=np.sin(Teta);
    Num=P[0];
    #Reading center of rotation
    RCp=P[2*Num+2][p]; RCq=P[2*Num+2][q];

    for n in range(1,Num+1): #Rotating front face
        Xp=(P[n][p]-RCp)*Cos_Teta \
            + (P[n][q]-RCq)*Sin_Teta +RCp;
        Xq=-(P[n][p]-RCp)*Sin_Teta \
            + (P[n][q]-RCq)*Cos_Teta +RCq;
        P[n][p]=Xp;
        P[n][q]=Xq;
    #Rotating Back face
    for n in range(Num+1,2*Num+1):
        Xp=(P[n][p]-RCp)*Cos_Teta \
            + (P[n][q]-RCq)*Sin_Teta +RCp;
```

```python
    Xq=-(P[n][p]-RCp)*Sin_Teta \
        + (P[n][q]-RCq)*Cos_Teta +RCq;
    P[n][p]=Xp;
    P[n][q]=Xq;

#-----------------------------------------------------
#Function for filling one polygon face, line by line
#Array to store intersection points
Intersect=np.zeros(30);
def FillPolygon(P, B):
    Num=P[0]; #Reading number of face edges +1
    r,g,b=P[2*Num+1]; #Reading colors
    #Calculating polygon YMin, Ymax
    #for limiting number of line scans
    Factor=(D-VZ)/(D-P[Num+1][2]-VZ);
    YMin=YC+Factor*(P[Num+1][1]-VY)+VY;
    YMax=YMin;
    for n in range(Num+1,2*Num):
        Factor=(D-VZ)/(D-P[n+1][2]-VZ);
        if YMin>YC+Factor*(P[n+1][1]-VY)+VY:
            YMin=YC+Factor*(P[n+1][1]-VY)+VY;
        if YMax<YC+Factor*(P[n+1][1]-VY)+VY:
            YMax=YC+Factor*(P[n+1][1]-VY)+VY;
    #We have now (YMin, YMax). We now proceed
    #filling lines between Ymin and Ymax
    for y in np.arange (YMin, YMax, 2):
        Counter=0;
        #We search line cuts, segment by segment
        for n in range(Num+1, 2*Num):
            #We first order the two vertices of each
            #segment such that Y1<Y2
```

```
Factor1=(D-VZ)/(D-P[n][2]-VZ);
YA=YC+Factor1*(P[n][1]-VY)+VY;

Factor2=(D-VZ)/(D-P[n+1][2]-VZ);
YB=YC+Factor2*(P[n+1][1]-VY)+VY;

if ( YA<YB ):
    Y1=YA;
    X1=XC+Factor1*(P[n][0]-VX)+VX;
    Y2=YB;
    X2=XC+Factor2*(P[n+1][0]-VX)+VX;
else:
    Y1=YB;
    X1=XC+Factor2*(P[n+1][0]-VX)+VX;
    Y2=YA;
    X2=XC+Factor1*(P[n][0]-VX)+VX;

if (Y1<=y and y<Y2):
    if (Y2-Y1)!=0:
        M=(X2-X1)/(Y2-Y1);
    else:
         #if Y1=Y2, the slope becomes
         #infinite. Therefore,
         #we assign to M a large value
         M=1.0e8;
    #We store the x value
    Intersect[Counter]=(y-Y1)*M+X1;
    #And we increment Counter as a
    #new value has being stored
    Counter=Counter+1;
#Our polygon is a closed figure. We ask If
#an even number of cuts have occurred
```

```
        if(Counter>1 and Counter %2==0):
            #Intersect1 stores ordered pairs of
            #x values
            Intersect1=np.sort(Intersect[0:Counter]);
            #We proceed tracing horizontal lines
            #between pairs of intersections
            for n in range(0,Counter,2):
                XIntersect1=int(Intersect1[n]);
                XIntersect2=int(Intersect1[n+1]);
                Y=int(y)
                #Picking the color and drawing the
                #horizontal line between x pairs
                B.ids.Screen1.canvas.add(
                    Color(r,g,b) );
                B.ids.Screen1.canvas.add( Line(
                    points=(XIntersect1,Y,
                    XIntersect2,Y), width=1.0) );
#-----------------------------------------------------

class Form1(FloatLayout):
    def __init__(Handle, **kwargs):
        super(Form1, Handle).__init__(**kwargs);
        Event1=Clock.schedule_once(
            Handle.Initialize);
        Event2=Clock.schedule_interval(
            Handle.Temporal,0.1);

    def Initialize(B, *args):
        global W,H, XC,YC;
        W,H=B.ids.Screen1.size;
        XI,YI=B.ids.Screen1.pos
        XC=XI+int (W/2);
        YC=YI+int(H/2);
```

```
def Temporal(B, *args):
    global Flag, NUMBER, p, q;
    if (Flag==True):
        if (B.ids.Button3.state=="down"):
            Sense=-1; p=0; q=1;
        if(B.ids.Button5.state=="down"):
            Sense=-1; p=0;q=2;
        if(B.ids.Button7.state=="down"):
            Sense=-1; p=1;q=2;

        if(B.ids.Button4.state=="down"):
            Sense=1; p=0;q=1;
        if(B.ids.Button6.state=="down"):
            Sense=1;p=0;q=2;
        if(B.ids.Button8.state=="down"):
            Sense=1;p=1;q=2;
        B.ids.Screen1.canvas.clear();
        if(NUMBER==0):
            Rotate(Cube, Sense);
        if (NUMBER==1):
            Rotate(Pentagon, Sense);
        DrawEdges(Cube,B);
        FillPolygon(Cube,B);
        DrawEdges(Pentagon,B);
        FillPolygon(Pentagon,B);

def Button1_Click(B):
    B.ids.Screen1.canvas.clear();
    DrawEdges(Cube, B);
    FillPolygon(Cube,B);

    DrawEdges(Pentagon, B);
    FillPolygon(Pentagon,B)
```

```
def Button2_Click(B):
    B.ids.Screen1.canvas.clear();

def Button3_Click(B):
    global Flag;
    Flag=True;

def Button3_Release(B):
    global Flag;
    Flag=False;

def Button4_Click(B):
    global Flag;
    Flag=True;

def Button4_Release(B):
    global Flag;
    Flag=False;

def Button5_Click(B):
    global Flag;
    Flag=True;

def Button5_Release(B):
    global Flag;
    Flag=False;

def Button6_Click(B):
    global Flag;
    Flag=True;

def Button6_Release(B):
    global Flag;
    Flag=False;
```

```python
    def Button7_Click(B):
        global Flag;
        Flag=True;

    def Button7_Release(B):
        global Flag;
        Flag=False;

    def Button8_Click(B):
        global Flag;
        Flag=True;

    def Button8_Release(B):
        global Flag;
        Flag=False;

    def Button9_Click(B):
        global NUMBER;
        NUMBER=(NUMBER+1)%2;
        B.ids.Label1.text=str(NUMBER);

# This is the Start Up code.
class StartUp (App):
    def build (BU):
        BU.title="Form1"
        return Form1();
if __name__ =="__main__":
    StartUp().run();
```

Listing 5-6. The File.kv Code Listing

```
#:set W 440
#:set H 440
<Form1>:
    id : Form1
    StencilView:
        id: Screen1
        size_hint: None,None
        pos_hint: {"x":0.04, "y":0.34}
        size: W,H
        canvas.before:
            Color:
                rgba: 0.9, 0.9, 0, 1
            RoundedRectangle:
                pos:  self.pos
                size: self.size
    Button:
        id: Button1
        on_press: Form1.Button1_Click()
        text: "Button1"
        size_hint: None,None
        pos_hint: {"x": 0.2, "y":0.03}
        size: 100,30

    Button:
        id: Button2
        on_press: Form1.Button2_Click()
        text: "Button2"
        size_hint: None,None
        pos_hint: {"x": 0.63, "y":0.03}
        size: 100,30
```

```
Button:
    id: Button3
    on_press: Form1.Button3_Click()
    on_release: Form1.Button3_Release()
    text: "Button3"
    size_hint: None,None
    pos_hint: {"x": 0.05, "y":0.12}
    size: 100,30
    always_release: True
Button:
    id: Button4
    on_press: Form1.Button4_Click()
    on_release:  Form1.Button4_Release()
    text: "Button4"
    size_hint: None,None
    pos_hint: {"x": 0.73, "y":0.12}
    size: 100,30

Button:
    id: Button5
    on_press: Form1.Button5_Click()
    on_release:  Form1.Button5_Release()
    text: "Button5"
    size_hint: None,None
    pos_hint: {"x": 0.05, "y":0.20}
    size: 100,30
Button:
    id: Button6
    on_press: Form1.Button6_Click()
    on_release:  Form1.Button6_Release()
    text: "Button6"
```

```
        size_hint: None,None
        pos_hint: {"x": 0.73, "y":0.20}
        size: 100,30
    Button:
        id: Button7
        on_press: Form1.Button7_Click()
        on_release:  Form1.Button7_Release()
        text: "Button7"
        size_hint: None,None
        pos_hint: {"x": 0.05, "y":0.28}
        size: 100,30
    Button:
        id: Button8
        on_press: Form1.Button8_Click()
        on_release:  Form1.Button8_Release()
        text: "Button8"
        size_hint: None,None
        pos_hint: {"x": 0.73, "y":0.28}
        size: 100,30

    Button:
        id: Button9
        on_press: Form1.Button9_Click()
        text: "Button9"
        size_hint: None,None
        pos_hint: {"x": 0.38, "y":0.12}
        size: 100,30

    Label:
        id: Label1
        text: "0"
        font_size: 30
```

```
color: 1,1,0,1
size_hint: None,None
pos_hint: {"x": 0.38, "y":0.20}
size: 100,30
```

5.3 Summary

In this chapter, we introduced the required structures and functions to construct and rotate three-dimensional polygons. We described how to map them on the computer's screen using the equations obtained in Chapter 4.

CHAPTER 6

Stereoscopic 3D Programming

In this chapter, we describe the basic programming tools needed to provide stereoscopic 3D views of the polygons.

6.1 Basics of a Stereoscopic Scene

To produce stereoscopic 3D views of polygons, we create two images of the three-dimensional objects. The first image is the projection of the three-dimensional polygons onto the screen, using the equations given in Chapter 4 and a point of projection with coordinates (VX1, VY1, VZ1). The second image uses a second point of projection with coordinates (VX2, VY2, VZ2), slightly shifted horizontally from the first. Note that VX2=VX1+⊗X, VY2=VY1, and VZ2=VZ1. Here, ⊗X represents a small shift.

The two images obtained will not be displayed on the screen. Instead, we store them in a memory region to be binary ORed. The resulting image will appear on the computer's screen. Therefore, this process requires us to allocate three binary images in a memory region.

To appreciate the stereoscopic effect, you need to observe the scene through colored filters, red for the left eye and cyan for the right eye. For this purpose, you can construct glasses made with red and cyan cellophane films, which are commercially available, or you can acquire commercially

© Moisés Cywiak, David Cywiak 2021
M. Cywiak and D. Cywiak, *Multi-Platform Graphics Programming with Kivy*,
https://doi.org/10.1007/978-1-4842-7113-1_6

available glasses specifically made for this purpose (often called 3D glasses). However, in both cases, we must ensure that each filter transmits only its corresponding color. In our experience, we had to add an extra film to the red filter. Additionally, we must take care of the properties of the cellophane films as we have found different transparency qualities among them.

The program will perform the required calculations and will be in charge of drawing the corresponding red and cyan images on the screen. Figure 6-1 shows a scene of the program running on an Android cell phone. As mentioned, you can see the stereoscopic effect only if you observe the scene through appropriate red-cyan filters.

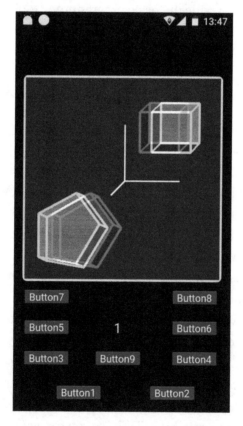

Figure 6-1. *Program screenshot obtained from an Android cell phone. Best viewed with 3D glasses*

6.2 Programming and ORing the Images

To calculate the binary OR between the left and right images, we have to import *Pillow* into our program, which is a specialized library for image processing. To verify if you have it installed on your computer, use the `pip3 list` directive. It should appear on the list. Otherwise, you can install it by typing the `pip3 install Pillow` command in your Terminal window.

We need three modules from Pillow, which will be available in the program by using the `from PIL import Image, ImageDraw, ImageFont` directive.

From the three libraries, Image will allow us to create the three images that this process requires. The second module, `ImageDraw`, provides tools for drawing lines. We will use straight lines to draw the edges of our polygons and to fill their faces. In our working example, we will fill only the back faces of our polygons. Finally, the last module, `ImageFont`, will allow us to display text.

Because the resulting image is a binary one, to be able to display it on the screen, we need to convert it into an appropriate image file. For our working example, we will use the png format. We will perform this conversion in a memory region. Therefore, we need to allocate memory and make it behave as a file. We will refer to a block of memory with this characteristic as an *in-memory file*. We will achieve this task using the library `io`, which we will incorporate into our program with the `import io` directive. Finally, the image stored in the in-memory file will be converted into a Kivy image to be displayed on the screen. We describe this process in detail in the following sections.

6.3 Projections

The program begins by creating the three required images by utilizing the Initialize(B, *args) function, which receives the handle B to access the widgets. Initialize(B, *args) uses the Image.new directive from PIL to create the three images, which we will name PilImage1, PilImage2, and PilImage3. The first image, PilImage1, will store the red image, while PilImage2 will store the cyan image. PilImage3 will store the result of the bitwise OR operation.

Additionally, to draw lines, we need to create two drawing instances, which we will name Draw1 and Draw2. These instances also allow us to display text.

We want to display a rounded frame like the one depicted in Figure 6-2, so the dimensions of our PIL images will be reduced by ten pixels in width and height compared to the Kivy image declared in the file.

When the program initiates, or when Button2 is pressed, the 3D Images text is displayed, as shown in Figure 6-2. To display text on the screen, we have to select one of the TrueType fonts available in Ubuntu, in the computer/usr/share/fonts/truetype folder. In this folder, we have several subfolders with names of the TrueType fonts. Copy the appropriate ttf file into your working folder. For our programs, we have selected Gargi.ttf.

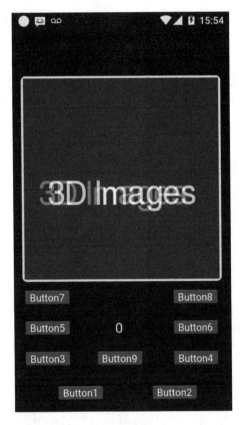

Figure 6-2. *Program screenshot showing text*

The code that corresponds to the Initialize(B, *args) function is shown in Listing 6-1.

Listing 6-1. The Initialize(B, *args) Function

```
def Initialize(B, *args):
        global W,H, XC,YC;
        global PilImage1,PilImage2, Draw1,Draw2;
        W,H=B.ids.Screen1.size;
        XC=int (W/2)
        YC=int(H/2)
```

```
PilImage1= Image.new('RGB', (W-10, H-10),
                               (60, 70, 30));
Draw1 = ImageDraw.Draw(PilImage1);
PilImage2= Image.new('RGB', (W-10, H-10),
                               (60, 70, 30));
Draw2 = ImageDraw.Draw(PilImage2);
Font = ImageFont.truetype('Gargi.ttf', 70)
Draw1.text( (30,200), "3D Images",
            fill =(255,0,0,1), font=Font);
Draw1.text( (50,200), "3D Images",
            fill =(0,255,255,1), font=Font);
ShowScene(B);
```

After creating the left and right images with their respective texts, Initialize(B, *args) calls the ShowScene(B) function. This function receives handle B to access the widgets declared in File.kv and performs the following tasks.

1. ShowScene(B) creates two NumPy arrays, called Array1 and Array2, resulting from the conversion of the data stored in PilImage1 and PilImage2.

2. An additional array, named Array3, is created as a result of bitwise ORing the elements of Array1 with Array2.

3. PilImage3 is created after converting Array3 into image data.

4. At this point, PilImage3 is converted into a Kivy image, following the procedure given at

    https://stackoverflow.com/questions/10762454/load-image-from-memory-in-kivy

The procedure is as follows.

a. A region of memory, behaving as a file, is allocated using the Memory=io.BytesIO() directive. This directive provides a memory region named Memory that can be used as a file. Now we can store our image in this memory block by means of the PilImage3.save(Memory, ext="png") directive.

b. As Memory behaves like a file, it has an inherent file pointer. Each time we access it for writing or reading, this file pointer is updated. Therefore, before copying the image to the Kivy widget, it is necessary to reload the file pointer to the beginning of the file, where our data will be stored. This is accomplished by using the Memory.seek(0) directive.

5.   We now proceed to convert the image into the png format by using the ImagePNG = CoreImage(Memory, ext="png") directive. Now, ImagePNG holds our result.

6.   The final step consists of copying ImagePNG to the Kivy image widget that is declared in the File. kv file. As ImagePNG has the appropriate format, it will be displayed on the screen simply by using the B.ids.Screen1.texture = ImagePNG.texture directive.

Before ShowScene(B) finishes, it must free the regions of memory that were dynamically allocated to accomplish this process. This is done by means of the directives shown in Listing 6-2.

Listing 6-2. Freeing Previously Allocated Resources

```
ImagePNG.remove_from_cache();
Memory.close();
PilImage3.close();
Array1=None;
Array2=None;
Array3=None.
```

The code for ShowScene(B) is shown in Listing 6-3.

Listing 6-3. Code for the ShowScene(B) Function

```
def ShowScene(B):
    Array1=np.array(PilImage1);
    Array2=np.array(PilImage2);
    Array3=Array1 | Array2;

    PilImage3=Image.fromarray(Array3);

    Memory=io.BytesIO();
    PilImage3.save(Memory, format="png");
    Memory.seek(0);
    ImagePNG=CoreImage(Memory, ext="png");

    B.ids.Screen1.texture=ImagePNG.texture;
    ImagePNG.remove_from_cache()
    Memory.close();
    PilImage3.close();
    Array1=None;
    Array2=None;
    Array3=None;
```

As our program allows the polygons to be rotated in real-time, we have to clean the previous scene before exhibiting the new one. The ClearObjects() function performs this task. This function draws in Draw1 and Draw2 rectangles with the same sizes as PilImage1 and PilImage2 using the background colors that we previously selected. As a result, the scene will appear to have been cleaned. The code for ClearObjects() is given in Listing 6-4.

Listing 6-4. Function to Clear the Screen

```
def ClearObjects():
    Draw1.rectangle( (0, 0, H-10, W-10),
                    fill=(60, 70, 30, 1) );
    Draw2.rectangle( (0, 0, H-10, W-10),
                    fill=(60, 70, 30, 1) );
```

6.4 Polygon Structure

To place the polygon in a stereoscopic scene, you can use the same polygon structure described in Chapter 5.

A stereoscopic scene provides depth perception, which means that small changes in the Z-coordinate can cause changes in the polygon position that can drive it off-screen. Therefore, it is convenient to devise a method to help position the polygons.

To visualize this situation, let's consider a point of projection VX1 situated on a plane of projection at a distance D from the screen, as depicted in Figure 6-3. The point X on the screen is the projection of the red point. We obtain point X by drawing a straight line that goes from VX1 through the red point up to the screen.

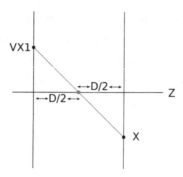

Figure 6-3. *Point X projected by the point of projection VX1. The red point, placed in the Z-axis, is in the middle of the two planes*

In Figure 6-3, the Z-axis passes through the center of the screen and the projected point, X, is shifted from this center. This method consists in calculating this shift. This quantity, calculated using properties of similar triangles, corresponds to VX1. An analog situation occurs for the y-direction. We will shift the whole scene using this value.

Before shifting the scene, we have to recall the equations for projecting a three-dimensional point given by Equations (5.1) and (5.2). Additionally, we have to rewrite these equations appropriately because the origin (0,0) of a PIL image is in the upper-left corner, in contrast to a Kivy image in which (0,0) corresponds to the bottom-left corner. Therefore, we have to maintain Equation (5.1) unaltered but, in Equation (5.2), the values added to Y_C should now be subtracted instead. The equations that correspond to Equations (5.1) and (5.2) for a PIL image read as follows:

$$X_p = X_C + \frac{D - V_Z}{D - Z_p - V_Z}(x - V_X) + V_X \tag{6.1}$$

$$Y_p = Y_C - \frac{D - V_Z}{D - Z_p - V_Z}(y - V_Y) - V_Y \tag{6.2}$$

Examining Equations (6.1) and (6.2) suggests the following parameter:

$$Factor = \frac{D - V_Z}{D - Z_p - V_Z} \qquad (6.3)$$

Now, as the red point depicted in Figure 6-3 is at $Z_p = \dfrac{D}{2}$, substituting this value in Equation (6.3) allows us to define the following constant factor:

$$Factor0 = \frac{D - V_Z}{\dfrac{D}{2} - V_Z} \qquad (6.4)$$

In Equation (6.4), *Factor0* * *VX1* will shift the projection of the red point, or equivalently, the point (0,0,0) precisely to the center of the screen.

Now, the Z distance is measured from the screen up to the plane of projection, as depicted in Figure 6-4. Therefore, Z=0 corresponds to points at the screen plane, while Z=D corresponds to points at the plane of projection. To proceed further, let's define a percentage value between 0 and 1, denoted as P. Then, we can position points at any distance between the screen and the plane of projection by using the formula Z=P*D. Let's focus on one of these points, depicted in blue in Figure 6-4.

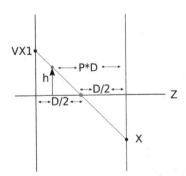

Figure 6-4. *Positioning an arbitrary point (blue point) to attain the same projection as the red point*

As indicated in Figure 6-4, the blue point is located at a distance Z= P*D, measured from the screen. Using triangle properties:

$$\frac{Vx}{\dfrac{D}{2}} = \frac{h}{\left(P*D - \dfrac{D}{2}\right)} \tag{6.5}$$

From Equation (6.5), the required shift h is given as follows:

$$h = (2P - 1)VX \tag{6.6}$$

Equation (6.6) specifies that, when the blue point is positioned at a vertical height h and at a distance Z=P*D from the screen, it will give the same projection X as the red point. The complete scene will be shifted by an amount equal to *Factor0* * *VX1*, so the red point and all the points satisfying Equation (6.6) will be projected at the center of the screen.

From this description, we can now describe our method for positioning the polygons at distances Z=P*D from the screen. The method consists of positioning the polygons first at the center of the screen using Equation (6.6), and then shifting them to a desired position.

Equation (6.6) does not depend on the parameter D, which means we can experiment with different stereoscopic perspectives using different D values, without the drawback of losing the polygons from the scene.

We can now proceed to program the polygons based on this description. We will first set the coordinates of the points of projection and the value of distance D. For the working example, we chose the following values.

```
D=8000;
VX1=1000; VY1=1000; VZ1=0;
VX2=970; VY2=1000; VZ2=0;
Factor0 =(D-VZ1) / (D/2-VZ1);
P=0.65;
```

Next, we provide the polygon data. For this example, the cube polygon has edges with a length equal to 15 pixels, placed at a distance of 0.65*D pixels from the screen, and centered at (30, 40). The corresponding code is shown in Listing 6-5.

Listing 6-5. Filling the Cube Polygon

```
P=0.65;
LX=15; LY=15; LZ=15; # Cube dimensions
#Offsets from the origin.
#OffZ is measured starting from the screen
OffX=(2*P-1)*VX1+30; OffY=(2*P-1)*VY1+40; OffZ=P*D;

Cube=[
    5,    #Number of vertexes +1
    #Front face
    [ LX+OffX,  LY+OffY,  LZ+OffZ],    #Vertex 1
    [ LX+OffX, -LY+OffY,  LZ+OffZ],    #Vertex 2
    [-LX+OffX, -LY+OffY,  LZ+OffZ],    #Vertex 3
    [-LX+OffX,  LY+OffY,  LZ+OffZ],    #Vertex 4
    [ LX+OffX,  LY+OffY,  LZ+OffZ],    #Vertex 1

    #Back face
    [ LX+OffX,  LY+OffY, -LZ+OffZ],    #Vertex 1
    [ LX+OffX, -LY+OffY, -LZ+OffZ],    #Vertex 2
    [-LX+OffX, -LY+OffY, -LZ+OffZ],    #Vertex 3
    [-LX+OffX,  LY+OffY, -LZ+OffZ],    #Vertex 4
    [ LX+OffX,  LY+OffY, -LZ+OffZ],    #Vertex 1

    ##Red, green, blue color. Entries must be
    #between 0 and 1. Entry = 2*Num+1
    [0,0,1],
    #Rotation Center RC; Entry = 2*Num+2
    [OffX,OffY,OffZ]
    ];
```

Although they are not used here, we maintain the polygon colors in the 2*Num+1 place of the structure, as in Chapter 5, for compatibility purposes.

6.5 DrawAxes Function

The DrawAxes (P, VX, VY ,VZ, Which) function is in charge of drawing the three-dimensional axes on the screen. This function receives a parameter P, corresponding to a polygon structure, and the three coordinates of a point of projection, (VX, VY, VZ). The parameter Which is 0 for the red projection and 1 for the cyan projection. In our program, VZ is always set to 0. This variable may be used in future applications. As described, the shifting values Factor0*VX and Factor0*VY are used to position the three-dimensional origin (0,0,0) at the center of the screen.

The code for DrawAxes(VX,VY,VZ,Which) is shown in Listing 6-6.

Listing 6-6. The DrawAxes(VX,VY,VZ,Which) Function

```
def DrawAxes(VX,VY,VZ,Which):
    global  Draw1,Draw2,Factor0;
    Length=60;
    if (Which==0):
        r,g,b = 255, 0, 0; #red Image
        Draw=Draw1;
    else:
        r,g,b = 0, 255, 255; #blue image
        Draw=Draw2;

    Z0=D/2; #Origin of the three-dimensional axis
    Factor=(D-VZ)/(D-Z0-VZ);
    x1=XC+Factor*(0-VX)+Factor0*VX;
    y1=YC-Factor*(0-VY)-Factor0*VY;
```

```
x2=XC+Factor*(Length-VX)+Factor0*VX;
y2=YC-Factor*(0-VY)-Factor0*VY;
#Drawing axis x
Draw.line( (x1,y1,x2,y2),fill=(r,g,b),width=3 );

x2=XC+Factor*(0-VX)+Factor0*VX;
y2=YC-Factor*(Length-VY)-Factor0*VY;
#Drawing axis y
Draw.line( (x1,y1,x2,y2),fill=(r,g,b),width=3 );

Z0=Z0+Length;
Factor=(D-VZ)/(D-Z0-VZ);
x2=XC+Factor*(0-VX)+Factor0*VX;
y2=YC-Factor*(0-VY)-Factor0*VY;
#Drawing axis z
Draw.line( (x1,y1,x2,y2),fill=(r,g,b),width=3 );
```

The DrawEdges(P, VX, VY, VZ, Which) and FillPolygon(P, VX, VY, VZ, Which) functions are similar to their respective functions described in Chapter 5, with the addition of the Which parameter.

6.6 Points of Projection

The points of projection for the red and cyan images have horizontal coordinates VX1 and VX2 and should differ slightly. In principle, increasing the difference between VX1 and VX2 produces a better stereoscopic appearance. However, there is a maximum difference allowed. It is advisable to experiment with different values.

Listing 6-7 shows the complete code for main.py and Listing 6-8 shows the complete code for File.kv.

Listing 6-7. Code Listing for main.py

```python
from kivy.app import App
from kivy.uix.floatlayout import FloatLayout
from kivy.graphics import Line, Color
from kivy.clock import Clock
from kivy.core.image import Image as CoreImage
from PIL import Image, ImageDraw, ImageFont

import io
import os
import numpy as np

from kivy.lang import Builder
Builder.load_file(
    os.path.join(os.path.dirname(os.path.abspath(
        __file__)), 'File.kv')
                );

#Avoid Form1 of being resizable
from kivy.config import Config
Config.set("graphics","resizable", False)
Config.set('graphics', 'width',  '480');
Config.set('graphics', 'height', '680');
#The width and height (W,H) and the
#center (XC,YC) of canvas are set by the
#function Initialize() after
#Clock.schedule_once has been executed.
Flag=False;
NUMBER=0;  #Polygon number
```

```
#============== Polygon structures =================
#The first entry corresponds to the
#number of vertexes+1.
#Following pair of entries correspond to the list
#of vertices ordered in clockwise direction.
#The first vertex is repeated as the last one.
#The next pair of entries corresponds to
#the center of rotation in screen coordinates
#The triplet before the end of the structure
#corresponds to the polygon color, red, green, blue.
D=8000;
VX1=1000; VY1=1000; VZ1=0;
VX2=970; VY2=1000; VZ2=0;
Factor0 =(D-VZ1) / (D/2-VZ1);

P=0.65;
LX=15; LY=15; LZ=15; # Cube dimensions
#Offsets from the origin.
#OffZ is measured starting from the screen
OffX=(2*P-1)*VX1+30; OffY=(2*P-1)*VY1+40; OffZ=P*D;

Cube=[
    5,    #Number of vertexes +1
    #Front face
    [ LX+OffX,  LY+OffY,  LZ+OffZ],    #Vertex 1
    [ LX+OffX, -LY+OffY,  LZ+OffZ],    #Vertex 2
    [-LX+OffX, -LY+OffY,  LZ+OffZ],    #Vertex 3
    [-LX+OffX,  LY+OffY,  LZ+OffZ],    #Vertex 4
    [ LX+OffX,  LY+OffY,  LZ+OffZ],    #Vertex 1
```

```
#Back face
[ LX+OffX,   LY+OffY,   -LZ+OffZ],      #Vertex 1
[ LX+OffX,  -LY+OffY,   -LZ+OffZ],      #Vertex 2
[-LX+OffX,  -LY+OffY,   -LZ+OffZ],      #Vertex 3
[-LX+OffX,   LY+OffY,   -LZ+OffZ],      #Vertex 4
[ LX+OffX,   LY+OffY,   -LZ+OffZ],      #Vertex 1

##Red, green, blue color. Entries must be
#between 0 and 1. Entry = 2*Num+1
[0,0,1],
#Rotation Center RC; Entry = 2*Num+2
[OffX,OffY,OffZ]
];

P=0.0;
L=80; LZ=20;  # Pentagon dimensions
#Offsets from the origin. OffZ measured starting at the screen
OffX=(2*P-1)*VX1-90; OffY=(2*P-1)*VY1-110; OffZ=P*D;

Pentagon=[
        6,   #Number of vertexes +1
        #Front face
        #Vertex 1
        [ 1*L+OffX,        0*L+OffY,      LZ+OffZ],
        #Vertex 2
        [ 0.309*L+OffX,  0.95*L+OffY,     LZ+OffZ],
        #Vertex 3
        [ -0.809*L+OffX,  0.58*L+OffY,   LZ+OffZ],
        #Vertex 4
        [ -0.809*L+OffX,  -0.58*L+OffY,  LZ+OffZ],
        #Vertex 5
        [ 0.309*L+OffX,  -0.95*L+OffY,   LZ+OffZ],
        #Vertex 1, repeated
        [ 1*L+OffX,        0*L+OffY,      LZ+OffZ],
```

```
#Back face
#Vertex 1
[ 1*L+OffX,        0*L+OffY,      -LZ+OffZ],
#Vertex 2
[ 0.309*L+OffX,  0.95*L+OffY,     -LZ+OffZ],
#Vertex 3
[ -0.809*L+OffX,  0.58*L+OffY,    -LZ+OffZ],
#Vertex 4
[ -0.809*L+OffX,  -0.58*L+OffY,   -LZ+OffZ],
#Vertex 5
[ 0.309*L+OffX,   -0.95*L+OffY,   -LZ+OffZ],
#Vertex 1, repeated
[ 1*L+OffX,        0*L+OffY,      -LZ+OffZ],

#Red, green, blue color. Entries must
#be between 0 and 1. Entry = 2*Num+1
[1,0,0],

#Rotation Center RC, Entry = 2*Num+2
[OffX,OffY,OffZ]

];

#------------------------------------------------------
def DrawAxes(VX,VY,VZ,Which):
    global  Draw1,Draw2,Factor0;
    Length=60;
    if (Which==0):
        r,g,b = 255, 0, 0; #red Image
        Draw=Draw1;
    else:
        r,g,b = 0, 255, 255; #blue image
        Draw=Draw2;
```

```
Z0=D/2; #Origin of the three-dimensional axis
Factor=(D-VZ)/(D-Z0-VZ);
x1=XC+Factor*(0-VX)+Factor0*VX;
y1=YC-Factor*(0-VY)-Factor0*VY;
x2=XC+Factor*(Length-VX)+Factor0*VX;
y2=YC-Factor*(0-VY)-Factor0*VY;
#Drawing axis x
Draw.line( (x1,y1,x2,y2),fill=(r,g,b),width=3 );

x2=XC+Factor*(0-VX)+Factor0*VX;
y2=YC-Factor*(Length-VY)-Factor0*VY;
#Drawing axis y
Draw.line( (x1,y1,x2,y2),fill=(r,g,b),width=3 );

Z0=Z0+Length;
Factor=(D-VZ)/(D-Z0-VZ);
x2=XC+Factor*(0-VX)+Factor0*VX;
y2=YC-Factor*(0-VY)-Factor0*VY;
#Drawing axis z
Draw.line( (x1,y1,x2,y2),fill=(r,g,b),width=3 );

def DrawEdges(P, VX, VY, VZ, Which):
    Num=P[0]; #Reading number of face edges +1
    if (Which==0):
        r,g,b =255, 0, 0; #red Image
        Draw=Draw1
    else:
        r,g,b = 0, 255 ,255;   #cyan image
        Draw=Draw2

    for n in range(1,Num): #Drawing front edges
        Factor=(D-VZ)/(D-P[n][2]-VZ);
        x1=XC+Factor*(P[n][0]-VX)+Factor0*VX;
        y1=YC-Factor*(P[n][1]-VY)-Factor0*VY;
```

```
    Factor=(D-VZ)/(D-P[n+1][2]-VZ);
    x2=XC+Factor*(P[n+1][0]-VX)+Factor0*VX;
    y2=YC-Factor*(P[n+1][1]-VY)-Factor0*VY;
    Draw.line( (x1,y1,x2,y2),fill=(r,g,b),
                              width=5 );

for n in range(Num+1,2*Num): #Drawing back edges
    Factor=(D-VZ)/(D-P[n][2]-VZ);
    x1=XC+Factor*(P[n][0]-VX)+Factor0*VX;
    y1=YC-Factor*(P[n][1]-VY)-Factor0*VY;
    Factor=(D-VZ)/(D-P[n+1][2]-VZ);
    x2=XC+Factor*(P[n+1][0]-VX)+Factor0*VX;
    y2=YC-Factor*(P[n+1][1]-VY)-Factor0*VY;
    Draw.line( (x1,y1,x2,y2),fill=(r,g,b),
                              width=5 );

#Drawing edges between back and front faces
for n in range(1,Num):
    Factor=(D-VZ)/(D-P[n][2]-VZ);
    x1=XC+Factor*(P[n][0]-VX)+Factor0*VX;
    y1=YC-Factor*(P[n][1]-VY)-Factor0*VY;
    Factor=(D-VZ)/(D-P[Num+n][2]-VZ);
    x2=XC+Factor*(P[Num+n][0]-VX)+Factor0*VX;
    y2=YC-Factor*(P[Num+n][1]-VY)-Factor0*VY;
    Draw.line( (x1,y1,x2,y2),  fill=(r,g,b),
                              width=5 );

#-----------------------------------------------------
def Rotate(P, Sense):
    global p,q;
    if Sense==-1:
        Teta=np.pi/180*(-5);
```

```python
    else:
        Teta=np.pi/180*(5);
    Cos_Teta=np.cos(Teta)
    Sin_Teta=np.sin(Teta);
    Num=P[0];
    # Center of rotation
    RCp=P[2*Num+2][p]; RCq=P[2*Num+2][q];

    #Rotating front face
    for n in range(1,Num+1):
        Xp=(P[n][p]-RCp)*Cos_Teta \
            +(P[n][q]-RCq)*Sin_Teta +RCp;
        Xq=-(P[n][p]-RCp)*Sin_Teta \
            +(P[n][q]-RCq)*Cos_Teta +RCq;
        P[n][p]=Xp;
        P[n][q]=Xq;

    #Rotating Back face
    for n in range(Num+1,2*Num+1):
        Xp=(P[n][p]-RCp)*Cos_Teta \
            + (P[n][q]-RCq)*Sin_Teta +RCp;
        Xq=-(P[n][p]-RCp)*Sin_Teta \
            + (P[n][q]-RCq)*Cos_Teta +RCq;
        P[n][p]=Xp;
        P[n][q]=Xq;

#------------------------------------------------------
#Function for filling the back polygon
#face, line by line
#Array to store intersection points
Intersect=np.zeros(30);
def FillPolygon(P, VX,VY,VZ,Which):
    Num=P[0]; #Reading number of face edges +1
```

```
if (Which==0):
    r,g,b = 200, 0, 0; #red Image
    Draw=Draw1
else:
    r,g,b= 0, 200, 200; #cyan image
    Draw=Draw2
#Calculating polygon YMin, Ymax for
#limiting number of line scans
Factor=(D-VZ)/(D-P[Num+1][2]-VZ);
YMin=YC-Factor*(P[Num+1][1]-VY)-VY;
YMax=YMin;
for n in range(Num+1,2*Num):
    Factor=(D-VZ)/(D-P[n+1][2]-VZ);
    if YMin>YC-Factor*(P[n+1][1]-VY)-Factor0*VY:
        YMin=YC-Factor*(P[n+1][1]-VY)-Factor0*VY;
    if YMax<YC-Factor*(P[n+1][1]-VY)-Factor0*VY:
        YMax=YC-Factor*(P[n+1][1]-VY)-Factor0*VY;
#We have now (YMin, YMax)
#We now proceed filling lines
#between Ymin and Ymax
for y in np.arange (YMin, YMax, 2):
    Counter=0;
    #We will search line cuts segment by segment
    for n in range(Num+1, 2*Num):
        # We first order the two vertices of
        #each segment such that Y1<Y2
        Factor1=(D-VZ)/(D-P[n][2]-VZ);
        YA=YC-Factor1*(P[n][1]-VY)-Factor0*VY;

        Factor2=(D-VZ)/(D-P[n+1][2]-VZ);
        YB=YC-Factor2*(P[n+1][1]-VY)-Factor0*VY;
```

```python
            if ( YA<YB ):
                Y1=YA;
                X1=XC+Factor1*(P[n][0]-VX) \
                        +Factor0*VX;
                Y2=YB;
                X2=XC+Factor2*(P[n+1][0]-VX) \
                        +Factor0*VX;
            else:
                Y1=YB;
                X1=XC+Factor2*(P[n+1][0]-VX) \
                        +Factor0*VX;
                Y2=YA;
                X2=XC+Factor1*(P[n][0]-VX) \
                        +Factor0*VX;

            if (Y1<=y and y<Y2):
                if (Y2-Y1)!=0:
                    M=(X2-X1)/(Y2-Y1);
                else:
                    # if Y1=Y2, the slope is infinite.
                    #We assign to M a large value
                    M=1.0e8;
                #We store the x value
                Intersect[Counter]=(y-Y1)*M+X1;
                # And we increment Counter as a new
                #value has being stored
                Counter=Counter+1;
        # Geometrical closed figure.
        #Only even number of cuts allowed
        if(Counter>1 and Counter %2 ==0):
            #Intersect1 contains ordered
            #pairs of x values
```

```
            Intersect1=np.sort(Intersect[0:Counter]);
            #We now trace lines between
            #pairs of intersections
            for n in range(0,Counter,2):
                XIntersect1=int(Intersect1[n]);
                XIntersect2=int(Intersect1[n+1]);
                Y=int(y)
                #Drawing an horizontal line
                #between x pairs
                Draw.line( (XIntersect1,
                           Y,XIntersect2,Y),
                           fill=(r,g,b), width=1 );
#----------------------------------------------------
def ShowScene(B):
    Array1=np.array(PilImage1);
    Array2=np.array(PilImage2);
    Array3=Array1 | Array2;

    PilImage3=Image.fromarray(Array3);

    Memory=io.BytesIO();
    PilImage3.save(Memory, format="png");
    Memory.seek(0);
    ImagePNG=CoreImage(Memory, ext="png");

    B.ids.Screen1.texture=ImagePNG.texture;
    ImagePNG.remove_from_cache()
    Memory.close();
    PilImage3.close();
    Array1=None;
    Array2=None;
    Array3=None;
```

```python
#-----------------------------------------------------
def ClearObjects():
    Draw1.rectangle( (0, 0, H-10, W-10),
                        fill=(60, 70, 30, 1) );
    Draw2.rectangle( (0, 0, H-10, W-10),
                        fill=(60, 70, 30, 1) );

class Form1(FloatLayout):
    def __init__(Handle, **kwargs):
        super(Form1, Handle).__init__(**kwargs);
        Event1=Clock.schedule_once(
                        Handle.Initialize);
        Event2=Clock.schedule_interval(
                        Handle.Temporal,0.1);

    def Initialize(B, *args):
        global W,H, XC,YC;
        global PilImage1,PilImage2, Draw1,Draw2;
        W,H=B.ids.Screen1.size;
        XC=int (W/2)
        YC=int(H/2)
        PilImage1= Image.new('RGB', (W-10, H-10),
                                (60, 70, 30));
        Draw1 = ImageDraw.Draw(PilImage1);
        PilImage2= Image.new('RGB', (W-10, H-10),
                                (60, 70, 30));
        Draw2 = ImageDraw.Draw(PilImage2);
        Font = ImageFont.truetype('Gargi.ttf', 70)
        Draw1.text( (30,200), "3D Images",
                    fill =(255,0,0,1), font=Font);
        Draw1.text( (50,200), "3D Images",
                    fill =(0,255,255,1), font=Font);
        ShowScene(B);
```

```python
def Temporal(B, *args):
    global Flag, NUMBER, p, q;
    if (Flag==True):
        if (B.ids.Button3.state=="down"):
            Sense=-1; p=0; q=1;
        if(B.ids.Button5.state=="down"):
            Sense=-1; p=0;q=2;
        if(B.ids.Button7.state=="down"):
            Sense=-1; p=1;q=2;

        if(B.ids.Button4.state=="down"):
            Sense=1; p=0;q=1;
        if(B.ids.Button6.state=="down"):
            Sense=1;p=0;q=2;
        if(B.ids.Button8.state=="down"):
            Sense=1;p=1;q=2;

        if(NUMBER==0):
            Rotate(Cube, Sense);
        if (NUMBER==1):
            Rotate(Pentagon, Sense);
        #  Clearing Draw1 and Draw2
        ClearObjects();

        DrawAxes(VX1,VY1,VZ1,0);
        DrawAxes(VX2,VY2,VZ2,1);

        FillPolygon(Cube,VX1,VY1,VZ1,0);
        DrawEdges(Cube,VX1,VY1,VZ1,0); #red cube

        FillPolygon(Cube,VX2,VY2,VZ2,1);
        DrawEdges(Cube,VX2,VY2,VZ2,1); #cyan cube
```

```
        #red pentagon
        FillPolygon(Pentagon,VX1,VY1,VZ1,0);
        DrawEdges(Pentagon,VX1,VY1,VZ1,0);

        #cyan pentagon
        FillPolygon(Pentagon,VX2,VY2,VZ2,1);
        DrawEdges(Pentagon,VX2,VY2,VZ2,1);

        ShowScene(B);
def Button1_Click(B):
    global Draw1, Draw2, PilImage1, PilImage2;
    #Clearing Draw1 and Draw2
    ClearObjects();

    DrawAxes(VX1,VY1,VZ1,0);
    DrawAxes(VX2,VY2,VZ2,1);

    FillPolygon(Cube,VX1,VY1,VZ1,0);
    DrawEdges(Cube,VX1,VY1,VZ1,0); #red cube

    FillPolygon(Cube,VX2,VY2,VZ2,1);
    DrawEdges(Cube,VX2,VY2,VZ2,1); #cyan cube

    #red pentagon
    FillPolygon(Pentagon,VX1,VY1,VZ1,0);
    DrawEdges(Pentagon,VX1,VY1,VZ1,0);

    #cyan pentagon
    FillPolygon(Pentagon,VX2,VY2,VZ2,1);
    DrawEdges(Pentagon,VX2,VY2,VZ2,1);

    ShowScene(B);
```

```python
def Button2_Click(B):
    #   Clearing Draw1 and Draw2
    ClearObjects();
    Font = ImageFont.truetype('Gargi.ttf', 70)
    Draw1.text( (30,200), "3D Images",
                  fill =(255,0,0,1), font=Font);
    Draw1.text( (50,200), "3D Images",
                  fill =(0,255,255,1), font=Font);
    ShowScene(B);

def Button3_Click(B):
    global Flag;
    Flag=True;

def Button3_Release(B):
    global Flag;
    Flag=False;

def Button4_Click(B):
    global Flag;
    Flag=True;

def Button4_Release(B):
    global Flag;
    Flag=False;

def Button5_Click(B):
    global Flag;
    Flag=True;

def Button5_Release(B):
    global Flag;
    Flag=False;
```

```python
    def Button6_Click(B):
        global Flag;
        Flag=True;

    def Button6_Release(B):
        global Flag;
        Flag=False;

    def Button7_Click(B):
        global Flag;
        Flag=True;

    def Button7_Release(B):
        global Flag;
        Flag=False;

    def Button8_Click(B):
        global Flag;
        Flag=True;

    def Button8_Release(B):
        global Flag;
        Flag=False;

    def Button9_Click(B):
        global NUMBER;
        NUMBER=(NUMBER+1)%2;
        B.ids.Label1.text=str(NUMBER);
# This is the Start Up code.
class StartUp (App):
    def build (BU):
        BU.title="Form1"
        return Form1();
if __name__ =="__main__":
    StartUp().run();
```

Listing 6-8. Code Listing for File.kv

```
#:set W 440
#:set H 440
<Form1>:
    id : Form1
    Image:
        id: Screen1
        size_hint: None,None
        pos_hint: {"x":0.04, "y":0.34}
        size: W,H
        canvas.before:
            Color:
                rgba: 0.8 ,0.8, 0.0 ,1
            RoundedRectangle:
                pos:   self.pos
                size: self.size
    Button:
        id: Button1
        on_press: Form1.Button1_Click()
        text: "Button1"
        size_hint: None,None
        pos_hint: {"x": 0.2, "y":0.03}
        size: 100,30

    Button:
        id: Button2
        on_press: Form1.Button2_Click()
        text: "Button2"
        size_hint: None,None
        pos_hint: {"x": 0.63, "y":0.03}
        size: 100,30
```

```
Button:
    id: Button3
    on_press: Form1.Button3_Click()
    on_release: Form1.Button3_Release()
    text: "Button3"
    size_hint: None,None
    pos_hint: {"x": 0.05, "y":0.12}
    size: 100,30
    always_release: True
Button:
    id: Button4
    on_press: Form1.Button4_Click()
    on_release:  Form1.Button4_Release()
    text: "Button4"
    size_hint: None,None
    pos_hint: {"x": 0.73, "y":0.12}
    size: 100,30

Button:
    id: Button5
    on_press: Form1.Button5_Click()
    on_release:  Form1.Button5_Release()
    text: "Button5"
    size_hint: None,None
    pos_hint: {"x": 0.05, "y":0.20}
    size: 100,30
Button:
    id: Button6
    on_press: Form1.Button6_Click()
    on_release:  Form1.Button6_Release()
```

```
    text: "Button6"
    size_hint: None,None
    pos_hint: {"x": 0.73, "y":0.20}
    size: 100,30
Button:
    id: Button7
    on_press: Form1.Button7_Click()
    on_release:  Form1.Button7_Release()
    text: "Button7"
    size_hint: None,None
    pos_hint: {"x": 0.05, "y":0.28}
    size: 100,30
Button:
    id: Button8
    on_press: Form1.Button8_Click()
    on_release:  Form1.Button8_Release()
    text: "Button8"
    size_hint: None,None
    pos_hint: {"x": 0.73, "y":0.28}
    size: 100,30

Button:
    id: Button9
    on_press: Form1.Button9_Click()
    text: "Button9"
    size_hint: None,None
    pos_hint: {"x": 0.38, "y":0.12}
    size: 100,30
```

```
Label:
    id: Label1
    text: "0"
    font_size: 30
    color: 1,1,0,1
    size_hint: None,None
    pos_hint: {"x": 0.38, "y":0.20}
    size: 100,30
```

6.7 Summary

In this chapter, we programmed the polygons in 3D stereoscopic scenes. We placed and rotated them using the three-dimensional projection equations derived in previous chapters. We created two images using Pillow and performed the logical OR between them using NumPy. Finally, the resulting ORed image was converted to a Kivy image and displayed on the screen.

CHAPTER 7

3D Plots Programming

In this chapter, we describe basic elements to create and plot functions of the form $f(x, y)$.

As an example, Figure 7-1 shows a circular Gaussian function of the program running on an Android cell phone.

© Moisés Cywiak, David Cywiak 2021
M. Cywiak and D. Cywiak, *Multi-Platform Graphics Programming with Kivy*,
https://doi.org/10.1007/978-1-4842-7113-1_7

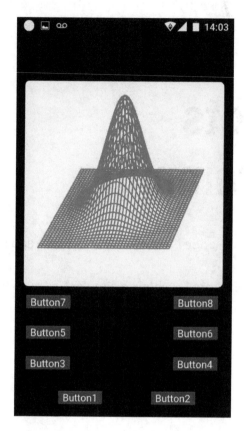

Figure 7-1. *Screenshot showing a 3D plot of a circular Gaussian function*

7.1 Programming the Basic Operations

The buttons in Figure 7-1 are used as follows.

Button1 shows the plot and Button2 clears the screen. Button3, Button5, and Button7 rotate and show the plot in a counterclockwise direction in steps of 5 degrees in the x-y, x-z, and y-z directions, respectively. Accordingly, Button4, Button6, and Button8 rotate the plot in clockwise directions.

In general, cell phones have limited speed capacities compared with computers. As a consequence, it is advisable to carefully press one of the buttons once and wait until the corresponding step completes.

7.2 Function Overview

The program can plot basically any function $f(x, y)$. For our example, we chose a circular Gaussian function, written as follows:

$$f(x,y) = A exp\left(-\frac{(x - x_0)^2 + (y - y_0)^2}{r_0^2}\right) \tag{7.1}$$

In Equation (7.1), A is the amplitude (or maximum vertical height) of the Gaussian function. The x_0 and y_0 parameters are used to shift the function from the origin. The r_0 parameter gives the semi-width of the function.

To display the plot in the screen, we need to take into account that the z-axis is normal to the screen, whereas the x- and y-axes are parallel to the screen. This is depicted in Figure 4-1, Chapter 4. Therefore, the vertical height distribution, given by $f(x, y)$ in Equation (7.1), must be rewritten as $y(x, z)$. This lets the y-coordinate take the roll of the vertical distribution function and the x- and z-coordinates take the roll of the horizontal and depth axes, respectively.

7.3 Generating the Axes, the Mesh, and the Function

To represent the function, it is convenient to start selecting an appropriate number of pixels, N. When setting this value, we must keep in mind that increasing N increases the precision of the plot at the cost of increasing the processing time. Conversely, decreasing N reduces the processing time, but lowers the accuracy of the results. Since we are dealing with three-dimensional data, a slight increment of N will only slightly improve the quality of the plots, but will drastically increase the processing time. According to our experience with the circular Gaussian function case, suitable graphs and processing times can be obtained when N ranges between 40 and 70.

The x- and z-axes are generated using the following code:

```
D=4000; L=140;

for n in range (0,N+1):
    x[n]=(n-N/2)/N*L;
    z[n]=(n-N/2)/N*L;
```

In this code, L represents the width of the plot and D is the distance between the plane of projection and the screen. Note that in the for loop, the $(n-N/2)/N*L$ equation will generate the x-axis ranging from $-L/2$ to $L/2$. In the for loop, when n equals 0, $x[0]$ takes the value $-L/2$. At the other end, when n is N, $x[N]$ takes the value $L/2$. Similarly, the z-axis ranges from $-L/2 +D/2$ to $L/2 +D/2$. This way, the z-axis represents an interval of length L, centered at $D/2$. These values will allow us to calculate the Gaussian function in the center of the screen and at a depth equal to $D/2$. This depth corresponds to the center point located between the plane of projection and the screen, as described in Chapter 6.

Now we proceed to calculate the two-dimensional array that corresponds to the $y[n][m]$ function with the following code:

```
for n in range(0,N+1):
    for m in range(0,N+1):
        y[n][m]=np.exp(- (x[n]**2 +z[m]**2)/r0**2 );
```

Note from this code that the amplitude (vertical height) of the Gaussian function is 1. The function is centered at x and z equal to 0.

Finally, to plot and rotate the function, we need to create the mesh. The code shown in Listing 7-1 creates and fills the mesh.

Listing 7-1. Creating and Filling the Mesh and the Vertical Coordinate

```
x1=np.zeros( (N+1,N+1) );
y1=np.zeros( (N+1,N+1) );
z1=np.zeros( (N+1,N+1) ); #Mesh
Scale_x=140; Scale_y=140; Scale_z=140;
for n in range (0,N+1):
    for m in range(0,N+1)
        x1[n][m]=Scale_x * x[n];
        z1[n][m]=Scale_z * z[m]+ZGO;
        y1[n][m]=Scale_y * y[n][m];
```

Arrays x1[n][m], y1[n][m], and z1[n][m] compose the mesh. All the arrays have sizes equal to that of y[n][m], which means a unique function value can be assigned to each point in the *x-z* plane. This condition is necessary to allow us to rotate the three-dimensional set of points represented by the function at the corresponding (x, z) values.

7.4 Plotting the Function on the Screen

The three-dimensional plot consists of drawing horizontal and vertical lines around a vicinity of the center of the function in the StencilView widget declared in the Kivy file called File.kv. To reduce the processing time as much as possible, instead of drawing individual lines between pairs of points in the screen, Kivy allows us to provide a list of points to draw lines in a sequential manner. This begins with the first point listed, to the last point in the list. We will take advantage of this property by defining an array that will store N+1 (x, y) points. The code to create this array is as follows:

```
#Array to store list of points
PointList=np.zeros( (N+1,2) );
```

To plot the function, we need values for *D*, *VX*, *VY*, *VZ*, and *N* as well as *x1*, *y*, and *z1*.

We use the following:

```
D=4000; VX=600; VY=1200; VZ=0;
Factor0 =(D-VZ) / (D/2-VZ);
N=40;
```

The *Factor0* parameter is used to position the function in the center of the screen.

Before placing the plot, we need to clear the screen. For this task, we use the following code:

```
B.ids.Screen1.canvas.clear(); #Clears the screen.
```

To plot the function, we use Equations (6.1), (6.2), and (6.3) to calculate each point in the screen, first in the horizontal direction and then in the vertical direction. Each calculation is stored in the array. The code for recording the horizontal lines in the *PointList* array is shown in Listing 7-2.

Listing 7-2. Code for Recording the Horizontal Lines in the PointList Array

```
for n in range (0,N+1):#Recording horizontal lines
        for m in range (0,N+1):
            Factor=(D-VZ)/(D-z1[n][m]-VZ);
            xA=XC+Factor*(x1[n][m]-VX)+Factor0*VX;
            yA=YC+Factor*(y[n][m]-VY)+Factor0*VY;
            PointList[m]=xA,yA;
```

Once a complete horizontal list of points is stored in the *PointList* array, the corresponding line is plotted by means of the following directive:

```
B.ids.Screen1.canvas.add(Line(points=
                    PointList.tolist(), width=1.3));
```

This process is repeated for the vertical lines.

GraphFunction(B) is in charge of drawing the plot. The parameter B is a handle to give us access to the widgets defined in *File.kv*.

The code that corresponds to GraphFunction(B)) is shown in Listing 7-3.

Listing 7-3. Code for GraphFunction(B)

```
def GraphFunction(B):
    global x1,y, z1, N, Step;
    B.ids.Screen1.canvas.clear(); #Clear the screen
    B.ids.Screen1.canvas.add( Color(1,0,0) ); #color

    for n in range (0,N+1):#Drawing horizontal lines
        for m in range (0,N+1):
            Factor=(D-VZ)/(D-z1[n][m]-VZ);
            xA=XC+Factor*(x1[n][m]-VX)+Factor0*VX;
            yA=YC+Factor*(y[n][m]-VY)+Factor0*VY;
            PointList[m]=xA,yA;
        B.ids.Screen1.canvas.add( Line(points=
                    PointList.tolist(), width=1.3));

    for n in range (0,N+1): #Drawing vertical lines
        for m in range (0,N+1, 1):
            Factor=(D-VZ)/(D-z1[m][n]-VZ);
            xA=XC+Factor*(x1[m][n]-VX)+Factor0*VX;
            yA=YC+Factor*(y[m][n]-VY)+Factor0*VY;
            PointList[m]=xA,yA;
        B.ids.Screen1.canvas.add( Line(points=
                    PointList.tolist(), width=1.3));
```

7.5 Rotating the Plot

Rotating the plot is performed by using Equations (4.26) and (4.27) for each direction of rotation. RotateFunction(B,Sense) receives the handle B to access the widgets and the parameter Sense, which takes the values 0 or 1 to indicate the sense of rotation. At each rotation, the code verifies which button is pressed and the requested sense of rotation. The code for RotateFunction(B,Sense) is shown in Listing 7-4.

Listing 7-4. Code for RotateFunction(B, Sense)

```
def RotateFunction(B, Sense):
    global p,q, x1, y, z1, D, N;
    if Sense==-1:
        Teta=np.pi/180*(-4.0);
    else:
        Teta=np.pi/180*(4.0);
    Cos_Teta=np.cos(Teta)
    Sin_Teta=np.sin(Teta);

    X0=0;  Y0=0;  Z0=D/2 # Center of rotation

    for n in range(0,N+1):
        for m in range(0,N+1):
            if (B.ids.Button3.state=="down" or
                    B.ids.Button4.state=="down"):
                yP=(y[n][m]-Y0)*Cos_Teta \
                    + (x1[n][m]-X0)*Sin_Teta + Y0;
                xP=-(y[n][m]-Y0)*Sin_Teta \
                    +(x1[n][m]-X0)*Cos_Teta + X0;
                y[n][m]=yP;
                x1[n][m]=xP;
```

```
    if (B.ids.Button5.state=="down" or
            B.ids.Button6.state=="down"):
        yP=(y[n][m]-Y0)*Cos_Teta \
            + (z1[n][m]-Z0)*Sin_Teta + Y0;
        zP=-(y[n][m]-Y0)*Sin_Teta \
            +(z1[n][m]-Z0)*Cos_Teta + Z0;
        y[n][m]=yP;
        z1[n][m]=zP;

    if (B.ids.Button7.state=="down" or
            B.ids.Button8.state=="down"):
        xP=(x1[n][m]-X0)*Cos_Teta \
            + (z1[n][m]-Z0)*Sin_Teta + X0;
        zP=-(x1[n][m]-X0)*Sin_Teta \
            +(z1[n][m]-Z0)*Cos_Teta + Z0;
        x1[n][m]=xP;
        z1[n][m]=zP;
```

The complete code listings for the main.py and File.kv files are shown in Listings 7-5 and 7-6, respectively.

Listing 7-5. Code for the main.py File

```
from kivy.app import App
from kivy.uix.floatlayout import FloatLayout
from kivy.graphics import Line, Ellipse, Color
from kivy.clock import Clock
import os
import numpy as np

from kivy.lang import Builder
Builder.load_file(
    os.path.join(os.path.dirname(os.path.abspath(
        __file__)), 'File.kv')
            );
```

```
#Avoid Form1 of being resizable
from kivy.config import Config
Config.set("graphics","resizable", False)
Config.set('graphics', 'width',  '480');
Config.set('graphics', 'height', '680');
#These values are adjusted by the function
#Initialize() after Clock.schedule_once has
#been executed.(XC,YC) = Canvas center,
#(W, H)= width, height of canvas

D=4000;
VX=600; VY=1200; VZ=0;
Factor0 =(D-VZ) / (D/2-VZ);
N=40;
#Coordinates arrays
x=np.zeros(N+1);
z=np.zeros(N+1); y=np.zeros( (N+1,N+1) );
#  Mesh
x1=np.zeros( (N+1,N+1) ); z1=np.zeros( (N+1,N+1) );
L=140;   r0=L/5;
for n in range (0,N+1):
    x[n]=(n-N/2)/N*L;
    z[n]=(n-N/2)/N*L+D/2;
for n in range(0,N+1):
    for m in range(0,N+1): #Create Gaussian function
        y[n][m]=120*np.exp(- ((x[n]-0)**2
                            +(z[m]-D/2)**2)/r0**2 );
for n in range (0,N+1):
    for m in range(0,N+1):#Filling Mesh
        x1[n][m]=x[n];
        z1[n][m]=z[m]
```

```python
PointList=np.zeros( (N+1,2) ); #Array to store list of points
def GraphFunction(B):
    global x1,y, z1, N, Step;
    B.ids.Screen1.canvas.clear(); #Clear the screen
    B.ids.Screen1.canvas.add( Color(1,0,0) ); #color

    for n in range (0,N+1):#Drawing horizontal lines
        for m in range (0,N+1):
            Factor=(D-VZ)/(D-z1[n][m]-VZ);
            xA=XC+Factor*(x1[n][m]-VX)+Factor0*VX;
            yA=YC+Factor*(y[n][m]-VY)+Factor0*VY;
            PointList[m]=xA,yA;
        B.ids.Screen1.canvas.add( Line(points=
                PointList.tolist(), width=1.3));

    for n in range (0,N+1): #Drawing vertical lines
        for m in range (0,N+1, 1):
            Factor=(D-VZ)/(D-z1[m][n]-VZ);
            xA=XC+Factor*(x1[m][n]-VX)+Factor0*VX;
            yA=YC+Factor*(y[m][n]-VY)+Factor0*VY;
            PointList[m]=xA,yA;
        B.ids.Screen1.canvas.add( Line(points=
                PointList.tolist(), width=1.3));

def RotateFunction(B, Sense):
    global p,q, x1, y, z1, D, N;
    if Sense===-1:
        Teta=np.pi/180*(-4.0);
    else:
        Teta=np.pi/180*(4.0);
    Cos_Teta=np.cos(Teta)
    Sin_Teta=np.sin(Teta);
```

```
    X0=0;   Y0=0;   Z0=D/2 # Center of rotation

for n in range(0,N+1):
    for m in range(0,N+1):
        if (B.ids.Button3.state=="down" or
                B.ids.Button4.state=="down"):
            yP=(y[n][m]-Y0)*Cos_Teta \
                + (x1[n][m]-X0)*Sin_Teta + Y0;
            xP=-(y[n][m]-Y0)*Sin_Teta \
                +(x1[n][m]-X0)*Cos_Teta + X0;
            y[n][m]=yP;
            x1[n][m]=xP;

        if (B.ids.Button5.state=="down" or
                B.ids.Button6.state=="down"):
            yP=(y[n][m]-Y0)*Cos_Teta \
                + (z1[n][m]-Z0)*Sin_Teta + Y0;
            zP=-(y[n][m]-Y0)*Sin_Teta \
                +(z1[n][m]-Z0)*Cos_Teta + Z0;
            y[n][m]=yP;
            z1[n][m]=zP;

        if (B.ids.Button7.state=="down" or
                B.ids.Button8.state=="down"):
            xP=(x1[n][m]-X0)*Cos_Teta \
                + (z1[n][m]-Z0)*Sin_Teta + X0;
            zP=-(x1[n][m]-X0)*Sin_Teta \
                +(z1[n][m]-Z0)*Cos_Teta + Z0;
            x1[n][m]=xP;
            z1[n][m]=zP;
```

```
class Form1(FloatLayout):
    def __init__(Handle, **kwargs):
        super(Form1, Handle).__init__(**kwargs);
        Event1=Clock.schedule_once(
                            Handle.Initialize);

    def Initialize(B, *args):
        global W,H, XC,YC;
        W,H=B.ids.Screen1.size;
        XI,YI=B.ids.Screen1.pos;
        XC=XI+int (W/2);
        YC=YI+int(H/2)-50;

    def Button1_Click(B):
        GraphFunction(B);

    def Button2_Click(B):
        B.ids.Screen1.canvas.clear();

    def Button3_Click(B):
        RotateFunction(B,1),
        GraphFunction(B);

    def Button4_Click(B):
        RotateFunction(B,-1),
        GraphFunction(B);

    def Button5_Click(B):
        RotateFunction(B,-1),
        GraphFunction(B);

    def Button6_Click(B):
        RotateFunction(B,1),
        GraphFunction(B);
```

```
    def Button7_Click(B):
        RotateFunction(B,-1),
        GraphFunction(B);

    def Button8_Click(B):
        RotateFunction(B,1),
        GraphFunction(B);

# This is the Start Up code.
class StartUp (App):
    def build (BU):
        BU.title="Form1"
        return Form1();
if __name__ =="__main__":
    StartUp().run();
```

Listing 7-6. Code for the File.kv File

```
#:set W 440
#:set H 440
<Form1>:
    id : Form1
    StencilView:
        id: Screen1
        size_hint: None,None
        pos_hint: {"x":0.04, "y":0.34}
        size: W,H
        canvas.before:
            Color:
                rgba: 0.9, 0.9, 0, 1
            RoundedRectangle:
                pos:  self.pos
                size: self.size
```

```
Button:
    id: Button1
    on_press: Form1.Button1_Click()
    text: "Button1"
    size_hint: None,None
    pos_hint: {"x": 0.2, "y":0.03}
    size: 100,30

Button:
    id: Button2
    on_press: Form1.Button2_Click()
    text: "Button2"
    size_hint: None,None
    pos_hint: {"x": 0.63, "y":0.03}
    size: 100,30

Button:
    id: Button3
    on_press: Form1.Button3_Click()
    text: "Button3"
    size_hint: None,None
    pos_hint: {"x": 0.05, "y":0.12}
    size: 100,30
    always_release: True
Button:
    id: Button4
    on_press: Form1.Button4_Click()
    text: "Button4"
    size_hint: None,None
    pos_hint: {"x": 0.73, "y":0.12}
    size: 100,30
```

```
Button:
    id: Button5
    on_press: Form1.Button5_Click()
    text: "Button5"
    size_hint: None,None
    pos_hint: {"x": 0.05, "y":0.20}
    size: 100,30
Button:
    id: Button6
    on_press: Form1.Button6_Click()
    text: "Button6"
    size_hint: None,None
    pos_hint: {"x": 0.73, "y":0.20}
    size: 100,30

Button:
    id: Button7
    on_press: Form1.Button7_Click()
    text: "Button7"
    size_hint: None,None
    pos_hint: {"x": 0.05, "y":0.28}
    size: 100,30
Button:
    id: Button8
    on_press: Form1.Button8_Click()
    text: "Button8"
    size_hint: None,None
    pos_hint: {"x": 0.73, "y":0.28}
    size: 100,30
```

As mentioned, this program can be used to plot distinct formulas. For example, instead of the Gaussian function, which is an even function, multiplying by x gives the following:

$$f(x,y) = A\, x\, exp\left(-\frac{x^2 + y^2}{r_0^2}\right) \tag{7.2}$$

Equation (7.2) is an odd function. The y[n][m] array to plot this function is filled, as shown in Listing 7-7.

Listing 7-7. Code for Filling y[n][m]

```
Amplitude =8;
for n in range(0,N+1):
    for m in range(0,N+1):
        y[n][m]=Amplitude*x[n]*np.exp(  - (x[n]**2 +z[m]**2)
        )/(r0**2 );
```

The corresponding plot obtained with this program is shown in Figure 7-2.

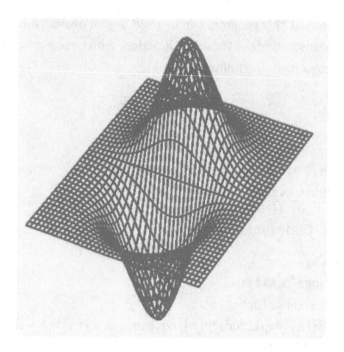

Figure 7-2. *Plot of a Gaussian function multiplied by x, obtained using this program*

7.6 Summary

In this chapter, we described basic elements to create and plot functions of the form $f(x, y)$. You learned how to generate the axes, the mesh, and the functions. You also learned how to rotate them and display them on the screen.

CHAPTER 8

Stereoscopic 3D Plots

In this chapter, we describe the basic elements for constructing stereoscopic 3D plots of analytical functions. A screenshot of this program obtained from an Android cell phone is shown in Figure 8-1.

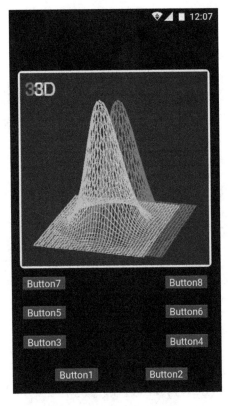

Figure 8-1. *Screenshot of the program running in an Android cell phone*

The functionality of the buttons is the same as in Chapter 7.

© Moisés Cywiak, David Cywiak 2021
M. Cywiak and D. Cywiak, *Multi-Platform Graphics Programming with Kivy*,
https://doi.org/10.1007/978-1-4842-7113-1_8

8.1 Creating the Function, Coordinates, and Mesh

The procedures to create the function, the coordinates, and the mesh are described in Chapter 7. The code is shown in Listing 8-1.

Listing 8-1. Creating the Mesh and the Discrete Function

```
P=0.5; # Function at z=D/2
N=40;   #Number of pixels for representing the function
#Arrays for filling function values
x=np.zeros(N+1);
z=np.zeros(N+1); y=np.zeros( (N+1,N+1) );
# Mesh
x1=np.zeros( (N+1,N+1) );
y1=np.zeros( (N+1,N+1) ); z1=np.zeros( (N+1,N+1) );
L=130;   r0=L/5; #L=Gaussian x-z scale. r0= semi-width
XG0=0; ZG0=P*D;
Amplitude=130; #Vertical scale

for n in range (0,N+1): #Filling the x-z axes
    x[n]=(n-N/2)/N*L;
    z[n]=(n-N/2)/N*L;
for n in range(0,N+1): #Filling function pixels
    for m in range(0,N+1):
        y[n][m]=Amplitude*np.exp(- (x[n]**2
                            +z[m]**2)/r0**2 );

Scale_x=1; Scale_y=1; Scale_z=1;
for n in range (0,N+1):
    for m in range(0,N+1):#Filling Mesh
        x1[n][m]=Scale_x* x[n];
        z1[n][m]=Scale_z*z[m]+ZG0;
        y1[n][m]=Scale_y*y[n][m];
```

As mentioned, this code is analogous to the code described in Chapter 7.

8.2 Creating Two Images for the Stereoscopic Effect

To produce the stereoscopic effect, we need to project the function onto two images using two points of projections that are slightly displaced horizontally. We use the parameters shown in Listing 8-2 for this purpose.

Listing 8-2. Setting Parameters for the Stereoscopic View

```
D=2000;
#Coordinates of the first point of projection.
VX1=-60; VY1=600; VZ1=0;
#Coordinates of the second point of projection.
VX2=60; VY2=600; VZ2=0;
P=0.5; # Percentage value of D; 50% places the function at z=D/2;
```

As in previous chapters, the parameter D is the distance from the plane of projection to the screen. The VX1 and VX2 parameters represent the horizontal coordinates of the point of projection and are displaced between them. The rest of the coordinates are given by VY1=VY2 and VZ1=VZ2. The P parameter represents a percentage of the distance, D, at which the function is placed. For the stereoscopic view, we will set P=0.5 to place the function in the middle, between the plane of projection and the screen.

Initialize(B, *args) is in charge of calculating the dimensions of the screen and of creating two PIL images with appropriate dimensions. These images are PilImage1 and PilImage2. Additionally, two drawing instances for the images are created, Draw1 and Draw2, to allow us to draw lines and text in the images. When the program starts, the 3D Images text is shown. Initialize(B, *args) is shown in Listing 8-3.

Listing 8-3. Code Initiating Variables When the Program Starts

```
def Initialize(B, *args):
        global W,H, XC,YC;
        global PilImage1,PilImage2, Draw1,Draw2;
        #P= Percentage of D distance
        global P, Amplitude;
        W,H=B.ids.Screen1.size;
        XC=int (W/2)+0;
        YC=int(H/2)+60;
        PilImage1= Image.new('RGB', (W-10, H-10),
                                (60, 70, 30));
        Draw1 = ImageDraw.Draw(PilImage1);
        PilImage2= Image.new('RGB', (W-10, H-10),
                                (60, 70, 30));
        Draw2 = ImageDraw.Draw(PilImage2);
        Font = ImageFont.truetype('Gargi.ttf', 70);
        Draw1.text( (30,200), "3D Images",
                    fill =(255,0,0,1), font=Font);
        Draw2.text( (50,200), "3D Images",
                    fill =(0,255,255,1), font=Font);
        ShowScene(B);
```

We need a third image, which we will name PilImage3, to store the result of bitwise ORing the left and right images. The ShowScene(B) function creates this array.

8.3 Drawing the Plot

GraphFunction(VX, VY, VZ, Which) is in charge of drawing the plot. The Which parameter selects the image to be used; PilImage1 if 0 and PilImage2 if 1. Accordingly, Draw1 or Draw2 will be used.

Drawing on the screen is a time-consuming process. Therefore, to plot the function, it is convenient to calculate the whole set of points of a horizontal or vertical line trace. We will store this set in an array. This way, we can plot the corresponding line with only one access to the screen memory, instead of drawing segment by segment between points. This way, we diminish the processing time.

We create the array by utilizing the PointList=np.zeros((N+1,2)) directive and proceed to calculate a line trace, which consists of N+1, (x, y) points, ranging from the position 0 to N. The points in the array cannot be displayed directly on the screen. We first have to create a list in the appropriate format. This list is created by means of the List=tuple(map(tuple,PointList)) directive. We proceed to draw the complete trace through the Draw.line(List, fill=(r,g,b), width=2) directive. The (r,g,b) parameters take the red or cyan color, according to the image selected, left or right, which is indicated by the Which parameter.

In the end, the function draws small text that reads 3D on the left corner of the scene.

The code for GraphFunction(VX,VY,VZ,Which) is shown in Listing 8-4.

Listing 8-4. Code for GraphFunction(VX,VY,VZ,Which)

```
def GraphFunction(VX,VY,VZ,Which):
    global x1,y1, z1, N;

    if (Which==0):
        r,g,b = 200, 0, 0; #red Image
        Draw=Draw1
```

```
    else:
        r,g,b= 0, 200, 200; #cyan image
        Draw=Draw2
    for n in range (0,N+1): #Horizontal Lines
        for m in range (0,N+1):
            Factor=(D-VZ)/(D-z1[n][m]-VZ);
            xA=XC+Factor*(x1[n][m]-VX)+VX \
                            +(P/(1-P))*VX;
            yA=YC-Factor*(y1[n][m]-VY)-VY \
                            -(P/(1-P))*VY;
            PointList[m]=xA,yA;
        List=tuple( map(tuple,PointList) );
        Draw.line( List, fill=(r,g,b), width=2 );

    for n in range (0,N+1): #Vertical Lines
        for m in range (0,N+1):
            Factor=(D-VZ)/(D-z1[m][n]-VZ);
            xA=XC+Factor*(x1[m][n]-VX)+VX \
                            + (P/(1-P))*VX;
            yA=YC-Factor*(y1[m][n]-VY)-VY \
                            -(P/(1-P))*VY;
            PointList[m]=xA,yA;
        List=tuple( map(tuple,PointList) );
        Draw.line( List, fill=(r,g,b), width=2 );

    Font = ImageFont.truetype('Gargi.ttf', 40);
    Draw1.text( (10,10), "3D", fill =
                    (255,0,0,1),font=Font);
    Draw2.text( (30,10), "3D", fill =
                    (0,255,255,1), font=Font);
```

The code listings for main.py and File.kv are shown in Listing 8-5 and 8-6, respectively.

Listing 8-5. The main.py Code

```
from kivy.app import App
from kivy.uix.floatlayout import FloatLayout
from kivy.graphics import Line, Ellipse, Color
from kivy.clock import Clock
from kivy.core.image import Image as CoreImage
from PIL import Image, ImageDraw, ImageFont
import io
import os
import numpy as np
from kivy.lang import Builder

Builder.load_file(
    os.path.join(os.path.dirname(os.path.abspath(
                        __file__)), 'File.kv')
            );
#Avoid Form1 of being resizable
from kivy.config import Config
Config.set("graphics","resizable", False);
Config.set('graphics', 'width',  '480');
Config.set('graphics', 'height', '680');
#These values are adjusted by the function
#Initialize() after Clock.schedule_once
#has been executed.
#Canvas center= (XC,YC) and width and height =(W,H);

D=2000;
VX1=-60; VY1=600; VZ1=0;
VX2=60; VY2=600; VZ2=0;

P=0.5; # Function at z=D/2
N=40;  #Number of pixels for representing the function
```

```
#Arrays for filling function values
x=np.zeros(N+1);
z=np.zeros(N+1); y=np.zeros( (N+1,N+1) );
# Mesh
x1=np.zeros( (N+1,N+1) );
y1=np.zeros( (N+1,N+1) ); z1=np.zeros( (N+1,N+1) );
L=130;   r0=L/5; #L=Gaussian x-z scale. r0= semi-width
XG0=0; ZG0=P*D;
Amplitude=130; #Vertical scale

for n in range (0,N+1): #Filling the x-z axes
    x[n]=(n-N/2)/N*L;
    z[n]=(n-N/2)/N*L;
for n in range(0,N+1): #Filling function pixels
    for m in range(0,N+1):
        y[n][m]=Amplitude*np.exp(- (x[n]**2
                            +z[m]**2)/r0**2 );

Scale_x=1; Scale_y=1; Scale_z=1;
for n in range (0,N+1):
    for m in range(0,N+1):#Filling Mesh
        x1[n][m]=Scale_x* x[n];
        z1[n][m]=Scale_z*z[m]+ZG0;
        y1[n][m]=Scale_y*y[n][m];

PointList=np.zeros( (N+1,2) );
def GraphFunction(VX,VY,VZ,Which):
    global x1,y1, z1, N;

    if (Which==0):
        r,g,b = 200, 0, 0; #red Image
        Draw=Draw1
```

```
else:
    r,g,b= 0, 200, 200; #cyan image
    Draw=Draw2
for n in range (0,N+1): #Horizontal Lines
    for m in range (0,N+1):
        Factor=(D-VZ)/(D-z1[n][m]-VZ);
        xA=XC+Factor*(x1[n][m]-VX)+VX \
                    +(P/(1-P))*VX;
        yA=YC-Factor*(y1[n][m]-VY)-VY \
                    -(P/(1-P))*VY;
        PointList[m]=xA,yA;
    List=tuple( map(tuple,PointList) );
    Draw.line( List, fill=(r,g,b), width=2 );

for n in range (0,N+1): #Vertical Lines
    for m in range (0,N+1):
        Factor=(D-VZ)/(D-z1[m][n]-VZ);
        xA=XC+Factor*(x1[m][n]-VX)+VX \
                    + (P/(1-P))*VX;
        yA=YC-Factor*(y1[m][n]-VY)-VY \
                    -(P/(1-P))*VY;
        PointList[m]=xA,yA;
    List=tuple( map(tuple,PointList) );
    Draw.line( List, fill=(r,g,b), width=2 );

Font = ImageFont.truetype('Gargi.ttf', 40);
Draw1.text( (10,10), "3D", fill =
            (255,0,0,1),font=Font);
Draw2.text( (30,10), "3D", fill =
            (0,255,255,1), font=Font);
```

```python
def ShowScene(B):
    Array1=np.array(PilImage1);
    Array2=np.array(PilImage2);
    Array3=Array1 | Array2;

    PilImage3=Image.fromarray(Array3);

    Memory=io.BytesIO();
    PilImage3.save(Memory, format="png");
    Memory.seek(0);
    ImagePNG=CoreImage(Memory, ext="png");

    B.ids.Screen1.texture=ImagePNG.texture;
    ImagePNG.remove_from_cache()
    Memory.close();
    PilImage3.close();
    Array1=None;
    Array2=None;
    Array3=None;

def ClearObjects():
    Draw1.rectangle( (0, 0, W-10, H-10),
                      fill=(60, 70, 30, 1) );
    Draw2.rectangle( (0, 0, W-10, H-10),
                      fill=(60, 70, 30, 1) );

def RotateFunction(B, Sense):
    global XGO, ZGO
    if Sense==-1:
        Teta=np.pi/180*(-4.0);
    else:
        Teta=np.pi/180*(4.0);
    Cos_Teta=np.cos(Teta)
    Sin_Teta=np.sin(Teta);
```

```
XO=XGO;  YO=0;  ZO=ZGO # Center of rotation

for n in range(0,N+1):
    for m in range(0,N+1):
        if (B.ids.Button3.state=="down" or
                B.ids.Button4.state=="down"):
            yP=(y1[n][m]-YO)*Cos_Teta \
                + (x1[n][m]-XO)*Sin_Teta + YO;
            xP=-(y1[n][m]-YO)*Sin_Teta \
                +(x1[n][m]-XO)*Cos_Teta + XO;
            y1[n][m]=yP;
            x1[n][m]=xP;

        if (B.ids.Button5.state=="down" or
                B.ids.Button6.state=="down"):
            yP=(y1[n][m]-YO)*Cos_Teta \
                + (z1[n][m]-ZO)*Sin_Teta + YO;
            zP=-(y1[n][m]-YO)*Sin_Teta \
                +(z1[n][m]-ZO)*Cos_Teta + ZO;
            y1[n][m]=yP;
            z1[n][m]=zP;

        if (B.ids.Button7.state=="down" or
                B.ids.Button8.state=="down"):
            xP=(x1[n][m]-XO)*Cos_Teta \
                + (z1[n][m]-ZO)*Sin_Teta + XO;
            zP=-(x1[n][m]-XO)*Sin_Teta \
                +(z1[n][m]-ZO)*Cos_Teta + ZO;
            x1[n][m]=xP;
            z1[n][m]=zP;
```

```python
class Form1(FloatLayout):
    def __init__(Handle, **kwargs):
        super(Form1, Handle).__init__(**kwargs);
        Event1=Clock.schedule_once(
                            Handle.Initialize);

    def Initialize(B, *args):
        global W,H, XC,YC;
        global PilImage1,PilImage2, Draw1,Draw2;
        #P= Percentage of D distance
        global P, Amplitude;
        W,H=B.ids.Screen1.size;
        XC=int (W/2)+0;
        YC=int(H/2)+60;
        PilImage1= Image.new('RGB', (W-10, H-10),
                                (60, 70, 30));
        Draw1 = ImageDraw.Draw(PilImage1);
        PilImage2= Image.new('RGB', (W-10, H-10),
                                (60, 70, 30));
        Draw2 = ImageDraw.Draw(PilImage2);
        Font = ImageFont.truetype('Gargi.ttf', 70);
        Draw1.text( (30,200), "3D Images",
                    fill =(255,0,0,1), font=Font);
        Draw2.text( (50,200), "3D Images",
                    fill =(0,255,255,1), font=Font);
        ShowScene(B);

    def Button1_Click(B):
        global Draw1, Draw2;
        ClearObjects(); # Clearing Draw1 and Draw2
        GraphFunction(VX1,VY1,VZ1,0);
        GraphFunction(VX2,VY2,VZ2,1);
        ShowScene(B);
```

```
def Button2_Click(B):
    ClearObjects(); # Clearing Draw1 and Draw2
    Font = ImageFont.truetype('Gargi.ttf', 70)
    Draw1.text( (30,200), "3D Images",
                fill =(255,0,0,1), font=Font);
    Draw2.text( (50,200), "3D Images",
                fill =(0,255,255,1), font=Font);
    ShowScene(B);

def Button3_Click(B):
    RotateFunction(B,1);
    ClearObjects(); # Clearing Draw1 and Draw2
    GraphFunction(VX1,VY1,VZ1,0);
    GraphFunction(VX2,VY2,VZ2,1);
    ShowScene(B);

def Button4_Click(B):
    RotateFunction(B,-1),
    ClearObjects();
    GraphFunction(VX1,VY1,VZ1,0);
    GraphFunction(VX2,VY2,VZ2,1);
    ShowScene(B);

def Button5_Click(B):
    RotateFunction(B,-1),
    ClearObjects();
    GraphFunction(VX1,VY1,VZ1,0);
    GraphFunction(VX2,VY2,VZ2,1);
    ShowScene(B);

def Button6_Click(B):
    RotateFunction(B,1),
    ClearObjects();
    GraphFunction(VX1,VY1,VZ1,0);
```

```
        GraphFunction(VX2,VY2,VZ2,1);
        ShowScene(B);

    def Button7_Click(B):
        RotateFunction(B,-1),
        ClearObjects();
        GraphFunction(VX1,VY1,VZ1,0);
        GraphFunction(VX2,VY2,VZ2,1);
        ShowScene(B);

    def Button8_Click(B):
        RotateFunction(B,1),
        ClearObjects();
        GraphFunction(VX1,VY1,VZ1,0);
        GraphFunction(VX2,VY2,VZ2,1);
        ShowScene(B);

# This is the Start Up code.
class StartUp (App):
    def build (BU):
        BU.title="Form1"
        return Form1();
if __name__ =="__main__":
    StartUp().run();
```

Listing 8-6. The file.kv Code

```
#:set W 440
#:set H 440
<Form1>:
    id : Form1
    Image:
        id: Screen1
        size_hint: None,None
```

```
    pos_hint: {"x":0.04, "y":0.34}
    size: W,H
    canvas.before:
        Color:
            rgba: 0.9, 0.9, 0, 1
        RoundedRectangle:
            pos:  self.pos
            size: self.size
Button:
    id: Button1
    on_press: Form1.Button1_Click()
    text: "Button1"
    size_hint: None,None
    pos_hint: {"x": 0.2, "y":0.03}
    size: 100,30

Button:
    id: Button2
    on_press: Form1.Button2_Click()
    text: "Button2"
    size_hint: None,None
    pos_hint: {"x": 0.63, "y":0.03}
    size: 100,30

Button:
    id: Button3
    on_press: Form1.Button3_Click()
    text: "Button3"
    size_hint: None,None
    pos_hint: {"x": 0.05, "y":0.12}
    size: 100,30
    always_release: True
```

```
Button:
    id: Button4
    on_press: Form1.Button4_Click()
    text: "Button4"
    size_hint: None,None
    pos_hint: {"x": 0.73, "y":0.12}
    size: 100,30

Button:
    id: Button5
    on_press: Form1.Button5_Click()
    text: "Button5"
    size_hint: None,None
    pos_hint: {"x": 0.05, "y":0.20}
    size: 100,30
Button:
    id: Button6
    on_press: Form1.Button6_Click()
    text: "Button6"
    size_hint: None,None
    pos_hint: {"x": 0.73, "y":0.20}
    size: 100,30

Button:
    id: Button7
    on_press: Form1.Button7_Click()
    text: "Button7"
    size_hint: None,None
    pos_hint: {"x": 0.05, "y":0.28}
    size: 100,30
```

```
Button:
    id: Button8
    on_press: Form1.Button8_Click()
    text: "Button8"
    size_hint: None,None
    pos_hint: {"x": 0.73, "y":0.28}
    size: 100,30
```

8.4 Surfaces with Saddle Points

In calculus and 3D geometry, an important field of surface studies deals with saddle points. A *saddle point* is a point of a surface that is a maximum of a linear path around the vicinity of the point along one direction and at the same time a minimum of another path along a different direction. A typical illustrative example of a surface with a saddle point is represented by this equation:

$$f(x,y) = x^3 - 3xz^2 \tag{8.1}$$

To plot Equation (8.1), we have to replace the code of the Gaussian function in the main.py listing with the code in Listing 8-7.

Listing 8-7. Code for Plotting Equation (8.1)

```
L=120;   LP=L/2;
XGO=0;  ZGO=P*D;
Amplitude=30; #Vertical scale

for n in range (0,N+1): #Filling the x-z axes
    x[n]=(n-N/2)/N*L;
    z[n]=(n-N/2)/N*L+ZGO;
```

```
for n in range(0,N+1): #Filling function pixels
    for m in range(0,N+1):
        y[n][m]=Amplitude*( (x[n]/LP)**3
                   -3*(x[n]/LP)*( (z[m]-ZGO)/LP )**2 );
for n in range (0,N+1):
    for m in range(0,N+1):#Filling Mesh
        x1[n][m]= x[n];
        z1[n][m]=z[m];
        y1[n][m]=y[n][m];
```

Figure 8-2 shows a plot obtained with this program.

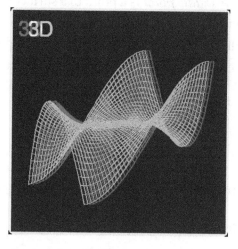

Figure 8-2. *Plot obtained with the program of Equation (8.1) showing a saddle point*

Another equation showing a typical saddle point is as follows:

$$f(x,y) = xy \qquad (8.2)$$

The corresponding plot obtained with this program is shown in Figure 8-3.

Figure 8-3. *Plot obtained with the program of Equation (8.2) showing a saddle point*

8.5 Summary

In this chapter, we described elements for constructing stereoscopic 3D plots of analytical functions. We showed how to incorporate the coordinates and the mesh. Additionally, we described how to create the required PIL images that are ORed and convert the resulting image into a Kivy one to display it on the screen.

CHAPTER 9

Parametric 3D Plotting

In this chapter, we present basic elements for parametric 3D plotting. A typical example on this subject consists of a three-dimensional circular helix, shown in Figure 9-1, which was obtained from a screenshot of this program running on an Android cell phone.

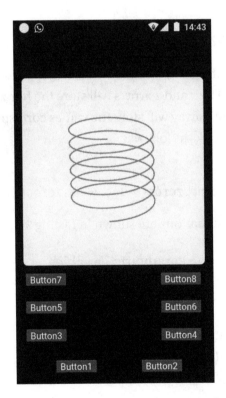

Figure 9-1. *Screenshot of the program showing a helix, obtained with 3D parametric equations*

© Moisés Cywiak, David Cywiak 2021
M. Cywiak and D. Cywiak, *Multi-Platform Graphics Programming with Kivy*,
https://doi.org/10.1007/978-1-4842-7113-1_9

The buttons in Figure 9-1 have the same functionality as described in Chapter 7.

9.1 Parametric Equations

Three-dimensional parametric equations consist of representing the three-dimensional spatial coordinates (x, y, z) as functions of a single parameter. For programming purposes, this parameter can be an integer that varies between 0 and a maximum value.

To begin with, as in previous chapters, we define the parameters, which are required to perform the projection:

```
D=4000;
VX=180; VY=200; VZ=0;
```

Next, we create three one-dimensional arrays of size N+1, ranging from entries 0 to N. The x and z arrays will store the horizontal and depth coordinates, and the y array will store the values corresponding to the function. The code looks as follows:

```
N=200;
x=np.zeros(N+1); z=np.zeros(N+1); y=np.zeros(N+1);
```

The parametric equations are shown in Listing 9-1.

Listing 9-1. Filling the Parametric Variables

```
Pi=np.pi;
L=50;
for n in range (0,N+1):
    x[n]=L*np.sin(12*Pi/N*n);
    z[n]=L*np.cos(12*Pi/N*n);
    y[n]=n/N*100;
```

In this code, the x[n] and z[n] arrays store the values that correspond to the parametric equations of a circle with radius equal to L. This can be verified by calculating $(x[n]^{**}2 + (z[n])^{**}2)$, which equals L^2. The number 12 in the sine and cosine arguments represents the speed of rotation of the helix. If this number is lowered, the helix will exhibit fewer turns.

In the for loop, the y[n]=n/N*100 directive fills the vertical array with values ranging from 0 to 100, which corresponds to the height of the helix.

To visualize how the helix is drawn, note that as n increases within the for loop, the path of a circle is generated on the x-z plane. At the same time, the vertical height, y, increases, thereby generating the circular helix.

9.2 Plotting

The plot is performed by the GraphFunction(B) function. First, the function creates an array to store the complete set of points that makes up the helix, using the PointList = np.zeros ((N + 1, 2)) directive. Then, we draw the lines that join the set of points, by utilizing this directive:

```
B.ids.Screen1.canvas.add( Line(points=
              PointList.tolist(), width=1.3)) ;
```

The corresponding code is shown in Listing 9-2.

Listing 9-2. Code for Plotting the Function

```
#Array to store list of points
PointList=np.zeros( (N+1,2) );

def GraphFunction(B):
    global x,y, z, N, D, VX, VY, VZ, Shift;

    B.ids.Screen1.canvas.clear(); #Clear the screen
    #Color to draw
```

```
B.ids.Screen1.canvas.add( Color(1,0,0) );
for n in range (0,N+1):      #Drawing
    Factor=(D-VZ)/(D-(z[n]+ZG0)-VZ);
    xA=XC+Factor*(x[n]-VX)+VX+ (P/(1-P))*VX;
    yA=YC+Factor*(y[n]-VY)+VY+ (P/(1-P))*VY;
    PointList[n]=xA,yA;
B.ids.Screen1.canvas.add( Line(points=
            PointList.tolist(), width=1.3)) ;
```

The code listings for main.py and File.kv are shown in Listings 9-3 and 9-4, respectively.

Listing 9-3. Code for the main.py File

```
from kivy.app import App
from kivy.uix.floatlayout import FloatLayout
from kivy.graphics import Line, Color
from kivy.clock import Clock
import os
import numpy as np

from kivy.lang import Builder
Builder.load_file(
    os.path.join(os.path.dirname(os.path.abspath(__file__)),
    'File.kv')
    )

#Avoid Form1 of being resizable
from kivy.config import Config
Config.set("graphics","resizable", False)
Config.set('graphics', 'width',  '480');
Config.set('graphics', 'height', '680');
#These values are adjusted by the function
#Initialize() after Clock.schedule_once
```

```
#has been executed.
#Canvas center= (XC,YC) and width and height =(W,H);

D=4000;
VX=180; VY=200; VZ=0;
#Factor0 =(D-VZ) / (D/2-VZ);

N=200;
x=np.zeros(N+1); z=np.zeros(N+1); y=np.zeros(N+1);
P=0.5;
ZG0=P*D;
Pi=np.pi;
L=50;
for n in range (0,N+1):
    x[n]=L*np.sin(12*Pi/N*n);
    z[n]=L*np.cos(12*Pi/N*n);
    y[n]=n/N*100;

#Array to store list of points
PointList=np.zeros( (N+1,2) );
def GraphFunction(B):
    global x,y, z, N, D, VX, VY, VZ, Shift;

    B.ids.Screen1.canvas.clear(); #Clear the screen
    #Color to draw
    B.ids.Screen1.canvas.add( Color(1,0,0) );
    for n in range (0,N+1):    #Drawing
        Factor=(D-VZ)/(D-(z[n]+ZG0)-VZ);
        xA=XC+Factor*(x[n]-VX)+VX+ (P/(1-P))*VX;
        yA=YC+Factor*(y[n]-VY)+VY+ (P/(1-P))*VY;
        PointList[n]=xA,yA;
    B.ids.Screen1.canvas.add( Line(points=
            PointList.tolist(), width=1.3)) ;
```

```python
def RotateFunction(B, Sense):
    global x, y, z, D, N;
    if Sense==-1:
        Teta=np.pi/180*(-4.0);
    else:
        Teta=np.pi/180*(4.0);
    Cos_Teta=np.cos(Teta)
    Sin_Teta=np.sin(Teta);

    X0=0;  Y0=0;  Z0=ZG0 # Center of rotation

    for n in range(0,N+1):
        if (B.ids.Button3.state=="down" or
                B.ids.Button4.state=="down"):
            yP=(y[n]-Y0)*Cos_Teta \
                    + (x[n]-X0)*Sin_Teta;
            xP=-(y[n]-Y0)*Sin_Teta \
                    +(x[n]-X0)*Cos_Teta;
            y[n]=yP;
            x[n]=xP;

        if (B.ids.Button5.state=="down" or
                B.ids.Button6.state=="down"):
            yP=(y[n]-Y0)*Cos_Teta \
                    + z[n]*Sin_Teta;
            zP=-(y[n]-Y0)*Sin_Teta \
                    +z[n]*Cos_Teta;
            y[n]=yP;
            z[n]=zP;

        if (B.ids.Button7.state=="down" or
                B.ids.Button8.state=="down"):
            xP=(x[n]-X0)*Cos_Teta \
                    + z[n]*Sin_Teta;
```

```
            zP=-(x[n]-X0)*Sin_Teta \
                        +z[n]*Cos_Teta;
            x[n]=xP;
            z[n]=zP;

class Form1(FloatLayout):
    def __init__(Handle, **kwargs):
        super(Form1, Handle).__init__(**kwargs);
        Event1=Clock.schedule_once(
                            Handle.Initialize);

    def Initialize(B, *args):
        global W,H, XC,YC;
        W,H=B.ids.Screen1.size;
        XI,YI=B.ids.Screen1.pos
        XC=XI+int (W/2);
        YC=YI+int(H/2)-80;

    def Button1_Click(B):
        GraphFunction(B);

    def Button2_Click(B):
        B.ids.Screen1.canvas.clear();

    def Button3_Click(B):
        RotateFunction(B,1),
        GraphFunction(B);

    def Button4_Click(B):
        RotateFunction(B,-1),
        GraphFunction(B);

    def Button5_Click(B):
        RotateFunction(B,-1),
        GraphFunction(B);
```

```
    def Button6_Click(B):
        RotateFunction(B,1),
        GraphFunction(B);

    def Button7_Click(B):

        RotateFunction(B,-1),
        GraphFunction(B);

    def Button8_Click(B):
        RotateFunction(B,1),
        GraphFunction(B);

# This is the Start Up code.
class StartUp (App):
    def build (BU):
        BU.title="Form1"
        return Form1();
if __name__ =="__main__":
    StartUp().run();
```

Listing 9-4. Code for the file.kv File

```
#:set W 440
#:set H 440
<Form1>:
    id : Form1
    StencilView:
        id: Screen1
        size_hint: None,None
        pos_hint: {"x":0.04, "y":0.34}
        size: W,H
        canvas.before:
            Color:
                rgba: 0.9, 0.9, 0, 1
```

```
        RoundedRectangle:
            pos:  self.pos
            size: self.size
Button:
    id: Button1
    on_press: Form1.Button1_Click()
    text: "Button1"
    size_hint: None,None
    pos_hint: {"x": 0.2, "y":0.03}
    size: 100,30

Button:
    id: Button2
    on_press: Form1.Button2_Click()
    text: "Button2"
    size_hint: None,None
    pos_hint: {"x": 0.63, "y":0.03}
    size: 100,30

Button:
    id: Button3
    on_press: Form1.Button3_Click()
    text: "Button3"
    size_hint: None,None
    pos_hint: {"x": 0.05, "y":0.12}
    size: 100,30
    always_release: True
Button:
    id: Button4
    on_press: Form1.Button4_Click()
    text: "Button4"
    size_hint: None,None
```

```
        pos_hint: {"x": 0.73, "y":0.12}
        size: 100,30
    Button:
        id: Button5
        on_press: Form1.Button5_Click()
        text: "Button5"
        size_hint: None,None
        pos_hint: {"x": 0.05, "y":0.20}
        size: 100,30
    Button:
        id: Button6
        on_press: Form1.Button6_Click()
        text: "Button6"
        size_hint: None,None
        pos_hint: {"x": 0.73, "y":0.20}
        size: 100,30
    Button:
        id: Button7
        on_press: Form1.Button7_Click()
        text: "Button7"
        size_hint: None,None
        pos_hint: {"x": 0.05, "y":0.28}
        size: 100,30
    Button:
        id: Button8
        on_press: Form1.Button8_Click()
        text: "Button8"
        size_hint: None,None
        pos_hint: {"x": 0.73, "y":0.28}
        size: 100,30
```

9.3 Summary

In this chapter, we described elements for parametric 3D plotting. As a typical example, we presented code for a three-dimensional circular helix.

CHAPTER 10

Stereoscopic parametric 3D Plots

In this chapter, we present basic elements for constructing parametric 3D plots. A screenshot of a circular helix generated with this program running on an Android cell phone is shown in Figure 10-1.

© Moisés Cywiak, David Cywiak 2021
M. Cywiak and D. Cywiak, *Multi-Platform Graphics Programming with Kivy*,
https://doi.org/10.1007/978-1-4842-7113-1_10

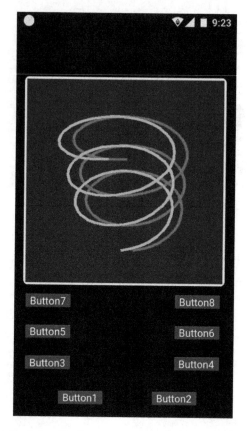

Figure 10-1. *Android cell phone screenshot of a circular helix generated with this program*

The buttons have the same functionality as described in Chapter 7.

10.1 Generating the Function

The code to generate the circular helix is shown in Listing 10-1.

Listing 10-1. Generating the Circular Helix

```
#Number of pixels for representing the function
N=100;
x=np.zeros(N+1); z=np.zeros(N+1); y=np.zeros(N+1);

L=50;  Pi=np.pi;
for n in range (0,N+1):
    x[n]=L*np.sin(6*Pi/N*n);
    z[n]=L*np.cos(6*Pi/N*n) +D/2;
for n in range(0,N+1):
    y[n]=n/N*100;
```

10.2 Creating the PIL Images for the Stereoscopic Effect

The Initialize(B, *args) function obtains the dimensions of the screen and creates PilImage1 and PilImage2. Additionally, the function creates the instances Draw1 and Draw2, where the left and right plots will be drawn. A TrueType Font (TTF) is selected to display the 3D Images text when the program starts. The code for Initialize(B, *args) is shown in Listing 10-2.

Listing 10-2. The Initialize Function

```
def Initialize(B, *args):
        global W,H, XC,YC;
        global PilImage1,PilImage2, Draw1,Draw2;
        # P= Percentage of the D distance
        global P, Amplitude;
        W,H=B.ids.Screen1.size;
```

```
XC=int (W/2)+20;
YC=int(H/2)+60;
PilImage1= Image.new('RGB', (W-10, H-10),
                          (60, 70, 30));
Draw1 = ImageDraw.Draw(PilImage1);
PilImage2= Image.new('RGB', (W-10, H-10),
                          (60, 70, 30));
Draw2 = ImageDraw.Draw(PilImage2);
Font = ImageFont.truetype('Gargi.ttf', 70);
Draw1.text( (30,200), "3D Images", fill =(
                   255,0,0,1), font=Font);
Draw2.text( (50,200), "3D Images", fill =
                (0,255,255,1), font=Font);
ShowScene(B);
```

10.3 Plotting the Function

As described in Chapter 8, drawing memory on the screen is a time-consuming process. Therefore, it is convenient to allocate a memory region of the appropriate size to store the complete set of consecutive points for circular helix. This way, we can draw the plot with only one access to the screen memory, reducing the processing time.

We create the array by means of this directive:

```
PointList=np.zeros( (N+1,2) )
```

Next, we fill the array with the list of points. After this, we use this directive to convert the data stored in the array into the appropriate tuple list required by PIL for drawing:

```
List=tuple( map(tuple,PointList) )
```

Finally, the following directive draws the plot:

```
Draw.line( List, fill=(r,g,b), width=6 )
```

As the helix aspect is similar to a wire, for better visualization, we set the drawing line width equal to 6.

These directives are enclosed in the GraphFunction(VX, VY, VZ, Which) function. This function receives the parameters corresponding to the left or to the right projections, depending on whether the variable Which receives the value 0 or 1. The code for GraphFunction(VX, VY, VZ, Which) is shown in Listing 10-3.

Listing 10-3. Code for Plotting the Function

```
PointList=np.zeros( (N+1,2) );
def GraphFunction(VX,VY,VZ,Which):
    global x,y, z, N;
    if (Which==0):
        r,g,b = 250, 0, 0; #red Image
        Draw=Draw1
    else:
        r,g,b= 0, 250, 250; #cyan image
        Draw=Draw2
    for n in range (0,N+1):     #Drawing
        Factor=(D-VZ)/(D-z[n]-VZ);
        xA=XC+Factor*(x[n]-VX)+VX+ShiftX;
        yA=YC-Factor*(y[n]-VY)-VY+ShiftY;
        PointList[n]=xA,yA;
    List=tuple( map(tuple,PointList) );
    Draw.line( List, fill=(r,g,b), width=6 );
```

This code generates the left and right images with the required plots. Now, the ShowScene(B) function will create the necessary arrays for ORing the PIL images and displaying the result on the screen, in the same manner as described in previous chapters. The code for **ShowScene(B)** is shown in Listing 10-4.

Listing 10-4. Code for Displaying the Scene

```
def ShowScene(B):
    Array1=np.array(PilImage1);
    Array2=np.array(PilImage2);
    Array3=Array1 | Array2;

    PilImage3=Image.fromarray(Array3);

    Memory=io.BytesIO();
    PilImage3.save(Memory, format="png");
    Memory.seek(0);
    ImagePNG=CoreImage(Memory, ext="png");

    B.ids.Screen1.texture=ImagePNG.texture;
    ImagePNG.remove_from_cache()
    Memory.close();
    PilImage3.close();
    Array1=None;
    Array2=None;
    Array3=None;
```

The code for main.py and File.kv are shown in Listings 10-5 and 10-6, respectively.

Listing 10-5. Code for the main.py File

```
from kivy.app import App
from kivy.uix.floatlayout import FloatLayout
from kivy.graphics import Line, Color
from kivy.clock import Clock
from kivy.core.image import Image as CoreImage
from PIL import Image, ImageDraw, ImageFont
import io
import os
import numpy as np
from kivy.lang import Builder

Builder.load_file(
    os.path.join(os.path.dirname(os.path.abspath(
                 __file__)), 'File.kv')
             );
#Avoid Form1 of being resizable
from kivy.config import Config
Config.set("graphics","resizable", False);
Config.set('graphics', 'width',  '480');
Config.set('graphics', 'height', '680');

D=1000;
VX1=180; VY1=200; VZ1=0;
VX2=200; VY2=200; VZ2=0;
ShiftX=VX1; ShiftY=-VY1;
#Number of pixels for representing the function
N=100;
x=np.zeros(N+1); z=np.zeros(N+1); y=np.zeros(N+1);
```

```
L=50;   Pi=np.pi;
for n in range (0,N+1):
    x[n]=L*np.sin(6*Pi/N*n);
    z[n]=L*np.cos(6*Pi/N*n) +D/2;
for n in range(0,N+1):
    y[n]=n/N*100;

PointList=np.zeros( (N+1,2) );
def GraphFunction(VX,VY,VZ,Which):
    global x,y, z, N;
    if (Which==0):
        r,g,b = 250, 0, 0; #red Image
        Draw=Draw1
    else:
        r,g,b= 0, 250, 250; #cyan image
        Draw=Draw2
    for n in range (0,N+1):     #Drawing
        Factor=(D-VZ)/(D-z[n]-VZ);
        xA=XC+Factor*(x[n]-VX)+VX+ShiftX;
        yA=YC-Factor*(y[n]-VY)-VY+ShiftY;
        PointList[n]=xA,yA;
    List=tuple( map(tuple,PointList) );
    Draw.line( List, fill=(r,g,b), width=6 );

def ShowScene(B):
    Array1=np.array(PilImage1);
    Array2=np.array(PilImage2);
    Array3=Array1 | Array2;

    PilImage3=Image.fromarray(Array3);

    Memory=io.BytesIO();
    PilImage3.save(Memory, format="png");
```

```
    Memory.seek(0);
    ImagePNG=CoreImage(Memory, ext="png");

    B.ids.Screen1.texture=ImagePNG.texture;
    ImagePNG.remove_from_cache()
    Memory.close();
    PilImage3.close();
    Array1=None;
    Array2=None;
    Array3=None;

def ClearObjects():
    Draw1.rectangle( (0, 0, W-10, H-10),
                     fill=(60, 70, 30, 1) );
    Draw2.rectangle( (0, 0, W-10, H-10),
                     fill=(60, 70, 30, 1) );

def RotateFunction(B, Sense):
    global x,y,z,D,N
    if Sense==-1:
        Teta=np.pi/180*(-0.1);
    else:
        Teta=np.pi/180*(0.1);
    Cos_Teta=np.cos(Teta)
    Sin_Teta=np.sin(Teta);

    X0=0;  Y0=0;  Z0=D/2 # Center of rotation

    for n in range(0,N+1):
        for m in range(0,N+1):
            if (B.ids.Button3.state=="down" or
                    B.ids.Button4.state=="down"):
                yP=(y[n]-Y0)*Cos_Teta \
                    + (x[n]-X0)*Sin_Teta +Y0;
```

165

```
            xP=-(y[n]-YO)*Sin_Teta \
                +(x[n]-XO)*Cos_Teta + XO;
            y[n]=yP;
            x[n]=xP;

        if (B.ids.Button5.state=="down" or
                    B.ids.Button6.state=="down"):
            yP=(y[n]-YO)*Cos_Teta \
                    + (z[n]-ZO)*Sin_Teta + YO;
            zP=-(y[n]-YO)*Sin_Teta \
                    +(z[n]-ZO)*Cos_Teta + ZO;
            y[n]=yP;
            z[n]=zP;

        if (B.ids.Button7.state=="down" or
                    B.ids.Button8.state=="down"):
            xP=(x[n]-XO)*Cos_Teta \
                    + (z[n]-ZO)*Sin_Teta + XO;
            zP=-(x[n]-XO)*Sin_Teta \
                    +(z[n]-ZO)*Cos_Teta + ZO;
            x[n]=xP;
            z[n]=zP;

class Form1(FloatLayout):
    def __init__(Handle, **kwargs):
        super(Form1, Handle).__init__(**kwargs);
        Event1=Clock.schedule_once(
                    Handle.Initialize);

    def Initialize(B, *args):
        global W,H, XC,YC;
        global PilImage1,PilImage2, Draw1,Draw2;
        # P= Percentage of the D distance
```

```
    global P, Amplitude;
    W,H=B.ids.Screen1.size;

    XC=int (W/2)+20;
    YC=int(H/2)+60;
    PilImage1= Image.new('RGB', (W-10, H-10),
                            (60, 70, 30));
    Draw1 = ImageDraw.Draw(PilImage1);
    PilImage2= Image.new('RGB', (W-10, H-10),
                            (60, 70, 30));
    Draw2 = ImageDraw.Draw(PilImage2);
    Font = ImageFont.truetype('Gargi.ttf', 70);
    Draw1.text( (30,200), "3D Images", fill =(
                    255,0,0,1), font=Font);
    Draw2.text( (50,200), "3D Images", fill =
                (0,255,255,1), font=Font);

    ShowScene(B);

def Button1_Click(B):
    global Draw1, Draw2;
    ClearObjects(); # Clearing Draw1 and Draw2
    GraphFunction(VX1,VY1,VZ1,0);
    GraphFunction(VX2,VY2,VZ2,1);
    ShowScene(B);

def Button2_Click(B):
    ClearObjects(); # Clearing Draw1 and Draw2
    Font = ImageFont.truetype('Gargi.ttf', 70)
    Draw1.text( (30,200), "3D Images", fill =
                    (255,0,0,1), font=Font);
    Draw2.text( (50,200), "3D Images", fill =
                (0,255,255,1), font=Font);

    ShowScene(B);
```

```
def Button3_Click(B):
    RotateFunction(B,1);
    ClearObjects(); # Clearing Draw1 and Draw2
    GraphFunction(VX1,VY1,VZ1,0);
    GraphFunction(VX2,VY2,VZ2,1);
    ShowScene(B);

def Button4_Click(B):
    RotateFunction(B,-1),
    ClearObjects();
    GraphFunction(VX1,VY1,VZ1,0);
    GraphFunction(VX2,VY2,VZ2,1);
    ShowScene(B);

def Button5_Click(B):
    RotateFunction(B,-1),
    ClearObjects();
    GraphFunction(VX1,VY1,VZ1,0);
    GraphFunction(VX2,VY2,VZ2,1);
    ShowScene(B);

def Button6_Click(B):
    RotateFunction(B,1),
    ClearObjects();
    GraphFunction(VX1,VY1,VZ1,0);
    GraphFunction(VX2,VY2,VZ2,1);
    ShowScene(B);

def Button7_Click(B):
    RotateFunction(B,-1),
    ClearObjects();
    GraphFunction(VX1,VY1,VZ1,0);
    GraphFunction(VX2,VY2,VZ2,1);
    ShowScene(B);
```

```
def Button8_Click(B):
    RotateFunction(B,1),
    ClearObjects();
    GraphFunction(VX1,VY1,VZ1,0);
    GraphFunction(VX2,VY2,VZ2,1);
    ShowScene(B);

# This is the Start Up code.
class StartUp (App):
    def build (BU):
        BU.title="Form1"
        return Form1();
if __name__ =="__main__":
    StartUp().run();
```

Listing 10-6. Code for the file.kv File

```
#:set W 440
#:set H 440
<Form1>:
    id : Form1
    Image:
        id: Screen1
        size_hint: None,None
        pos_hint: {"x":0.04, "y":0.34}
        size: W,H
        canvas.before:
            Color:
                rgba: 0.9, 0.9, 0, 1
            RoundedRectangle:
                pos:  self.pos
                size: self.size
```

```
Button:
    id: Button1
    on_press: Form1.Button1_Click()
    text: "Button1"
    size_hint: None,None
    pos_hint: {"x": 0.2, "y":0.03}
    size: 100,30

Button:
    id: Button2
    on_press: Form1.Button2_Click()
    text: "Button2"
    size_hint: None,None
    pos_hint: {"x": 0.63, "y":0.03}
    size: 100,30

Button:
    id: Button3
    on_press: Form1.Button3_Click()
    text: "Button3"
    size_hint: None,None
    pos_hint: {"x": 0.05, "y":0.12}
    size: 100,30
    always_release: True
Button:
    id: Button4
    on_press: Form1.Button4_Click()
    text: "Button4"
    size_hint: None,None
    pos_hint: {"x": 0.73, "y":0.12}
    size: 100,30
```

```
Button:
    id: Button5
    on_press: Form1.Button5_Click()
    text: "Button5"
    size_hint: None,None
    pos_hint: {"x": 0.05, "y":0.20}
    size: 100,30
Button:
    id: Button6
    on_press: Form1.Button6_Click()
    text: "Button6"
    size_hint: None,None
    pos_hint: {"x": 0.73, "y":0.20}
    size: 100,30

Button:
    id: Button7
    on_press: Form1.Button7_Click()
    text: "Button7"
    size_hint: None,None
    pos_hint: {"x": 0.05, "y":0.28}
    size: 100,30
Button:
    id: Button8
    on_press: Form1.Button8_Click()
    text: "Button8"
    size_hint: None,None
    pos_hint: {"x": 0.73, "y":0.28}
    size: 100,30
```

When plotting curves described by parametric equations, it can be hard to follow their paths from the proper perspective. You can see this in the plot in Figure 10-2. For these cases, stereoscopy can provide a better perception of the graph. The code to generate this function is shown in Listing 10-7.

Listing 10-7. Another Parametric Function Used as an Illustrative Example

```
for n in range (0,N+1):
    x[n]=L*np.sin(6*Pi/N*n);
    z[n]=L*np.cos(6*Pi/N*n);
    y[n]=60*np.sin(4*Pi/N*n)
```

Figure 10-2. *Stereoscopic 3D plot obtained with the program for a parametric function*

10.4 Summary

In this chapter, we described elements for constructing stereoscopic parametric 3D plots. We also included two working examples.

CHAPTER 11

SymPy

In the previous chapters, we used NumPy to program our arrays, along with mathematical capabilities. In this chapter, we introduce SymPy. This Python library provides special mathematical functions and polynomials as well as powerful symbolic mathematics. You can include SymPy in your programs by means of the following directive:

```
import sympy as sp.
```

Now, your program can access SymPy functions through the local name sp and the dot operator. For example, we can obtain the symbolic value of π and assign it to a variable, which we will name Pi by utilizing the following directive:

```
Pi=sp.pi.
```

After executing this directive, the variable Pi will represent the symbolic value of π, not precisely its numerical value. As a result, if we now perform the print (Pi) directive, we will obtain pi instead of its numerical value. Furthermore, the print (Pi**2) directive will give pi**2. Notice that we have incorporated symbolic mathematics into our programs.

Now, if we need the numerical value stored in our variable Pi, we can use the following directive:

```
print (Pi.evalf()).
```

© Moisés Cywiak, David Cywiak 2021
M. Cywiak and D. Cywiak, *Multi-Platform Graphics Programming with Kivy*,
https://doi.org/10.1007/978-1-4842-7113-1_11

This directive will display the value 3.14159265358979 on the screen. Furthermore, the following directive:

```
print (Pi.evalf(100)),
```

will display this:

```
3.1415926535897932384626433832795028841971693993751058209749445
9230781640628620899862803482534211708.
```

11.1 Analytical Expressions and Symbols

To use analytical expressions in our programs, we need to declare symbols. For example, the code for the equation $2x^2 + 5 + x + 1$ is shown in Listing 11-1.

Listing 11-1. Code for the $2x^2 + 5 + x + 1$ Equation

```
import sympy as sp
x=sp.symbols("x");
Q=2*x**2+5+x+1;
print(Q);
```

After executing this code, we obtain the following:

```
2*x**2 + x + 6
```

In this code, the following directive:

```
x=sp.symbols("x")
```

declares x as a symbolic variable. In turn, this directive:

```
Q=2*x**2+5+x+1
```

creates Q as a symbolic expression. It is worth noticing in this code that you don't have to declare Q as a symbolic variable.

At this point, based on our programming experience with numerical functions, we might think that this directive:

```
print ( Q(1) )
```

would print the numerical value of Q, calculated at x=1. However, we will see that this assumption is incorrect. In response to this, we would obtain a list of errors, including the following error:

```
TypeError: 'Add' object is not callable.
```

Up to this point, we have learned that Q is not the usual numerical function that would allow us to calculate the numerical values of our expressions, but rather is a *symbolic representation* of an algebraic equation.

Let's also try to obtain numerical values of Q by following the idea of the first example, using the code shown in Listing 11-2.

Listing 11-2. Incorrect Way to Obtain Numerical Q Values

```
import sympy as sp
x=sp.symbols("x")
Q=2*x**2+5+x+1;
print ( Q(1).evalf() );
```

In Listing 11-2, we intended to extend our previous notion in the first example, in which we successfully obtained the value of π. However, in this case, we will obtain several errors, including this one:

```
TypeError: 'Add' object is not callable.
```

With this outcome, we should now realize that the variable Pi in the first example holds only one value. In contrast, the Q variable is a function of x, which means it can take an infinite set of values.

The correct way to obtain a numerical value of Q, evaluated at some x, is to use the substitute property, abbreviated subs. For example, to calculate Q(1), we can use the following:

```
Q.subs(x,1).
```

This way, we can obtain numerical values of our symbolic Q equation. However, this is not exactly what we want, as we are looking for a numerical function.

Fortunately, there is a more versatile solution provided by SymPy. It utilizes a built-in function, referred to as lambdify. This function allows us to convert symbolic expressions into numerical formulas. To clarify this concept, take a look at the code in Listing 11-3.

Listing 11-3. Converting a Symbolic Function to a Numeric Function

```
import sympy as sp
x=sp.symbols("x");
Q=2*x**2+5+x+1;
R=sp.lambdify(x,Q);
print( R(1) );
```

In this code, the following directive:

```
R=sp.lambdify(x,Q)
```

assigns to the variable R the properties of a typical numerical function according to our symbolic Q equation. Therefore, R becomes a numerical function, and we can proceed to calculate values of it. For example, R(1) gives the value of the equation at x=1. The previous code prints the requested result to the screen, which in this case is 9.

11.2 Declaring Functions with Analytical Expressions

In general, it is hard to write large mathematical expressions. For these cases, it's convenient to break the symbolic function code into several parts. As an example, let's consider the following algebraic expression:

$$\frac{100}{\left(5x^2+3x+2\right)}\left(75x^3+2x^2+3\right)\frac{\left(50x-3\right)}{\left(12x+5\right)} \tag{11.1}$$

The code in Listing 11-4 splits the symbolic expression into several lines, making the code simpler.

Listing 11-4. Splitting a Symbolic Expression Into Several Code Lines

```
def f():
    N1=100/(5*x**2+3*x+2);
    N2=(75*x**3+2*x**2+3);
    N3=(50*x-3)/(12*x+5)
    return N1*N2*N3;
Q=f();
```

If we now use the print (Q) directive, we obtain the following:

```
100*(50*x - 3)*(75*x**3 + 2*x**2 + 3)/((12*x + 5)*(5*x**2 +
3*x + 2))
```

From this result, we can see that Q symbolically represents our algebraic expression. We can obtain the corresponding numerical formula by using the sp.lambdify(Q) directive. The complete code is shown in Listing 11-5.

Listing 11-5. Example of a Symbolic Expression with Several Lines
of Code

```
import sympy as sp
x=sp.symbols("x");
def f():
    N1=100/(5*x**2+3*x+2);
    N2=(75*x**3+2*x**2+3);
    N3=(50*x-3)/(12*x+5)
    return N1*N2*N3;
Q=f();
R=sp.lambdify(x,Q);
print( R(-2) ); # Calculate the function at x=-2
```

In this code, we defined the function f(), which does not receive any
parameters and returns the symbolic algebraic expression. After this, we
can execute the Q=f() directive to assign the symbolic function to the
variable Q. Finally, this directive:

```
R=sp.lambdify(x,Q);
```

creates the numerical function R corresponding to the algebraic
expression. R now allows numerical evaluation.

After executing this code, print(R(-2)) will give the value -19956.25.
This is the correct value of our symbolic equation, evaluated at x=-2.

At this point, note that we could avoid using Q by using this directive:

```
R=sp.lambdify( x,f() );
```

11.3 Solving Equations

Let's consider the simple code in Listing 11-6, which can solve the equation $ax + b = 0$, where a and b are constant terms.

Listing 11-6. Code for Solving $ax + b = 0$ Symbolically

```
import sympy as sp
x,a,b =sp.symbols("x a b");
Q=a*x+b
R=sp.solve (Q,x);
print(R);
```

In this code, x, a, and b are symbolic variables. After running the code, the program will give the result [-b/a], which is correct.

Now let's consider using the code in Listing 11-7 to solve $ax^2 + bx + c = 0$.

Listing 11-7. Symbolically Solving $ax^2 + bx + c = 0$

```
import sympy as sp
x,a,b,c =sp.symbols("x a b c");
Q=a*x**2+b*x+c
R1,R2=sp.solve (Q,x);
print(R1);
print(R2);
```

After executing this code, we obtain the following:

```
(-b + sqrt(-4*a*c + b**2))/(2*a)
-(b + sqrt(-4*a*c + b**2))/(2*a)
```

In this code, we anticipated that the quadratic equation has two solutions. Therefore, we assigned each solution to the variables R1 and R2. Equivalently, if we had not known the number of solutions beforehand, we could have combined NumPy and SymPy, as illustrated in Listing 11-8.

Listing 11-8. Alternative Code for Solving $ax^2 + bx + c = 0$

```
import sympy as sp
import numpy as np
x,a,b,c =sp.symbols("x a b c");
Q=a*x**2+b*x+c
R=sp.solve (Q,x);
N=np.size(R);
print(N);
for n in range(0, int(N) ):
    print( R[n] );
```

In this code, R takes the form of an array to store the complete set of solutions. Now, we use NumPy to obtain the number of solutions. Then, the for loop goes from 0 to N to print R[0], which holds one of the solutions, and R[1], which holds the second one. To investigate what R looks like, let's print R, R[0], and R[1]. We obtain the following:

```
[(-b + sqrt(-4*a*c + b**2))/(2*a), -(b + sqrt(-4*a*c + b**2))/
(2*a)],
(-b + sqrt(-4*a*c + b**2))/(2*a),
-(b + sqrt(-4*a*c + b**2))/(2*a).
```

For the cubic equation, we want to solve $ax^3 + bx^2 + cx + d = 0$. The corresponding code is shown in Listing 11-9.

Listing 11-9. Symbolically Solving $ax^3 + bx^2 + cx + d = 0$

```
import sympy as sp
x,a,b,c,d =sp.symbols("x a b c d");
Q=a*x**3 + b*x**2 + c*x + d;
R=sp.solve (Q,x);
for n in range(0,3):
    print(R[n]);
    print("\n");
```

We know in advance that the cubic equation has three solutions. Therefore, we used a for loop to print each one. We added the directive print ("\n") to add carriage returns to separate the solutions. The results follow:

```
-(-3*c/a + b**2/a**2)/(3*(sqrt(-4*(-3*c/a + b**2/a**2)**3
+ (27*d/a - 9*b*c/a**2 + 2*b**3/a**3)**2)/2 + 27*d/(2*a) -
9*b*c/(2*a**2) + b**3/a**3)**(1/3)) - (sqrt(-4*(-3*c/a +
b**2/a**2)**3 + (27*d/a - 9*b*c/a**2 + 2*b**3/a**3)**2)/2 +
27*d/(2*a) - 9*b*c/(2*a**2) + b**3/a**3)**(1/3)/3 - b/(3*a),

-(-3*c/a + b**2/a**2)/(3*(-1/2 - sqrt(3)*I/2)*(sqrt(-4*(-3*c/a
+ b**2/a**2)**3 + (27*d/a - 9*b*c/a**2 + 2*b**3/a**3)**2)/2
+ 27*d/(2*a) - 9*b*c/(2*a**2) + b**3/a**3)**(1/3)) - (-1/2 -
sqrt(3)*I/2)*(sqrt(-4*(-3*c/a + b**2/a**2)**3 + (27*d/a -
9*b*c/a**2 + 2*b**3/a**3)**2)/2 + 27*d/(2*a) - 9*b*c/(2*a**2) +
b**3/a**3)**(1/3)/3 - b/(3*a),

-(-3*c/a + b**2/a**2)/(3*(-1/2 + sqrt(3)*I/2)*(sqrt(-4*(-3*c/a
+ b**2/a**2)**3 + (27*d/a - 9*b*c/a**2 + 2*b**3/a**3)**2)/2
+ 27*d/(2*a) - 9*b*c/(2*a**2) + b**3/a**3)**(1/3)) - (-1/2
+ sqrt(3)*I/2)*(sqrt(-4*(-3*c/a + b**2/a**2)**3 + (27*d/a -
9*b*c/a**2 + 2*b**3/a**3)**2)/2 + 27*d/(2*a) - 9*b*c/(2*a**2) +
b**3/a**3)**(1/3)/3 - b/(3*a).
```

This code gives the three roots of the cubic algebraic equation. As you can see, it will not be straightforward to demonstrate the correctness of the results. One approach consists of substituting the roots into the algebraic equation and using the simplify directive. Alternatively, you can test for some particular cases. For example, let's test the a=b=c=d=1 case using the code in Listing 11-10.

Listing 11-10. Printing Numerical Values to the Symbolic Solution of $ax^3 + bx^2 + cx + d = 0$ for Specific Values

```
import sympy as sp
x,a,b,c,d =sp.symbols("x a b c d");
Q=a*x**3 + b*x**2 +c*x+d
R=sp.solve (Q,x);
T0=sp.lambdify([a,b,c,d ], R[0]);
T1=sp.lambdify([a,b,c,d ], R[1]);
T2=sp.lambdify([a,b,c,d ], R[2]);
x0=T0(1,1,1,1);
x1=T1(1,1,1,1);
x2=T2(1,1,1,1);
print(x0);
print(x1);
print(x2);
```

We will focus on the following three directives:

```
T0=sp.lambdify([a,b,c,d ], R[0]);
T1=sp.lambdify([a,b,c,d ], R[1]);
T2=sp.lambdify([a,b,c,d ], R[2]);
```

Each directive converts the symbolic expressions R[0], R[1], and R[2] into the numerical parameters T0, T1, and T2. These are actually numerical functions that we will express as T0(a,b,c,d), T1(a,b,c,d), and T2(a,b,c,d), respectively. We can calculate the roots for specific values of a, b, c, and d. For example, for the case a=b=c=d=1, the results are as follows:

```
-0.9999999999999998
(-5.551115123125783e-17+0.9999999999999999j)
(-5.551115123125783e-17-0.9999999999999999j)
```

Note that the first root is a real number, while the other two solutions are complex, accomplished using the complex conjugate roots theorem. The parameter j represents the imaginary unit.

To verify that the three roots are indeed solutions of our equation, we can add the code in Listing 11-11 to the end of the previous program.

Listing 11-11. Verifying Specific Solutions for $ax^3 + bx^2 + cx + d = 0$

```
a=1; b=1; c=1; d=1;
S0=a*x0**3 + b*x0**2 +c*x0+d
S1=a*x1**3 + b*x1**2 +c*x1+d
S2=a*x2**3 + b*x2**2 +c*x2+d
print(S0); print(S1); print(S2);
```

From this code, we obtain the following values:

```
.440892098500626e-16
(2.220446049250313e-16+1.1102230246251565e-16j)
(2.220446049250313e-16-1.1102230246251565e-16j)
```

Each calculated root should satisfy the cubic equation, rigorously speaking, so the three values should be 0. Although they are not precisely equal to 0, the three numerical values are, for practical purposes, negligible (in the order of 10^{-16}). This confirms that, within the numerical precision of the processor, these three roots are indeed solutions of the cubic equation.

Finally, let's investigate if SymPy can solve the algebraic quartic equation written in the form $ax^4 + bx^3 + cx^2 + dx + e = 0$.

The corresponding code is shown Listing 11-12.

Listing 11-12. Symbolically Solving $ax^4 + bx^3 + cx^2 + dx + e = 0$

```
import sympy as sp
x,a,b,c,d, e =sp.symbols("x a b c d e");
Q=a*x**4 + b*x**3 + c*x**2 + d*x + e;
```

```
R=sp.solve (Q,x);
for n in range(0,4):
    print(R[n]);
    print("\n");
```

After executing this code, we obtain four messages with the following text:

```
Squeezed text (51 lines).
```

We can print the symbolic results by double-clicking each one of these messages. However, the results are lengthy. Therefore, as in the previous case, we need to verify their correctness by testing particular values.

11.4 Solving Simultaneous Equations

Let's consider the following pair of simultaneous algebraic equations.

$$ax + by = C1 \tag{11.2}$$

$$cx + dy = C2 \tag{11.3}$$

Listing 11-13 obtains the solutions symbolically.

Listing 11-13. Symbolically Solving Two Simultaneous Linear Equations

```
import sympy as sp
x, y, a, b, c, d, C1, C2=sp.symbols("x y a b c d C1 C2");
Eq1=sp.Eq(a*x+b*y,C1);
Eq2=sp.Eq(c*x**2+d*y**2, C2);
R=sp.solve( [Eq1,Eq2],(x,y) );
print(R[0]);
print("\n");
print(R[1]);
```

As the solutions are lengthy, we can proceed as in the previous example to test some particular solutions.

11.5 Symbolic Differentiation

Let's consider the following expression:

$$b\,exp(-ax) \tag{11.4}$$

Listing 11-14 will print the symbolic derivative of the expression with respect to the variable x.

Listing 11-14. Example of Symbolic Differentiation

```
import sympy as sp
x,a,b=sp.symbols("x a b");
f=b*sp.exp(-a*x);
R=sp.diff(f,x); # first order derivative
print(R);
```

We obtain the following:

```
-a*b*exp(-a*x)
```

To code to obtain the second derivative is shown in Listing 11-15.

Listing 11-15. Second Symbolic Derivative Example

```
import sympy as sp
x,a,b=sp.symbols("x a b");
f=b*sp.exp(-a*x);
R=sp.diff(f,x,2);
print(R);
```

After executing this code, we obtain:

```
a**2*b*exp(-a*x)
```

Let's now consider a two-dimensional expression, as follows:

$$c\,exp(-ax-by) \tag{11.5}$$

We want to symbolically calculate the following derivative:

$$\frac{\partial^2}{\partial y^2}\frac{\partial}{\partial x}\Big[c\,exp(-ax-by)\Big] \tag{11.6}$$

This expression requires us to calculate three derivatives. The first one with respect to the variable x, and the first and second derivative with respect to the variable y. The code is shown in Listing 11-16.

Listing 11-16. Symbolic Third Order with Partial Derivatives

```
import sympy as sp
x,y,a,b,c=sp.symbols("x y a b c");
f=c*sp.exp(-a*x-b*y);
#Perform first derivative respect to x and then, second
derivatives respect to y.
R=sp.diff(f,x,1, y,2);
print(R);
```

The result obtained with this code reads as follows:

```
-a*b**2*c*exp(-a*x - b*y
```

11.6 Integration

Let's now symbolically calculate the following integral:

$$\int_{b}^{c}\left(ax^2+3\right)dx \qquad (11.7)$$

The corresponding code is shown in Listing 11-17.

Listing 11-17. Symbolic Integration Example

```
import sympy as sp
x,a,b,c=sp.symbols("x a b c");
f=a*x**2 + 3;
R=sp.integrate(f, (x,b,c)); #Integrate f with  respect to x
from b to c.
print(R);
```

After executing the code, we obtain the following:

```
-a*b**3/3 + a*c**3/3 - 3*b + 3*c
```

Let's investigate if SymPy can calculate some improper integrals. In these types of integrals, one or both of the integration limits is infinity. As an example, consider the following improper integral:

$$\int_{-\infty}^{\infty}exp\left(-x^2\right)dx \qquad (11.8)$$

It is well known that the result of this integral equals $\pi^{\frac{1}{2}}$.

The corresponding code to calculate the integral is shown in Listing 11-18.

Listing 11-18. Symbolic Improper Integral Calculation

```
import sympy as sp
x=sp.symbols("x");
Infinity=sp.oo; #Read sympy infinity and assign it to the
parameter Infinity.
f=sp.exp(-x**2);
R=sp.integrate(f, (x,-Infinity,Infinity)); #Calculate the
integral
print (R); # Print the result
```

After executing this code, the program prints the following result:

```
sqrt(pi)
```

This result confirms the capability of SymPy to calculate improper integrals.

Let's now extend the integral to the two-dimensional case:

$$\int\limits_{-\infty}^{\infty}\int\limits_{-\infty}^{\infty} exp\left(-\left(x^2+y^2\right)\right)dx\,dy \qquad (11.9)$$

The code to calculate this integral is shown in Listing 11-19.

Listing 11-19. Symbolic Two-Dimensional Improper Integral Calculation

```
import sympy as sp
x,y=sp.symbols("x y");
Infinity=sp.oo; #Assigning the value of infinity to a variable.
f=sp.exp(-x**2-y**2);
#Calculating the integral
R=sp.integrate(f,(x,-Infinity,Infinity), (y,-Infinity,Infinity));
print(R);
```

After executing this code, we obtain the result, `pi`, as expected.

In the following chapters, you will use some SymPy functions. In the next subsection, we describe the procedure to incorporate SymPy into Android projects.

11.7 Incorporating SymPy Into Android Projects

Now you learn how to incorporate SymPy into your Android projects. At first glance, you might think that it will suffice to add SymPy to the end of the requirements line in the `buildozer.spec` file, in the same manner as you did with NumPy and Pillow. However, if you do so, Buildozer will fail in the conversion process. Among the list of errors, you will see: `"mpmath with version larger or equal to 0.19 is required."`

To verify if mpath is installed on your computer, open a Terminal window and type `pip3 list`. In our case, we had mpmath version 1.1.0.

At this point, you might conclude that SymPy, apparently, is not compatible with Buildozer. Fortunately, this is not the case. At `https://github.com/kivy/python-for-android/issues/2303`, we found a solution posted by Robert Flatt to solve this problem. The solution consists of adding mpmath, instead of SymPy, to the row that corresponds to requirements in the `buildozer.spec` file, as follows:

```
requirements = python3,kivy,numpy,pillow,mpmath
```

Then you need to copy SymPy's source code into the working folder. In Ubuntu, you'll find the code in the following folder:

```
/home/ComputerName/.local/lib/python3.8/site-packages
```

In this path, the term `ComputerName` has to be replaced with the name you assigned to your computer when Ubuntu was installed.

The source code we are looking for corresponds to the folder named sympy. Therefore, you must copy this folder into your working one.

After accomplishing this procedure, you can use Buildozer as usual to create the Android APK. Type the following:

```
buildozer -v android debug
```

In the following chapters, you will need SymPy.

11.8 Summary

In this chapter, we introduced SymPy to symbolically access special mathematical functions and polynomials. We described how to incorporate SymPy into your projects, and we described its functionality by using working examples.

CHAPTER 12

Plotting Functions in Spherical Coordinates

In this chapter, we describe fundamental elements for calculating and plotting functions in spherical coordinates. For the working examples, we focus on the so-called spherical harmonics polynomials, encountered on diverse physical problems, as is the case with electron orbitals derived from Schrödinger's differential equation. These polynomials, represented as $Y_{l,m}$, are characterized by two positive integers, l and m, with $|m| \leq l$. The polynomials are functions of the zenithal and azimuthal coordinates, as described in the following sections.

Figure 12-1 shows a screenshot of the program running on an Android cell phone with a plot of $\|Re(Y_{3,2})\|^2$.

© Moisés Cywiak, David Cywiak 2021
M. Cywiak and D. Cywiak, *Multi-Platform Graphics Programming with Kivy*,
https://doi.org/10.1007/978-1-4842-7113-1_12

Figure 12-1. *Screenshot of the program running on an Android cell phone showing a plot of* $\|Re(Y_{3,2})\|^2$

To begin, we describe the spherical-coordinate system in the following section.

12.1 Overview of Spherical Coordinates

Figure 12-2 depicts a typical three-dimensional spherical-coordinate system.

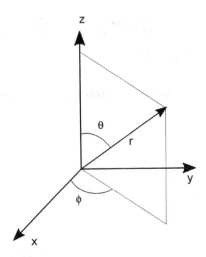

Figure 12-2. *Typical spherical-coordinate system*

In Figure 12-2, the parameters θ and ϕ represent the zenithal or polar and azimuthal angular coordinates, respectively. To generate points over a complete sphere, we need $0 < \theta < \pi$ and $0 < \phi < 2\pi$. The r parameter is referred to as the radial distance.

From Figure 12-2, the coordinates of a point can be written as follows:

$$x = r\sin(\theta)\cos(\phi) \tag{12.1}$$

$$y = r\sin(\theta)\sin(\phi) \tag{12.2}$$

$$z = r\cos(\theta) \tag{12.3}$$

Equations (12.1)-(12.3) will be used to transform a three-dimensional differential equation from Cartesian coordinates into spherical coordinates.

In the following section, we present our working example, which consists of solving the well-known Schrödinger's differential equation expressed in spherical coordinates.

12.2 Spherical Differential Equation Working Example

Consider the three-dimensional Schrödinger's differential equation in Cartesian coordinates:

$$\frac{-\hbar2}{2M}\left(\frac{\partial^2\psi\left(x,y,z\right)}{\partial x^2}+\frac{\partial^2\psi\left(x,y,z\right)}{\partial y^2}+\frac{\partial^2\psi\left(x,y,z\right)}{\partial z^2}\right)+$$

$$\frac{q}{4\pi\epsilon_0 r}\psi\left(x,y,z\right)=E\psi\left(x,y,z\right) \tag{12.4}$$

In Equation (12.4), the $\psi(x, y, z)$ function will represent, in principle, all the possible spatial positions that a charged particle, with charge q and mass M, can take under the influence of a potential distribution function equal to $\frac{q}{r}$. The term $\hbar$ is the well-known Plank's constant. The parameter ϵ_0 represents vacuum permittivity.

By using Equations (12.1)-(12.3), we can express Equation (12.4) in spherical coordinates, as follows:

$$\frac{-\hbar^2}{2M}[\frac{\partial^2\psi\left(r,\theta,\phi\right)}{\partial r^2}+\frac{2}{r}\frac{\partial\psi\left(r,\theta,\phi\right)}{\partial r}+\frac{1}{r^2}\frac{\partial^2\psi\left(r,\theta,\phi\right)}{\partial\theta^2}+\frac{cos\left(\theta\right)}{r^2 sin\left(\theta\right)}$$

$$\frac{\partial\psi\left(r,\theta,\phi\right)}{\partial\theta}+\frac{1}{r^2 sin^2\left(\theta\right)}\frac{\partial^2\psi\left(r,\theta,\phi\right)}{\partial\phi^2}]+\frac{q}{4\pi\epsilon_0 r}\psi\left(r,\theta,\phi\right)=E\psi\left(r,\theta,\phi\right) \tag{12.5}$$

Analogous to Equation (12.4), $\psi(r, \theta, \phi)$ in Equation (12.5) gives valid spatial positions expressed in spherical coordinates for a particle with energy E, charge q, and mass M in a hydrogen-like atom with attractive potential equal to q/r.

Equation (12.5) can be solved using the method of separation of variables, proposing a solution of the product of three functions, as follows:

$$\psi\left(r,\theta,\phi\right)=R\left(r\right)T\left(\theta\right)F\left(\phi\right) \tag{12.6}$$

After substituting Equation (12.6) into Equation (12.5), we see that the differential equations that correspond to the functions $R(r)$ and $T(\theta)$ are not common ones, and therefore, they must be solved by suitable methods referred to as series expansion methods. Under these conditions, the overall solution corresponds to the product of three differential equations, as follows.

- Solutions for $R(r)$ are spherical Bessel functions.

- Solutions for $T(\theta)$ are associated Legendre polynomials, typically written as $P_{l,m}(cos(\theta))$.

- Solutions for $F(\phi)$ are exponentials in the form $exp(im\phi)$. The parameter i represents the imaginary unit.

For our example, we will focus on the case r equal to a constant. Therefore, $\psi(r,\theta,\phi)$ becomes a function of only θ and ϕ. This condition will permit us to focus on the orbitals that the electrons follow in hydrogen-like atoms. These orbitals correspond to spherical-harmonics functions, defined as follows:

$$Y_{l,m}\left(\theta,\phi\right)=\sqrt{\frac{2l+1}{4\pi}\frac{\left(l-m\right)!}{\left(l+m\right)!}}P_{l,m}\left(cos\left(\theta\right)\right)exp\left(im\phi\right) \tag{12.7}$$

In Equation (12.7), the square root is a normalization factor.

The atomic orbitals correspond to probabilistic spatial distributions, which analytically correspond to the square of the absolute real value of the harmonics functions, expressed as follows:

$$\left| Re\left(Y_{l,m}\left(\theta, \phi \right) \right) \right|^2 = \left| \sqrt{\frac{2l+1}{4\pi}\frac{(l-m)!}{(l+m)!}} P_{l,m}\left(cos\left(\theta \right) \right) cos\left(m\phi \right) \right|^2 \tag{12.8}$$

To plot Equation (12.8) for a set of different l, m values, we need to calculate $P_{l,m}(\theta, \phi)$. In the following section, we focus on this subject. For illustrative purposes, the normalization factor will not be considered.

12.3 The Associated Legendre Polynomials

It can be analytically demonstrated that the associated Legendre polynomials can be generated using the following equation:

$$P_{l,m} = \frac{1}{2^l l!}\left(1 - x^2\right)^{\frac{m}{2}}\frac{d^{m+l}}{dx^{m+l}}\left(x^2 - 1\right)^l \tag{12.9}$$

In Equation (12.9), we used the change of variable, $x = cos\left(\theta \right)$. The $l!$ expression represents the factorial of the integer l, calculated by the following expression, $l! = l(l-1)(l-2)\cdots(1)$.

In this case, we will use SymPy to symbolically calculate derivatives and factorials. The code in Listing 12-1 allows us to generate some Legendre polynomials.

Listing 12-1. Generating Legendre polynomials

```
import sympy as sp
x=sp.symbols("x");
def Plm(l,m ):
    N=( 1/(2**l) )*(1 /sp.factorial(l) )
```

```
    return N * (  (1-x**2)**(m/2)  ) \
           * sp.diff( (x**2-1)**l, x,m+l );
L_Num=3; M_Num=2; #Legendre l,m orders
R=sp.lambdify( x, Plm(L_Num,M_Num) );
```

In this code, `x=sp.symbols("x")` declares the variable x as symbolic, as described in Chapter 11. As a consequence, as `Plm(l,m)` function uses this variable for symbolic calculations, the function itself is, in turn a symbolic function.

The `R=sp.lambdify( x, Plm(L_Num,M_Num) )` directive assigns to l, the value L_Num and m, the value M_NUM, respectively, 3 and 2 in this example. After executing `sp.lambdify`, we obtain the numerical function `R(x)`.

At this point, it may be interesting to inspect the analytical expression of some associated Legendre polynomials. Listing 12-2 converts the equations given in the previous code to LaTeX. This expression can be visualized in a text editor.

Listing 12-2. Code for Visualizing Symbolic Equations with LaTeX

```
import sympy as sp
x=sp.symbols("x");
#Associated Legendre l, m orders

L_Num=3; M_Num=3; # l, m orders
def Plm(l,m ):
    N=( 1/(2**l) )*(1 /sp.factorial(l) );
    return N * (  (1-x**2)**(m/2)  ) \
* sp.diff( (x**2-1)**l, x,m+l );
R=  Plm(L_Num,M_Num);
R1=sp.simplify(R);
T=sp.latex(R1); # Convert expression to LaTeX
# Replace \ symbols by spaces to allow printing the equation.
A=T.replace("\\"," ");
# A can be printed in a text editor
```

In this code, the following directive:

```
T=sp.latex(R1),
```

converts the symbolic expression R into a LaTeX expression T. However, to print the corresponding formulas in a text editor, we remove the symbol \\ by using the following code:

```
A=T.replace("\\"," ").
```

Listing 12-3 gives some associated Legendre polynomials obtained with the code in Listing 12-2. When required, we have replaced rational exponents with their equivalent fractions.

Listing 12-3. List of Some Associated Legendre Polynomials

$P_{0,\,0}(x) = 1;$

$$P_{1,0}(x)=x;\ P_{1,1}(x)=1\left(1-x^2\right)^{\frac{1}{2}}$$

$$P_{2,0}(x)=\frac{3}{2}x^2-\frac{1}{2};P_{2,1}(x)=3x\left(1-x^2\right)^{\frac{1}{2}}P_{2,2}(x)=3\left(1-x^2\right)$$

$$P_{3,0}(x)=x\left(\frac{5}{2}x^2-372\right);P_{3,1}(x)=\left(1-x^2\right)^{\frac{1}{2}}\left(\frac{15}{2}x^2-\frac{3}{2}\right);P_{3,2}(x)$$

$$=15x\left(1-x^2\right);\ P_{3,3}(x)=15\left(1-x^2\right)^{\frac{3}{2}}$$

As indicated, $x = cos(\theta)$. Therefore, we will use NumPy to create a one-dimensional array for θ with entries in the range $0 < \theta < \pi$, to substitute x with its corresponding cosine values. Similarly, we will create a second array for ϕ, with values between 0 and 2π. The corresponding code is shown in Listing 12-4.

Listing 12-4. Creating and Filling the Angular Axes

```
import numpy as np
N=40;
Pi=np.pi;
Theta=np.zeros(N+1);
Phi=np.zeros(N+1);
for n in range(0,N+1):
    Theta[n]=n/N*Pi;
    Phi[n]=n/N*2*Pi;
```

In this code, we generate the arrays Theta and Phi, each with 41 entries. The first array holds numbers ranging from 0 to π in equally spaced steps. The second array stores numbers from 0 to 2π. The first entry, called Theta[0], is equal to 0, while the last entry, Theta[40], is equal to π. In turn, Phi[0] is equal to 0 and Phi[40] is 2π.

To calculate the values of the associated Legendre polynomials, we use the following directive within a for loop, with n ranging from 0 to N:

```
R( np.cos(Theta[n]) )
```

The complete code needed to print the corresponding values is shown in Listing 12-5.

Listing 12-5. Code for Printing Numerical Values of the Symbolic Function

```
import numpy as np
import sympy as sp
x=sp.symbols("x");
def Plm(l,m ):
    N=( 1/(2**l) )*(1 /sp.factorial(l) )
    return N * (  (1-x**2)**(m/2)  ) \
            * sp.diff( (x**2-1)**l, x,m+l );
```

```
L_Num=3; M_Num=2; #Legendre l,m orders
R=sp.lambdify( x, Plm(L_Num,M_Num) );

N=40;
Pi=np.pi;
Theta=np.zeros(N+1); Phi=np.zeros(N+1);
for n in range(0,N+1):
    Theta[n]=n/N*Pi;
    Phi[n]=n/N*2*Pi;
for n in range(0,N+1):
    print( R(np.cos(Theta[n])) );
```

At this point, we are ready to calculate the values corresponding to Equation (12.9). However, we may wonder if SymPy has a built-in function for the associated Legendre polynomials. The answer is yes. Therefore, instead of the code listed previously, we could use this:

```
Plm=sp.assoc_legendre(L_Num,M_Num, x);
R=sp.lambdify(x,Plm);
```

We can verify that both methods give the same results by comparing some values.

We are now in the position of plotting some spherical harmonics functions. In the following section, we describe our method for plotting the orbitals given in Equation (12.8).

12.4 Plotting Functions in Spherical Coordinates

The program generates the associated Legendre polynomials using the code shown in Listing 12-1, which creates the numerical function R(x) to provide the associated Legendre polynomials, $P_{l,m}(x)$.

To create the 3D perspective, as in previous chapters, we use the required perspective parameters with the following values:

```
D=4000;
VX=600; VY=120; VZ=0;
Factor0 =(D-VZ) / (D/2-VZ);
```

The Factor0 variable is used to shift the plot to the center of the screen.

To calculate the spherical harmonics as functions of θ and ϕ, we use the code in Listing 12-6.

Listing 12-6. Creating the Angular Arrays

```
N=40;
Pi=np.pi;
Theta=np.zeros(N+1); Phi=np.zeros(N+1);
for n in range(0,N+1):
    Theta[n]=n/N*Pi;
    Phi[n]=n/N*2*Pi;
```

The code creates two arrays, each with 41 entries for the angular variables with $0 < \theta < \pi$ and $0 < \phi < 2\pi$.

Now, we proceed to calculate the orbitals given by Equation (12.8) with the code in Listing 12-7.

Listing 12-7. Calculating Orbitals

```
import numpy as np
import sympy as sp
x=sp.symbols("x");
def Plm(l,m ):
    N=( 1/(2**l) )*(1 /sp.factorial(l) )
    return N * (  (1-x**2)**(m/2)  ) \
            * sp.diff( (x**2-1)**l, x,m+l );
```

```
L_Num=3; M_Num=2; #Legendre l,m orders
R=sp.lambdify( x, Plm(L_Num,M_Num) );
N=40;
Pi=np.pi;
Theta=np.zeros(N+1); Phi=np.zeros(N+1);
for n in range(0,N+1):
    Theta[n]=n/N*Pi;
    Phi[n]=n/N*2*Pi;
F=np.zeros( (N+1,N+1) );
for n in range(0,N+1):
    for m in range(0,N+1):
        F[n][m]=np.abs( R(np.cos(Theta[n])) \
            *np.cos(M_Num*Phi[m]) )**2;
print(F);
```

In this code, the F=np.zeros((N+1,N+1)) directive creates the variable F, representing a two-dimensional $(N+1)*(N+1)$ array to store the absolute square real values of $Y_{l,m}(\theta, \phi)$.

To plot F, we create the mesh arrays with appropriate dimensions using the following code.

```
x1=np.zeros( (N+1,N+1) );
y=np.zeros( (N+1,N+1) );
z1=np.zeros( (N+1,N+1) );
```

Now, we will use Equations (12.1)-(12.3) to create the plot. In these equations, the radial distance r is considered constant.

We have to assign the appropriate role to each variable, as described in previous chapters. The vertical height corresponds to the y-axis, the horizontal length corresponds to the x-axis, and the depth to the z-axis. The code in Listing 12-8 assigns the corresponding parameters appropriately.

Listing 12-8. Filling Mesh and Vertical Coordinates

```
x1=np.zeros( (N+1,N+1) );
y=np.zeros( (N+1,N+1) );
z1=np.zeros( (N+1,N+1) );
L=2.5;
for n in range(0,N+1):
    for m in range(0,N+1):
        x1[n][m]=L*F[n][m]*np.sin(Theta[n]) \
        *np.cos(Phi[m]);
        z1[n][m]=L*F [n][m]*np.sin(Theta[n]) \
        *np.sin(Phi[m])+D/2;
        y[n][m]=L*F[n][m]*np.cos(Theta[n]);
```

In this code, we included a scale factor L for enlarging or shrinking the plot as required. Finally, GraphFunction(B) and RotateFunction(B, Sense) are in charge of plotting and rotating the function, similarly to the previous chapters.

The code for main.py and File.kv is shown in Listings 12-9 and 12-10, respectively.

Listing 12-9. Code for the main.py File

```
from kivy.app import App
from kivy.uix.floatlayout import FloatLayout
from kivy.graphics import Line, Color
from kivy.clock import Clock
import os
import numpy as np
import sympy as sp
from kivy.lang import Builder
```

```
Builder.load_file(
    os.path.join(os.path.dirname(os.path.abspath(
                __file__)), 'File.kv')
                );

#Avoid Form1 of being resizable
from kivy.config import Config
Config.set("graphics","resizable", False)
Config.set('graphics', 'width',  '480');
Config.set('graphics', 'height', '680');

x=sp.symbols("x");
def Plm(l,m ):
    N=( 1/(2**l) )*(1 /sp.factorial(l) )
    return N * (   (1-x**2)**(m/2)   ) \
            * sp.diff( (x**2-1)**l, x,m+l );
L_Num=3; M_Num=2; #Legendre l,m orders
R=sp.lambdify( x, Plm(L_Num,M_Num) );

D=4000;
VX=600; VY=1200; VZ=0;
Factor0 =(D-VZ) / (D/2-VZ);
N=40;
Pi=np.pi;
Theta=np.zeros(N+1); Phi=np.zeros(N+1);
for n in range(0,N+1):
    Theta[n]=n/N*Pi;
    Phi[n]=n/N*2*Pi;
M_Num=2; N_Num=3; #Legendre m,n orders
F=np.zeros( (N+1,N+1) );
for n in range(0,N+1):
    for m in range(0,N+1):
        F[n,m]=np.abs( R(np.cos(Theta[n])) \
                    *np.cos(M_Num*Phi[m]) )**2;
```

```python
x1=np.zeros( (N+1,N+1) );
y=np.zeros( (N+1,N+1) );
z1=np.zeros( (N+1,N+1) );
L=2.4;
for n in range(0,N+1):
    for m in range(0,N+1):
        x1[n][m]=L*F[n][m]*np.sin(Theta[n]) \
                *np.cos(Phi[m]);
        z1[n][m]=L*F [n][m]*np.sin(Theta[n]) \
                *np.sin(Phi[m])+D/2;
        y[n][m]=L*F[n][m]*np.cos(Theta[n]);

 #Array to store list of points
PointList=np.zeros( (N+1,2) );
def GraphFunction(B):
    global x1,y, z1, N, D, VX, VY, VZ;
    B.ids.Screen1.canvas.clear(); #Clear the screen
    #Choose color to draw
    B.ids.Screen1.canvas.add( Color(1,0,0) );
    for n in range (0,N+1): #Draw horizontal lines
        for m in range (0,N+1):
            Factor=(D-VZ)/(D-z1[n][m]-VZ);
            xA=XC+Factor*(x1[n][m]-VX)+Factor0*VX;
            yA=YC+Factor*(y[n][m]-VY)+Factor0*VY;
            PointList[m]=xA,yA;
        B.ids.Screen1.canvas.add( Line(points=
                PointList.tolist(), width=1.3));

    for n in range (0,N+1): #Drawing vertical lines
        for m in range (0,N+1, 1):
            Factor=(D-VZ)/(D-z1[m][n]-VZ);
            xA=XC+Factor*(x1[m][n]-VX)+Factor0*VX;
```

```
                yA=YC+Factor*(y[m][n]-VY)+FactorO*VY;
                PointList[m]=xA,yA;
           B.ids.Screen1.canvas.add( Line(points=
                    PointList.tolist(), width=1.3));
def RotateFunction(B, Sense):
    global x1, y, z1, D, N;
    if Sense==-1:
        Theta=np.pi/180*(-4.0);
    else:
        Theta=np.pi/180*(4.0);
    Cos_Theta=np.cos(Theta)
    Sin_Theta=np.sin(Theta);

    XO=0;  YO=0;  ZO=D/2 # Center of rotation

    for n in range(0,N+1):
        for m in range(0,N+1):
            if (B.ids.Button3.state=="down" or
                    B.ids.Button4.state=="down"):
                yP=(y[n][m]-YO)*Cos_Theta \
                    + (x1[n][m]-XO)*Sin_Theta + YO;
                xP=-(y[n][m]-YO)*Sin_Theta \
                    +(x1[n][m]-XO)*Cos_Theta + XO;
                y[n][m]=yP;
                x1[n][m]=xP;

            if (B.ids.Button5.state=="down" or
                    B.ids.Button6.state=="down"):
                yP=(y[n][m]-YO)*Cos_Theta \
                    + (z1[n][m]-ZO)*Sin_Theta + YO;
                zP=-(y[n][m]-YO)*Sin_Theta \
                    +(z1[n][m]-ZO)*Cos_Theta + ZO;
```

```
                y[n][m]=yP;
                z1[n][m]=zP;

        if (B.ids.Button7.state=="down" or
                B.ids.Button8.state=="down"):
            xP=(x1[n][m]-XO)*Cos_Theta \
                + (z1[n][m]-ZO)*Sin_Theta + XO;
            zP=-(x1[n][m]-XO)*Sin_Theta \
                +(z1[n][m]-ZO)*Cos_Theta + ZO;
            x1[n][m]=xP;
            z1[n][m]=zP;

class Form1(FloatLayout):
    def __init__(Handle, **kwargs):
        super(Form1, Handle).__init__(**kwargs);
        Event1=Clock.schedule_once(Handle.Initialize);

    def Initialize(B, *args):
        global W,H, XC,YC;
        W,H=B.ids.Screen1.size;
        XI,YI=B.ids.Screen1.pos
        XC=XI+int (W/2);
        YC=YI+int(H/2);

    def Button1_Click(B):
        GraphFunction(B);

    def Button2_Click(B):
        B.ids.Screen1.canvas.clear();

    def Button3_Click(B):
        RotateFunction(B,1),
        GraphFunction(B);
```

```
    def Button4_Click(B):
        RotateFunction(B,-1),
        GraphFunction(B);

    def Button5_Click(B):
        RotateFunction(B,-1),
        GraphFunction(B);

    def Button6_Click(B):
        RotateFunction(B,1),
        GraphFunction(B);

    def Button7_Click(B):

        RotateFunction(B,-1),
        GraphFunction(B);

    def Button8_Click(B):
        RotateFunction(B,1),
        GraphFunction(B);

# This is the Start Up code.
class StartUp (App):
    def build (BU):
        BU.title="Form1"
        return Form1();
if __name__ =="__main__":
    StartUp().run();
```

Listing 12-10. Code for the file.kv File

```
#:set W 440
#:set H 440
<Form1>:
    id : Form1
    StencilView:
        id: Screen1
        size_hint: None,None
        pos_hint: {"x":0.04, "y":0.34}
        size: W,H
        canvas.before:
            Color:
                rgba: 0.9, 0.9, 0, 1
            RoundedRectangle:
                pos:   self.pos
                size: self.size
    Button:
        id: Button1
        on_press: Form1.Button1_Click()
        text: "Button1"
        size_hint: None,None
        pos_hint: {"x": 0.2, "y":0.03}
        size: 100,30

    Button:
        id: Button2
        on_press: Form1.Button2_Click()
        text: "Button2"
        size_hint: None,None
        pos_hint: {"x": 0.63, "y":0.03}
        size: 100,30
```

```
Button:
    id: Button3
    on_press: Form1.Button3_Click()
    text: "Button3"
    size_hint: None,None
    pos_hint: {"x": 0.05, "y":0.12}
    size: 100,30
    always_release: True
Button:
    id: Button4
    on_press: Form1.Button4_Click()
    text: "Button4"
    size_hint: None,None
    pos_hint: {"x": 0.73, "y":0.12}
    size: 100,30

Button:
    id: Button5
    on_press: Form1.Button5_Click()
    text: "Button5"
    size_hint: None,None
    pos_hint: {"x": 0.05, "y":0.20}
    size: 100,30
Button:
    id: Button6
    on_press: Form1.Button6_Click()
    text: "Button6"
    size_hint: None,None
    pos_hint: {"x": 0.73, "y":0.20}
    size: 100,30
```

```
Button:
    id: Button7
    on_press: Form1.Button7_Click()
    text: "Button7"
    size_hint: None,None
    pos_hint: {"x": 0.05, "y":0.28}
    size: 100,30
Button:
    id: Button8
    on_press: Form1.Button8_Click()
    text: "Button8"
    size_hint: None,None
    pos_hint: {"x": 0.73, "y":0.28}
    size: 100,30
```

Using this code, we generated the plots of $|P_{l,m}(cos(\theta))\ cos\ (m\phi)|^2$ shown in Figure 12-3.

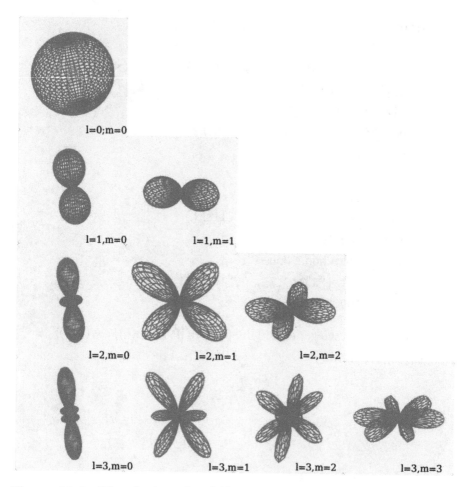

Figure 12-3. *Plots for $|P_{l,m}(cos(\theta))\ cos\ (m\phi)|^2$ obtained with this chapter's code*

12.5 Summary

In this chapter, we introduced elements for plotting functions in spherical coordinates. We introduced analytical concepts on three-dimensional spherical coordinates and illustrated the programming methods with working examples of spherical harmonics polynomials.

CHAPTER 13

Stereoscopic Plots in Spherical Coordinates

In this chapter, we describe elements for creating stereoscopic scenes of functions expressed in spherical coordinates. As in Chapter 12, we focus on spherical harmonics.

Figure 13-1 shows a screenshot of the program running on an Android cell phone. It shows a plot of the square of the absolute real value of the spherical harmonic l=3 and m=2, written as $|P_{l,m}(cos(\theta)) \, cos\,(m\phi)|^2$.

© Moisés Cywiak, David Cywiak 2021
M. Cywiak and D. Cywiak, *Multi-Platform Graphics Programming with Kivy*,
https://doi.org/10.1007/978-1-4842-7113-1_13

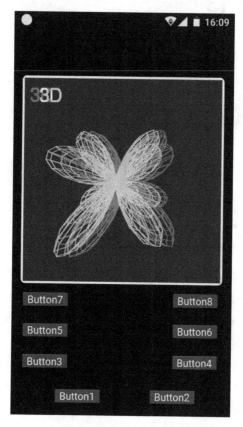

Figure 13-1. *Screenshot on an Android cell phone showing a stereoscopic 3D plot of $|P_{3,2}(cos(\theta))\,cos(2\phi)|^2$ obtained with the program*

In the following sections, we describe this program.

13.1 Creating the Stereoscopic Scenes

As in previous chapters, to create the stereoscopic perception, we need two images slightly displaced horizontally. In our program, this is accomplished by using two points of projection. The corresponding parameters are as follows:

```
D=500;
VX1=60;  VY1=60;  VZ1=0;
VX2=80;  VY2=60;  VZ2=0;
```

In this code, D is the normal distance between the screen and the plane of projection.

To create stereoscopic views of our spherical harmonics plots, we will treat our graphs as three-dimensional objects. We will project them similarly as we did with the polygons. We will place them, centered, between the plane of projection and the screen by utilizing the percentage variable P, introduced in previous chapters, with a value of 0.5.

We will calculate the associated Legendre polynomials using Equation (12.9). As this equation involves factorials and derivatives, we will need to create its corresponding symbolic expression. The code in Listing 13-1 creates the required formula.

Listing 13-1. Symbolically Calculating the Associated Legendre Polynomials Using Equation (12.9)

```
x=sp.symbols("x");
def Plm(l,m ):
    N=( 1/(2**l) )*(1 /sp.factorial(l) )
    return N * (  (1-x**2)**(m/2)  ) \
            * sp.diff( (x**2-1)**l, x,m+l );
```

Next, we apply the lambdify directive to obtain the corresponding numerical function, as in Chapter 12. The code looks as follows:

```
L_Num=3;  M_Num=2  #Legendre l, m orders
R=sp.lambdify( x, Plm(L_Num,M_Num) );
```

As in Chapter 12, the numerical function R(x) gives the values of $P_{l,m}(x)$. For example, R(x) in the previous code gives $P_{3,2}(x)$.

We will now create three arrays. The first two arrays, Theta and Phi, will store the angular variables, and the F array will store the associated Legendre polynomials, as shown in Listing 13-2.

Listing 13-2. Creating the Angle Arrays and the Function

```
N=40;  # Number of pixels to represent the function
Pi=np.pi;
Theta=np.zeros(N+1); Phi=np.zeros(N+1);
for n in range(0,N+1):
    Theta[n]=n/N*Pi;
    Phi[n]=n/N*2*Pi;
F=np.zeros( (N+1,N+1) );
for n in range(0,N+1):
    for m in range(0,N+1):
        F[n,m]=np.abs( R(np.cos(Theta[n]))*np.cos(M_Num*Phi[m])
        )**2;
```

It is worth noticing that the Theta and Phi arrays are one-dimensional arrays with sizes N+1. In contrast, F is a two-dimensional (N+1) x (N+1) array.

To continue, we create the mesh in the same manner as in Chapter 12, using the following code:

```
x1=np.zeros( (N+1,N+1) );
y=np.zeros( (N+1,N+1) );
z1=np.zeros( (N+1,N+1) );
```

Now we create the plot, as shown in Listing 13-3.

Listing 13-3. Filling the Mesh and Vertical Coordinate

```
L=2.4; D=500;
for n in range(0,N+1):
    for m in range(0,N+1):
        x1[n][m]=L*F[n][m]*np.sin(Theta[n]) \
                        *np.cos(Phi[m]);
        z1[n][m]=L*F [n][m]*np.sin(Theta[n])\
                        *np.sin(Phi[m])+D/2;
        y[n][m]=L*F[n][m]*np.cos(Theta[n]);
```

When the program starts, `Initialize(B, *args)` creates two PIL images, called `PilImage1` and `PilImage2`, to store the left and right images required for our stereoscopic program. Additionally, two instances, `Draw1` and `Draw2`, are created for drawing. `PilImage1` will store the red image, while `PilImage2` will store the cyan image. A third image, `PilImage3`, will hold the result of the bitwise OR operation between the two images.

We will need an array to store the set of points that composes each horizontal or vertical line of the plot. Therefore, we will create `PointList` with size `(N+1)x2` using this directive:

```
PointList=np.zeros( (N+1,2) )
```

`GraphFunction(VX, VY, VZ, Which)` will now plot the function on its corresponding instance, according to the `Which` value. If the point of projection corresponds to the left one, the parameter called `Which` is 0 and the plotting color is red. If the point of projection corresponds to the one placed at the right, the `Which` parameter is 1 and the plotting color is cyan.

The code listings for `main.py` and `file.kv` are shown in Listing 13-4 and Listing 13-5, respectively.

Listing 13-4. Code for the main.py File

```python
from kivy.app import App
from kivy.uix.floatlayout import FloatLayout
from kivy.clock import Clock
from kivy.core.image import Image as CoreImage
from PIL import Image, ImageDraw, ImageFont
import io
import os
import numpy as np
import sympy as sp
from kivy.lang import Builder

Builder.load_file(
    os.path.join(os.path.dirname(os.path.abspath(
                 __file__)), 'File.kv')
                );
#import scipy.special as Special
#Avoid Form1 of being resizable
from kivy.config import Config
Config.set("graphics","resizable", False);
Config.set('graphics', 'width',  '480');
Config.set('graphics', 'height', '680');

x=sp.symbols("x");
def Plm(l,m ):
    N=( 1/(2**l) )*(1 /sp.factorial(l) )
    return N * (  (1-x**2)**(m/2)  ) \
          * sp.diff( (x**2-1)**l, x,m+l );
R=sp.lambdify( x, Plm(3,2) );

def P2(x):
    return 15*x*(1-x**2);
XC=0; YC=0; W=0; H=0;
```

```
D=500;
VX1=60; VY1=60; VZ1=0;
VX2=80; VY2=60; VZ2=0;

P=0.5; #Place the function at z=D/2
N=40;   #Number of pixels to represent the function
Pi=np.pi;
Theta=np.zeros(N+1); Phi=np.zeros(N+1);
for n in range(0,N+1):
    Theta[n]=n/N*Pi;
    Phi[n]=n/N*2*Pi;
M_Num=2; N_Num=3; #Legendre m,n orders

F=np.zeros( (N+1,N+1) );
for n in range(0,N+1):
    for m in range(0,N+1):
        F[n,m]=np.abs( R(np.cos(Theta[n])) \
                    *np.cos(M_Num*Phi[m]) )**2;

x1=np.zeros( (N+1,N+1) );
y=np.zeros( (N+1,N+1) );
z1=np.zeros( (N+1,N+1) );
L=2.4;
for n in range(0,N+1):
    for m in range(0,N+1):
        x1[n][m]=L*F[n][m]*np.sin(Theta[n]) \
                        *np.cos(Phi[m]);
        z1[n][m]=L*F [n][m]*np.sin(Theta[n])\
                        *np.sin(Phi[m])+D/2;
        y[n][m]=L*F[n][m]*np.cos(Theta[n]);
```

```python
PointList=np.zeros( (N+1,2) );
def GraphFunction(VX,VY,VZ,Which):
    global x1,y, z1, N;
    #MaxY=np.max(y)

    if (Which==0):
        r,g,b = 255, 0, 0; #red Image
        Draw=Draw1
    else:
        r,g,b= 0, 200, 200; #cyan image
        Draw=Draw2
    for n in range (0,N+1): #Horizontal Lines
        for m in range (0,N+1):
            Factor=(D-VZ)/(D-z1[n][m]-VZ);
            xA=XC+Factor*(x1[n][m]-VX)+VX;
            yA=YC-Factor*(y[n][m]-VY)-VY;
            PointList[m]=xA,yA;
        List=tuple( map(tuple,PointList) );
        Draw.line( List, fill=(r,g,b), width=2 );

    for n in range (0,N+1): #Vertical Lines
        for m in range (0,N+1):
            Factor=(D-VZ)/(D-z1[m][n]-VZ);
            xA=XC+Factor*(x1[m][n]-VX)+VX;
            yA=YC-Factor*(y[m][n]-VY)-VY;
            PointList[m]=xA,yA;
        List=tuple( map(tuple,PointList) );
        Draw.line( List, fill=(r,g,b), width=2 );

        Font = ImageFont.truetype('Gargi.ttf', 40)
        Draw1.text( (10,10), "3D", fill =
                        (255,0,0,1), font=Font);
        Draw2.text( (30,10), "3D", fill =
                        (0,255,255,1), font=Font);
```

```python
def ShowScene(B):
    Array1=np.array(PilImage1);
    Array2=np.array(PilImage2);
    Array3=Array1 | Array2;

    PilImage3=Image.fromarray(Array3);

    Memory=io.BytesIO();
    PilImage3.save(Memory, format="png");
    Memory.seek(0);
    ImagePNG=CoreImage(Memory, ext="png");

    B.ids.Screen1.texture=ImagePNG.texture;
    ImagePNG.remove_from_cache()
    Memory.close();
    PilImage3.close();
    Array1=None;
    Array2=None;
    Array3=None;

def ClearObjects():
    Draw1.rectangle( (0, 0, W-10, H-10), fill=
                                (60, 70, 30, 1) );
    Draw2.rectangle( (0, 0, W-10, H-10), fill=
                                (60, 70, 30, 1) );

def RotateFunction(B, Sense):
    global XGO, ZGO
    if Sense==-1:
        Theta=np.pi/180*(-4.0);
    else:
        Theta=np.pi/180*(4.0);
    Cos_Theta=np.cos(Theta)
    Sin_Theta=np.sin(Theta);
```

```
X0=0;   Y0=0;   Z0=D/2 # Center of rotation

for n in range(0,N+1):
    for m in range(0,N+1):
        if (B.ids.Button3.state=="down" or
                B.ids.Button4.state=="down"):
            yP=(y[n][m]-Y0)*Cos_Theta \
                + (x1[n][m]-X0)*Sin_Theta + Y0;
            xP=-(y[n][m]-Y0)*Sin_Theta \
                +(x1[n][m]-X0)*Cos_Theta + X0;
            y[n][m]=yP;
            x1[n][m]=xP;

        if (B.ids.Button5.state=="down" or
                B.ids.Button6.state=="down"):
            yP=(y[n][m]-Y0)*Cos_Theta \
                + (z1[n][m]-Z0)*Sin_Theta + Y0;
            zP=-(y[n][m]-Y0)*Sin_Theta \
                +(z1[n][m]-Z0)*Cos_Theta + Z0;
            y[n][m]=yP;
            z1[n][m]=zP;

        if (B.ids.Button7.state=="down" or
                B.ids.Button8.state=="down"):
            xP=(x1[n][m]-X0)*Cos_Theta \
                + (z1[n][m]-Z0)*Sin_Theta + X0;
            zP=-(x1[n][m]-X0)*Sin_Theta \
                +(z1[n][m]-Z0)*Cos_Theta + Z0;
            x1[n][m]=xP;
            z1[n][m]=zP;
```

```python
class Form1(FloatLayout):
    def __init__(Handle, **kwargs):
        super(Form1, Handle).__init__(**kwargs);
        Event1=Clock.schedule_once(Handle.Initialize);

    def Initialize(B, *args):
        global W,H, XC,YC;
        global PilImage1,PilImage2, Draw1,Draw2;
        #P= Percentage of the D distance
        global P, Amplitude;
        W,H=B.ids.Screen1.size;
        XC=int (W/2)+P/(1-P)*VX1;
        YC=int(H/2)-P/(1-P)*VY1;
        PilImage1= Image.new('RGB', (W-10, H-10),
                                    (60, 70, 30));
        Draw1 = ImageDraw.Draw(PilImage1);
        PilImage2= Image.new('RGB', (W-10, H-10),
                                    (60, 70, 30));
        Draw2 = ImageDraw.Draw(PilImage2);
        Font = ImageFont.truetype('Gargi.ttf', 70)
        Draw1.text( (30,200), "3D Images", fill =
                                (255,0,0,1), font=Font);
        Draw2.text( (50,200), "3D Images", fill =
                                (0,255,255,1), font=Font);
        ShowScene(B);

    def Button1_Click(B):
        global Draw1, Draw2;
        ClearObjects(); # Clearing Draw1 and Draw2
        GraphFunction(VX1,VY1,VZ1,0);
        GraphFunction(VX2,VY2,VZ2,1);
        ShowScene(B);
```

```python
def Button2_Click(B):
    ClearObjects(); # Clearing Draw1 and Draw2
    Font = ImageFont.truetype('Gargi.ttf', 70)
    Draw1.text( (30,200), "3D Images", fill =
                            (255,0,0,1), font=Font);
    Draw2.text( (50,200), "3D Images", fill =
                            (0,255,255,1), font=Font);
    ShowScene(B);

def Button3_Click(B):
    RotateFunction(B,1);
    ClearObjects(); # Clearing Draw1 and Draw2
    GraphFunction(VX1,VY1,VZ1,0);
    GraphFunction(VX2,VY2,VZ2,1);
    ShowScene(B);

def Button4_Click(B):
    RotateFunction(B,-1),
    ClearObjects();
    GraphFunction(VX1,VY1,VZ1,0);
    GraphFunction(VX2,VY2,VZ2,1);
    ShowScene(B);

def Button5_Click(B):
    RotateFunction(B,-1),
    ClearObjects();
    GraphFunction(VX1,VY1,VZ1,0);
    GraphFunction(VX2,VY2,VZ2,1);
    ShowScene(B);

def Button6_Click(B):
    RotateFunction(B,1),
    ClearObjects();
```

```python
        GraphFunction(VX1,VY1,VZ1,0);
        GraphFunction(VX2,VY2,VZ2,1);
        ShowScene(B);

    def Button7_Click(B):
        RotateFunction(B,-1),
        ClearObjects();
        GraphFunction(VX1,VY1,VZ1,0);
        GraphFunction(VX2,VY2,VZ2,1);
        ShowScene(B);

    def Button8_Click(B):
        RotateFunction(B,1),
        ClearObjects();
        GraphFunction(VX1,VY1,VZ1,0);
        GraphFunction(VX2,VY2,VZ2,1);
        ShowScene(B);

# This is the Start Up code.
class StartUp (App):
    def build (BU):
        BU.title="Form1"
        return Form1();
if __name__ =="__main__":
    StartUp().run();
```

Listing 13-5. Code for the file.kv File

```
#:set W 440
#:set H 440
<Form1>:
    id : Form1
    Image:
        id: Screen1
```

```
        size_hint: None,None
        pos_hint: {"x":0.04, "y":0.34}
        size: W,H
        canvas.before:
            Color:
                rgba: 0.9, 0.9, 0, 1
            RoundedRectangle:
                pos:  self.pos
                size: self.size
    Button:
        id: Button1
        on_press: Form1.Button1_Click()
        text: "Button1"
        size_hint: None,None
        pos_hint: {"x": 0.2, "y":0.03}
        size: 100,30

    Button:
        id: Button2
        on_press: Form1.Button2_Click()
        text: "Button2"
        size_hint: None,None
        pos_hint: {"x": 0.63, "y":0.03}
        size: 100,30

    Button:
        id: Button3
        on_press: Form1.Button3_Click()
        text: "Button3"
        size_hint: None,None
        pos_hint: {"x": 0.05, "y":0.12}
        size: 100,30
        always_release: True
```

```
Button:
    id: Button4
    on_press: Form1.Button4_Click()
    text: "Button4"
    size_hint: None,None
    pos_hint: {"x": 0.73, "y":0.12}
    size: 100,30

Button:
    id: Button5
    on_press: Form1.Button5_Click()
    text: "Button5"
    size_hint: None,None
    pos_hint: {"x": 0.05, "y":0.20}
    size: 100,30
Button:
    id: Button6
    on_press: Form1.Button6_Click()
    text: "Button6"
    size_hint: None,None
    pos_hint: {"x": 0.73, "y":0.20}
    size: 100,30

Button:
    id: Button7
    on_press: Form1.Button7_Click()
    text: "Button7"
    size_hint: None,None
    pos_hint: {"x": 0.05, "y":0.28}
    size: 100,30
Button:
    id: Button8
    on_press: Form1.Button8_Click()
```

```
text: "Button8"
size_hint: None,None
pos_hint: {"x": 0.73, "y":0.28}
size: 100,30
```

Figure 13-2 shows plots of $|P_{l,m}(cos(\theta))\ cos\ (m\phi)|^2$ for different $l.\ m,$ values, obtained with the code listed previously.

Figure 13-2. *Plots of $|P_{l,m}(cos(\theta))\ cos\ (m\phi)|^2$ obtained with the chapter's code*

13.2 Summary

In this chapter, we introduced elements for creating stereoscopic scenes of functions expressed in spherical coordinates. We provided working examples for creating the required images, ORing them, and displayed them on a Kivy screen.

CHAPTER 14

Stereoscopic Simple Numerical Method for Gravitational N-body

In this chapter, we provide a simple numerical approach to the gravitational N-body problem to be observed in a stereoscopic view. A screenshot of the program running on an Android cell phone is shown in Figure 14-1.

© Moisés Cywiak, David Cywiak 2021
M. Cywiak and D. Cywiak, *Multi-Platform Graphics Programming with Kivy*,
https://doi.org/10.1007/978-1-4842-7113-1_14

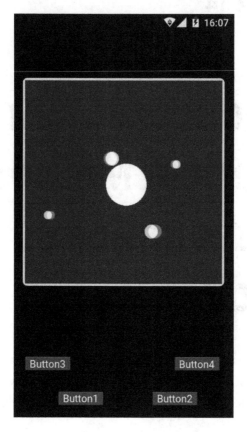

Figure 14-1. *Screenshot of the program running on an Android cell phone*

The functionality of the buttons is described as follows.

Button1 shows the scene. It does not suspend calculations. Button2 stops the calculations, clears the scene, and displays a text message on the screen. Button3 reactivates computations to show the evolution of the masses orbiting in real-time. Finally, Button4 suspends the calculations so that the last scene remains on the screen.

In the following section, we describe the N-body problem.

14.1 The Gravitational N-body Problem

The gravitational N-body-problem consists of determining the dynamic parameters of N masses whose interaction is described by Newton's gravitational law. Let's exemplify the physical situation by considering three of these masses in a three-dimensional Cartesian coordinate system, depicted in Figure 14-2.

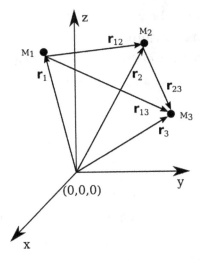

Figure 14-2. *Three punctual masses and their corresponding position vectors in a three-dimensional Cartesian coordinate system*

Figure 14-2 depicts three punctual masses, M_1, M_2, and M_3, pointed by position vectors r_1, r_2, and r_3, respectively. The relative position vectors between them are $r_{1,2}$, $r_{1,3}$, and $r_{2,3}$.

Let i, j, and k represent the unit director vectors in the x-, y-, and z-directions, respectively. Then, each position vector in Figure 14-2 can be expressed as follows:

$$r_n = x_n i + y_n j + z_n k \tag{14.1}$$

In Equation (14.1), the value of n ranges between 1 and 3.

Analogously, the relative position vectors between masse, can be written as follows:

$$r_{n,m} = (x_m - x_n)i + (y_m - y_n)j + (z_m - z_n)k \tag{14.2}$$

In Equation (14.2) n, m can take the values 1, 2, 3, and $n \neq m$.

In the gravitational N-body problem, we assume that the masses are in a three-dimensional free space. No other forces are acting on them except for the gravitational forces between them. For example, mass M_1 interacts only with masses M_2 and M_3 through Newton's gravitational law. Therefore, to calculate the total force exerted on mass M_1, we have to sum the forces due to M_2 and M_3 on M_1. The analytical equation to calculate this force is written as follows:

$$F_1 = G\,M_1 M_2 \frac{r_{1,2}}{\|r_{1,2}\|^3} + G\,M_1 M_3 \frac{r_{1,3}}{\|r_{1,3}\|^3} \tag{14.3}$$

In Equation (14.3), F_1 represents the total force acting on mass M_1. We emphasize that the forces between masses are attractive. The $\|\ \|^3$ symbol represents the cube of the magnitude of a vector. For example, for the case of vector $r_{1,2}$, we can write the following:

$$\|r_{1,2}\|^3 = \left[(x_2 - x_1)^2 + (y_2 - y_1)^2 + (z_2 - z_1)^2\right]^{3/2} \tag{14.4}$$

For two masses, M_n and M_m, the general expression of Equation (14.4) can be written as follows:

$$\|r_{n,m}\|^3 = \left[(x_m - x_n)^2 + (y_m - y_n)^2 + (z_m - z_n)^2\right]^{3/2} \tag{14.5}$$

In Equation (14.5), $m \neq n$ should hold; otherwise, we would have the trivial case in which the distance from one particle to itself is zero.

Now that the net force acting on M_1 has been calculated, we apply Newton's law of motion to this mass, as follows.

$$F_1 = M_1 \frac{d^2 r_1(t)}{dt^2} \qquad (14.6)$$

In Equation (14.6), we have explicitly expressed r_1 as a function of time. The second derivative of this vector gives the three components of the acceleration vector that correspond to M_1.

14.2 Motion Equations

We will now focus on calculating the dynamic conditions of M_1. Equating Equations (14.3) and (14.6) gives this:

$$\frac{d^2 r_1(t)}{dt^2} = G M_2 \frac{r_{1,2}}{\| r_{1,2} \|^3} + G M_3 \frac{r_{1,3}}{\| r_{1,3} \|^3} \qquad (14.7)$$

In Equation (14.7), the second derivative of the position vector represents the acceleration vector acting on M_1. For programming purposes, it will be useful to note that this expression is independent of M_1. Therefore, we conclude that, in general, the formula for calculating the acceleration vector acting on a given mass is a function of all the others present in the system and, in turn, independent of its value.

We now express vector Equation (14.7) in terms of their spatial components, as follows:

$$\frac{d^2 x_1(t)}{dt^2} = \frac{G M_2 (x_2 - x_1)}{\left((x_2 - x_1)^2 + (y_2 - y_1)^2 + (z_2 - z_1)^2 \right)^{\frac{3}{2}}} +$$
$$\frac{G M_3 (x_3 - x_1)}{\left((x_3 - x_1)^2 + (y_3 - y_1)^2 + (z_3 - z_1)^2 \right)^{\frac{3}{2}}} \qquad (14.8)$$

$$\frac{d^2 y_1(t)}{dt^2} = \frac{G M_2 (y_2 - y_1)}{\left((x_2 - x_1)^2 + (y_2 - y_1)^2 + (z_2 - z_1)^2 \right)^{\frac{3}{2}}} +$$

$$\frac{G M_3 (y_3 - y_1)}{\left((x_3 - x_1)^2 + (y_3 - y_1)^2 + (z_3 - z_1)^2 \right)^{\frac{3}{2}}} \tag{14.9}$$

$$\frac{d^2 z_1(t)}{dt^2} = \frac{G M_2 (z_2 - z_1)}{\left((x_2 - x_1)^2 + (y_2 - y_1)^2 + (z_2 - z_1)^2 \right)^{\frac{3}{2}}} +$$

$$\frac{G M_3 (z_3 - z_1)}{\left((x_3 - x_1)^2 + (y_3 - y_1)^2 + (z_3 - z_1)^2 \right)^{\frac{3}{2}}} \tag{14.10}$$

Equations (14.8) through (14.10) are the dynamic equations for M_1. Analog equations can be derived for M_2 and M_3. It is straightforward to extend this derivation to the case of N masses.

In the following section, we describe the method to numerically solve the dynamic equations.

14.3 Numerical Solution to the Dynamic Equations

We now continue with our example of three masses. We will numerically solve the dynamic equations that correspond to mass M_1. For the description, let's associate the following acceleration components to M_1:

$$a_{x1} = \frac{d^2 x_1(t)}{dt^2} \tag{14.11}$$

$$a_{y1} = \frac{d^2 y_1(t)}{dt^2} \qquad (14.12)$$

$$a_{z1} = \frac{d^2 z_1(t)}{dt^2} \qquad (14.13)$$

Now, let's introduce the components of velocity of mass M_1 as follows:

$$v_{x1}(t) = \frac{dx_1(t)}{dt} = \frac{x_1(t+\Delta t) - x_1(t)}{\Delta t} \qquad (14.14)$$

$$v_{y1}(t) = \frac{dy_1(t)}{dt} = \frac{y_1(t+\Delta t) - y_1(t)}{\Delta t} \qquad (14.15)$$

$$v_{z1}(t) = \frac{dz_1(t)}{dt} = \frac{z_1(t+\Delta t) - z_1(t)}{\Delta t} \qquad (14.16)$$

In writing Equations (14.14) through (14.16), we have approximated the derivatives using a small increment value, called Δt.

We will represent the path followed by mass M_1 by the discrete sequence, $x_1(0)$, $x_1(1)$.. $x_1(n)$. Here, n corresponds to an integer. Equations (14.14)-(14.16) give the following recurrence equations:

$$x_1(n+1) = x_1(n) + v_{x1}(n)\Delta t \qquad (14.17)$$

$$y_1(n+1) = y_1(n) + v_{y1}(n)\Delta t \qquad (14.18)$$

$$z_1(n+1) = z_1(n) + v_{z1}(n)\Delta t \qquad (14.19)$$

Now, if the initial spatial coordinates and component velocities at state $n=0$ are known, we can use Equations (14.17) through (14.19) to calculate the position of mass M_1 at the state $n=1$. However, for the state $n=2$, we need the values of the component velocities of state $n=1$. These values can be calculated as follows.

First, we rewrite Equations (14.11) through (14.13) as follows:

$$a_{x1} = \frac{d^2 x_1(t)}{dt^2} = \frac{dv_{x1}}{dt} = \frac{v_{x1}(t+\Delta t) - v_{x1}(t)}{\Delta t} \tag{14.20}$$

$$a_{y1} = \frac{d^2 y_1(t)}{dt^2} = \frac{dv_{y1}}{dt} = \frac{v_{y1}(t+\Delta t) - v_{y1}(t)}{\Delta t} \tag{14.21}$$

$$a_{z1} = \frac{d^2 z_1(t)}{dt^2} = \frac{dv_{z1}}{dt} = \frac{v_{z1}(t+\Delta t) - v_{z1}(t)}{\Delta t} \tag{14.22}$$

Equations (14.20) through (14.22) lead to this:

$$v_{x1}(n+1) = v_{x1}(n) + a_{x1}(n)\Delta t \tag{14.23}$$

$$v_{y1}(n+1) = v_{y1}(n) + a_{y1}(n)\Delta t \tag{14.24}$$

$$v_{z1}(n+1) = v_{z1}(n) + a_{z1}(n)\Delta t \tag{14.25}$$

In Equations (14.23) through (14.25), the values for the component accelerations in the n-state are calculated by means of Equations (14.8) through (14.10).

This procedure allows us to calculate the dynamic components of M_1. To obtain the dynamic equations for the other masses, we proceed in a similar way. The method can be applied, in principle, to any number of masses.

In the following section, we describe the numerical approach to calculating the dynamic parameters of the N-body problem.

14.4 Capturing Numerical Data

To visualize how we perform the calculations, we present an example with five planets, which corresponds to the screenshot in Figure 14-1.

To track all of the parameters described in the previous section, we need a memory region for storing the values that correspond to the position, velocity, and acceleration components that correspond to each mass. We also need to track the three-dimensional values calculated with Equations (14.17) through (14.25). Finally, we also need the value of each mass. All this data can be manageable if we associate a one-dimensional array to each mass.

We use NumPy to create N one-dimensional arrays, with 16 entries each, to store all the values required for each punctual mass. The arrays will be numbered from 0 to N-1. The code corresponding to the case N=5 is shown in Listing 14-1.

Listing 14-1. Creating Array Planets

```
import numpy as np
N=5; #Number of planets
# Array Planet:
# [x,y,z,   vx,vy,vz,   Mass,
# xP,yP,zP,  vxP,vyP,vzP,  ax,ay,az]
Planet=np.zeros( (N,16) );
```

In this code, we refer to each array as a planet. In this example, we set the parameter N=5 to generate five planets in the system, each with 16 entries, as follows:

- The first three entries, 0 to 2, correspond to the position of the planet, given by coordinates (x,y,z).

- The second three entries, 3 to 5, correspond to the three velocity components, given by (vx,vy,vz).

- Entry 6 corresponds to the mass of the planet.

- Entries 7 to 9 correspond to the (xP, yP, zP) values calculated using Equations (14.17)-(14.19). These values will replace (x, y, z), entries 0 to 2. However, we will perform this action only after finishing all the calculations over all the planets. Otherwise, we would disturb the system, and the results would be incorrect.

- Entries 10 to 12 store the new velocity components, (vxP,vyP,vzP), calculated with Equations (14.23)-(14.25). These values will replace the values stored in entries 3 to 5, after completing the calculations over all the planets.

Entries 13 to 15 store the three acceleration components, (ax,ay,az), calculated by Equations (14.8) through (14.10). These values will be used in Equations (14.23) through (14.25) to calculate the new velocity components.

This program will keep track of all the relative distances between the masses. To store them, we create a two-dimensional array of size NxN. However, Equation (14.7) suggests storing $\|r_{n,m}\|^3$ instead of $\|r_{n,m}\|$ in the array. To illustrate how the array looks, let's define $S_{n,m} = \|r_{n,m}\|^3$. Table 14-1 depicts the array for the case N=5.

Table 14-1. *5x5 Array Storing $S_{n,m}$ Values for the Case N=5*

mass	0	1	2	3	4
0	X	$S_{0,1}$	$S_{0,2}$	$S_{0,3}$	$S_{0,4}$
1	$S_{1,0}$	X	S	$Sr_{1,3}$	$S_{1,4}$
2	$S_{2,0}$	$S_{2,1}$	X	$S_{2,3}$	$S_{2,4}$
3	$S_{3,0}$	$S_{3,1}$	$S_{3,2}$	X	$S_{3,4}$
4	$S_{4,0}$	$S_{4,1}$	$S_{4,2}$	$S_{4,3}$	X

In Table 14-1, there are N=5 masses present in the system, numbered from 0 to 4. The 5x5 array stores all possible combinations of parameter $S_{n,m}$. Since $S_{n,m} = S_{m,n}$, the array stores redundant entries that we will keep to simplify the code. Additionally, we will not use the entries marked with the X symbol.

The following section discusses the working example.

14.5 Five Planets Working Example

In principle, there is no restriction on the number of punctual masses our N-body program can handle. In our working example, N=5.

The initial values that we provide to our planets must be based on our geometrical situation. We have assigned to the horizontal and vertical axes the coordinates (x and y), respectively. The z-axis corresponds to the depth.

For simplicity, in our working example, we will position the planets on the x-z plane. The initial velocities will only have components in the z-direction. Additionally, in trying to mimic the solar system, we will position one of the planets at the center and the rest of them will orbit around this one. The masses of the orbiting planets will be small compared with the one placed at the center.

As it is not simple to provide initial conditions that guarantee stable orbits, we will try some values obtained with the following simple approach. Given the fact that each orbiting mass follows a circular path, we will equate the centrifugal force corresponding to its gravitational one. The corresponding analytical expression reads as follows:

$$\frac{GM_0 M_1}{r^2} = \frac{M_1 v^2}{r} \tag{14.26}$$

In writing Equation (14.26), we assume that $M_0 \gg M_1$, and as mentioned, that the small mass orbits around the biggest one following approximately a circular path. The left side of the equation represents the attractive force between the two masses. The right side of the equation represents the centrifugal force acting on mass M_1.

For our working example, we will normalize the value of the gravitational constant to $G=1$. Next, we will assign a large value to the mass at the center; in this example, 10.0×10^4. Next, we will provide some distances to the planets in the x-z plane. Finally, using Equation (14.26), we will provide initial velocities to the five planets. The corresponding code is shown in Listing 14-2.

Listing 14-2. Setting the Initial Conditions for the Planets

```
import numpy as np
D=400; # Perspective distance
P=0.5; # Percentage distance from screen
N=5; # Number of planets
# Array Planet:
# [x,y,z,  vx,vy,vz,  Mass,
# xP,yP,zP, vxP,vyP,vzP, ax,ay,az]
Planet=np.zeros( (N,16) );
Planet[0]=( 0,0,P*D,    0,0,0,   10.0e4,
                        0,0,0,  0,0,0, 0,0,0 );
Planet[1]=( -40,0,P*D,  0,0,50,   14.0,
                        0,0,0,  0,0,0, 0,0,0 );
Planet[2]=( 40,0,P*D,   0,0,-50,  14.0,
                        0,0,0,  0,0,0, 0,0,0 );
Planet[3]=( 60,0,P*D,   0,0, -41,  8.0,
                        0,0,0,  0,0,0, 0,0,0 );
```

```
Planet[4]=(  -60,0,P*D,    0,0, 41,  8.0,
                        0,0,0,  0,0,0, 0,0,0  );
#Array to store distances between planets: r(n,m)
R=np.zeros( (N,N) );
```

In this code, we have assigned to the percentage variable P the value 0.5, as in previous chapters. This value will place the initial z-coordinate of the planets centered between the screen and the plane of projection. The first planet, Planet[0], is placed at the center of the screen and it is initially static, with zero velocity. The other four, Planet[1] to Planet[4], have been assigned initial speeds different from zero. Their masses are small compared to Planet[0].

The NxN array, R, will store the relative distances between planets, each elevated to 3. The code that assigns the corresponding values is shown in Listing 14-3.

Listing 14-3. Calculating the Initial Distances Between Planets

```
#Filling array R with values r(n,m)**3/2
    for n in range(0,N):
        for m in range(0,N):
            if (n>=m):
                continue;
            R[n][m]=((Planet[n][0]-Planet[m][0])**2 \
                    +(Planet[n][1]-Planet[m][1])**2 \
        +(Planet[n][2]-Planet[m][2])**2  )**(3/2);
            R[m][n]=R[n][m];
```

The DrawPlanets(VX, VY, VZ, Which) function is in charge of drawing the planets. As in previous chapters, two PIL images are used for the stereoscopic scene. If the Which parameter is equal to 0, the left image is drawn in red using the left point of projection. If the Which parameter is equal to 1, the right point of projection is used and the right PIL image is colored in cyan. The function starts by reading the value stored in entry 6, which corresponds to the mass. If the mass is greater than 1000, a value equal to 44 is assigned to the local variable M; otherwise, this variable takes the integer value of the mass. The variable M is used to indicate the radius of the circles, depending on the mass of the planet. The directive that draws a planet looks as follows:

```
Draw.ellipse( (x1-M,y1-M,x1+M,y1+M),  fill=(r,g,b) )
```

This directive draws a circle with radius equal to M, filled with the corresponding red or cyan color.

The code for drawing the planets is shown in Listing 14-4.

Listing 14-4. Code for Representing Planets with Ellipses

```
Factor0 =(D-VZ1)/(D/2-VZ1);
N=5; D=400;
for n in range(0,N):
    M=int(Planet[n][6]);
    if (M>1000):
        M=44;
    else:
        M=int(M);
    Factor=(D-VZ)/(D-Planet[n][2]-VZ);
    x1=XC+Factor*(Planet[n][0]-VX)+Factor0*VX;
    y1=YC-Factor*(Planet[n][1]-VY)-Factor0*VY;
    Draw.ellipse( (x1-M,y1-M,x1+M,y1+M),
        fill=(r,g,b));
```

In this code, the function utilizes the coordinates of one of the two points of projection given in (VX, VY, VZ) together with the x-, y-, and z-coordinates available in the Planet array to draw the corresponding circle in Draw1 or Draw2, according to the value of the parameter Which.

The MovePlanets() function, at every clock tick, updates all the parameters of the planets. The function uses a normalized gravitational constant with a value of 1 and a positive parameter dt with a value equal to 0.02. This parameter corresponds to Δt in the analytical equations in Section 14.3.

The value of dt must be as small as possible to attain accurate solutions of the differential equations. However, lowering this value too much will reduce the rate of change in the planet's position, so that the displacements may not be appreciated.

The first task for MovePlanets() is to calculate the values of the new positions using Equations (14.17) through (14.19) and then store them in their corresponding array. The code is shown in Listing 14-5.

Listing 14-5. Calculating Planets with the New Position

```
for n in range(0,N):
    Planet[n][7]=Planet[n][0]+Planet[n][3]*dt;
    Planet[n][8]=Planet[n][1]+Planet[n][4]*dt;
    Planet[n][9]=Planet[n][2]+Planet[n][5]*dt;
```

MovePlanets() now calculates all the distances between planets. According to Equations (14.8) through (14.10), the values that will be stored in the R array correspond to $\|r_{n,m}\|^3$. The code is shown in Listing 14-6.

Listing 14-6. Calculating Dynamic Distances Between Planets

```
#Filling array R with values r(n,m)**3/2
    for n in range(0,N):
        for m in range(0,N):
            if (n>=m):
                continue;
```

```
      R[n][m]=((Planet[n][0]-Planet[m][0])**2 \
              +(Planet[n][1]-Planet[m][1])**2 \
  +(Planet[n][2]-Planet[m][2])**2  )**(3/2);
      R[m][n]=R[n][m];
```

MovePlanets() will now use Equations (14.8) through (14.10) to calculate the three acceleration components for each planet. The calculations require us to sum the contributions over all the planets. The corresponding code is shown in Listing 14-7.

Listing 14-7. Calculating Acceleration Terms ax, ay, and az for Each Planet Using the Gravitational Formula (Positions 13, 14, and 15)

```
for n in range(0,N):
    Planet[n][13]=0;
    Planet[n][14]=0;
    Planet[n][15]=0;
    for m in range(0,N):
        if (n==m):
            continue;
        Planet[n][13]=Planet[n][13]\
                    + G*Planet[m][6]\
          *(Planet[m][0]-Planet[n][0])/R[m][n];
        Planet[n][14]=Planet[n][14]\
                    + G*Planet[m][6]\
          *(Planet[m][1]-Planet[n][1])/R[m][n];
        Planet[n][15]=Planet[n][15]\
            + G*Planet[m][6]\
            *(Planet[m][2]-Planet[n][2])/R[m][n];
```

MovePlanets() now calculates the new velocities with the code shown in Listing 14-8.

Listing 14-8. Calculating the New Velocities: vxP=vx+ax*dt, vyP=vy+ay*dt, and vzP=vz+az*dt, (Positions 10, 11, and 12)

```
for n in range(0,N):
    Planet[n][10]=Planet[n][3]+Planet[n][13]*dt;
    Planet[n][11]=Planet[n][4]+Planet[n][14]*dt;
    Planet[n][12]=Planet[n][5]+Planet[n][15]*dt;
```

Finally, the new position and velocity of each planet can be updated at its corresponding position in the array, using the code in Listing 14-9.

Listing 14-9. Actualizing the Positions and Velocities of the Planets

```
#Actualizing (x,y,z) and  (vx,vy,vz).
for n in range(0,N):
    Planet[n][0:6]=(Planet[n][7],
    Planet[n][8], Planet[n][9],
    Planet[n][10],Planet[n][11],
    Planet[n][12]);
```

At each clock tick, MovePlanets() repeats the actions described previously. Next, DrawPlanets(VX,VY,VZ,Which) clears the old scene and updates the screen with the new values, giving the appearance of real-time movement. The Temporal(B *args) function is in charge of coordinating these actions by using the code in Listing 14-10.

Listing 14-10. Function to Process the Movements of the Planets

```
def Temporal(B, *args):
    global Flag, NUMBER, p, q;
    if (Flag==True):
        ClearObjects();
        MovePlanets();
```

```
DrawPlanets(VX1,VY1,VZ1,0);
DrawPlanets(VX2,VY2,VZ2,1);
ShowScene(B);
```

The code listings for the main.py and File.kv files are shown in Listings 14-11 and 14-12, respectively.

Listing 14-11. Code for the main.py File

```
from kivy.app import App
from kivy.uix.floatlayout import FloatLayout
from kivy.graphics import Line, Color
from kivy.clock import Clock
from kivy.core.image import Image as CoreImage
from PIL import Image, ImageDraw, ImageFont

import io
import os
import numpy as np

from kivy.lang import Builder
Builder.load_file(
    os.path.join(os.path.dirname(os.path.abspath(
                            __file__)), 'File.kv')
                );

#Avoid Form1 of being resizable
from kivy.config import Config
Config.set("graphics","resizable", False)
Config.set('graphics', 'width',  '480');
Config.set('graphics', 'height', '680');

Flag=False; # Do not move planets until requested.
```

```
D=400;
VX1=-5; VY1=120; VZ1=0;
VX2=5; VY2=120; VZ2=0;
Factor0 =(D-VZ1) / (D/2-VZ1);

P=0.5; #percentage distance from screen
N=5; #Number of planets
# Array Planet:
# [x,y,z,  vx,vy,vz,  Mass,
# xP,yP,zP, vxP,vyP,vzP, ax,ay,az]
Planet=np.zeros( (N,16) );
Planet[0]=(  0,0,P*D,    0,0,0,   10.0e4,
                         0,0,0,  0,0,0, 0,0,0 );
Planet[1]=( -40,0,P*D,   0,0,50,   14.0,
                         0,0,0,  0,0,0, 0,0,0 );
Planet[2]=(  40,0,P*D,   0,0,-50,  14.0,
                         0,0,0,  0,0,0, 0,0,0 );
Planet[3]=(  60,0,P*D,   0,0, -41,  8.0,
                         0,0,0,  0,0,0, 0,0,0 );
Planet[4]=(  -60,0,P*D,   0,0, 41,  8.0,
                         0,0,0,  0,0,0, 0,0,0 );
#Array to store distances between planets: r(n,m)
R=np.zeros( (N,N) )

#-----------------------------------------------------
def DrawPlanets(VX,VY,VZ,Which):
    global  Draw1,Draw2,Factor0;
    if (Which==0):
        r,g,b = 255, 0, 0; #red Image
        Draw=Draw1;
    else:
        r,g,b = 0, 255, 255; #blue image
        Draw=Draw2;
```

```python
    for n in range(0,N):
        M=int(Planet[n][6]);
        if (M>1000):
            M=44;
        else:
            M=int(M);
        Factor=(D-VZ)/(D-Planet[n][2]-VZ);
        x1=XC+Factor*(Planet[n][0]-VX)+Factor0*VX;
        y1=YC-Factor*(Planet[n][1]-VY)-Factor0*VY;
        Draw.ellipse( (x1-M,y1-M,x1+M,y1+M), fill=(r,g,b));

def MovePlanets():
    G=1; dt=0.02;
    #Calculating x(n+1), y(n+1) and z(n+1).
    #values are stored in their
    #corresponding Planet array.
    #x(n+1)=x(n) +vx(n)*dt;
    #y(n+1)=y(n)+vy(n)*dt;
    #z(n+1)=z(n)+vz(n)*dt
    #These values will be stored at the end of
    #the calculations, in the initial positions.
    for n in range(0,N):
        Planet[n][7]=Planet[n][0]+Planet[n][3]*dt;
        Planet[n][8]=Planet[n][1]+Planet[n][4]*dt;
        Planet[n][9]=Planet[n][2]+Planet[n][5]*dt;
    #Filling array R with values r(n,m)**3/2
    for n in range(0,N):
        for m in range(0,N):
            if (n>=m):
                continue;
```

```
        R[n][m]=((Planet[n][0]-Planet[m][0])**2 \
                +(Planet[n][1]-Planet[m][1])**2 \
     +(Planet[n][2]-Planet[m][2])**2  )**(3/2);
        R[m][n]=R[n][m];
#Calculating acceleration terms ax,ay,az,
#for each planet using the gravitational formula.
for n in range(0,N):
    Planet[n][13]=0;
    Planet[n][14]=0;
    Planet[n][15]=0;
    for m in range(0,N):
        if (n==m):
            continue;
        Planet[n][13]=Planet[n][13]\
                    + G*Planet[m][6]\
          *(Planet[m][0]-Planet[n][0])/R[m][n];
        Planet[n][14]=Planet[n][14]\
                    + G*Planet[m][6]\
          *(Planet[m][1]-Planet[n][1])/R[m][n];
        Planet[n][15]=Planet[n][15]\
            + G*Planet[m][6]\
            *(Planet[m][2]-Planet[n][2])/R[m][n];

#Calculating the new velocities vxP= vx+ ax*dt,
#vyP=vy+ay*dt, and vzP=vz+az*dt.
for n in range(0,N):
    Planet[n][10]=Planet[n][3]+Planet[n][13]*dt;
    Planet[n][11]=Planet[n][4]+Planet[n][14]*dt;
    Planet[n][12]=Planet[n][5]+Planet[n][15]*dt;
```

```
        #Actualizing (x,y,z) and  (vx,vy,vz).
        for n in range(0,N):
            Planet[n][0:6]=(Planet[n][7],
                            Planet[n][8],
                            Planet[n][9],
                            Planet[n][10],
                            Planet[n][11],
                            Planet[n][12]);

def ShowScene(B):
    Array1=np.array(PilImage1);
    Array2=np.array(PilImage2);
    Array3=Array1 | Array2;

    PilImage3=Image.fromarray(Array3);

    Memory=io.BytesIO();
    PilImage3.save(Memory, format="png");
    Memory.seek(0);
    ImagePNG=CoreImage(Memory, ext="png");

    B.ids.Screen1.texture=ImagePNG.texture;
    ImagePNG.remove_from_cache()
    Memory.close();
    PilImage3.close();
    Array1=None;
    Array2=None;
    Array3=None;
#-------------------------------------------------------
def ClearObjects():
    Draw1.rectangle( (0, 0, H-10, W-10),
                                fill=(60, 70, 30, 1) );
    Draw2.rectangle( (0, 0, H-10, W-10),
                                fill=(60, 70, 30, 1) );
```

```
class Form1(FloatLayout):
    def __init__(Handle, **kwargs):
        super(Form1, Handle).__init__(**kwargs);
        Event1=Clock.schedule_once(Handle.Initialize);
        Event2=Clock.schedule_interval(
                            Handle.Temporal,0.1);

    def Initialize(B, *args):
        global W,H, XC,YC;
        global PilImage1,PilImage2, Draw1,Draw2;
        W,H=B.ids.Screen1.size;
        XC=int (W/2)
        YC=int(H/2)
        PilImage1= Image.new('RGB', (W-10, H-10),
                                    (60, 70, 30));
        Draw1 = ImageDraw.Draw(PilImage1);
        PilImage2= Image.new('RGB', (W-10, H-10),
                                    (60, 70, 30));
        Draw2 = ImageDraw.Draw(PilImage2);
        Font = ImageFont.truetype('Gargi.ttf', 70)
        Draw1.text( (30,200), "3D Images", fill =
                            (255,0,0,1), font=Font);
        Draw2.text( (50,200), "3D Images", fill =
                            (0,255,255,1), font=Font);
        ShowScene(B);

    def Temporal(B, *args):
        global Flag, NUMBER, p, q;
        if (Flag==True):
            ClearObjects();
            MovePlanets();
```

```
            DrawPlanets(VX1,VY1,VZ1,0);
            DrawPlanets(VX2,VY2,VZ2,1);
            ShowScene(B);

#-------------------------------------------------------------------
    def Button1_Click(B):
        global Draw1, Draw2, Flag;
        Flag=False;
        #  Clearing Draw1 and Draw2
        ClearObjects();
        DrawPlanets(VX1,VY1,VZ1,0);
        DrawPlanets(VX2,VY2,VZ2,1);
        ShowScene(B);

    def Button2_Click(B):
        global Draw1, Draw2, Flag;
        Flag=False;
        ClearObjects(); #  Clearing Draw1 and Draw2
        Font = ImageFont.truetype('Gargi.ttf', 70);
        Draw1.text( (30,200), "3D Images", fill =
                            (255,0,0,1), font=Font);
        Draw2.text( (50,200), "3D Images", fill =
                            (0,255,255,1), font=Font);
        ShowScene(B);

    def Button3_Click(B):
        global Flag;
        Flag=True;

    def Button4_Click(B):
        global Flag;
        Flag=False;
```

```
# This is the Start Up code.
class StartUp (App):
    def build (BU):
        BU.title="Form1"
        return Form1();
if __name__ =="__main__":
    StartUp().run();
```

Listing 14-12. Code for the file.kv File

```
#:set W 440
#:set H 440
<Form1>:
    id : Form1
    Image:
        id: Screen1
        size_hint: None,None
        pos_hint: {"x":0.04, "y":0.34}
        size: W,H
        canvas.before:
            Color:
                rgba: 0.8 ,0.8, 0.0 ,1
            RoundedRectangle:
                pos:  self.pos
                size: self.size
    Button:
        id: Button1
        on_press: Form1.Button1_Click()
        text: "Button1"
        size_hint: None,None
        pos_hint: {"x": 0.2, "y":0.03}
        size: 100,30
```

```
Button:
    id: Button2
    on_press: Form1.Button2_Click()
    text: "Button2"
    size_hint: None,None
    pos_hint: {"x": 0.63, "y":0.03}
    size: 100,30

Button:
    id: Button3
    on_press: Form1.Button3_Click()
    text: "Button3"
    size_hint: None,None
    pos_hint: {"x": 0.05, "y":0.12}
    size: 100,30

Button:
    id: Button4
    on_press: Form1.Button4_Click()
    text: "Button4"
    size_hint: None,None
    pos_hint: {"x": 0.73, "y":0.12}
    size: 100,30
```

14.6 Summary

In this chapter, we described a simple numerical approach to the gravitational N-body problem. We derived basic equations for calculating the interaction between masses under the influence of Newton's gravitational law. We presented numerical solutions of the dynamic equations and illustrated their use by employing a working five-planet example. This approach allows us to appreciate the dynamics of the system in stereoscopic view.

CHAPTER 15

Stereoscopic Cylindrical Coordinates Plotting

In this chapter, we describe elements for plotting stereoscopic 3D cylindrical functions. For this purpose, we focus on the so-called aberrations of optical lenses, also referred to as *Seidel aberrations*.

Figure 15-1 shows the program running on an Android cell phone with a stereoscopic plot of one of these terms, referred to as spherical aberration.

© Moisés Cywiak, David Cywiak 2021
M. Cywiak and D. Cywiak, *Multi-Platform Graphics Programming with Kivy*,
https://doi.org/10.1007/978-1-4842-7113-1_15

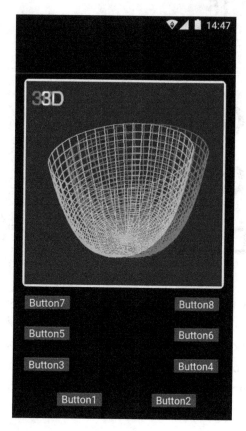

Figure 15-1. *Screenshot of the program on an Android cell phone showing a plot of a spherical aberration term*

The functionality of the buttons is the same as in previous chapters.

Seidel aberrations consist of algebraic terms, expressed as typical cylindrical coordinate functions, which can be obtained by expanding the transmittance phase function of an ideal lens by a Taylor series. According to the wave theory of light, in the process of focusing an illuminating light source by a lens, the interaction of the lens with the wavefronts of light prevents the lens from focusing on a single point, generating instead a spatial light distribution around the focal point. A precise analytical tool to calculate the spatial distribution of the focused profiles is given by the

Fresnel diffraction integral, which allows one to introduce the concept of the phase transmittance function of a lens. In the next section, we provide an introductory analytical description of this subject.

15.1 Ideal Lens Focusing: The Fresnel Diffraction Integral

In Figure 15-2, an illuminating beam is located at an initial plane with coordinates (x, y). The spatial amplitude distribution of the illuminating beam at the initial plane is represented by $\psi(x, y)$. The light propagates to the right, from plane (x, y) to an observation plane with coordinates (ξ, η), placed at a distance z. The planes are parallel. The amplitude distribution of the propagated field is given by $\psi_F(\xi, \eta)$.

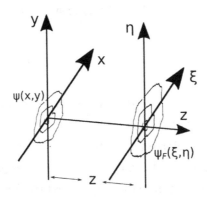

Figure 15-2. *An initial field with amplitude distribution $\psi(x, y)$ propagates a distance z toward an observation plane. The parameter $\psi_F(\xi, \eta)$ represents the amplitude distribution at the plane of observation*

As mentioned, an accurate tool to calculate the amplitude distribution of the field at the observation plane is given by the Fresnel diffraction integral, expressed as follows:

$$\psi_F(\xi,\eta) = \frac{exp\left(i\dfrac{2\pi z}{\lambda}\right)}{i\lambda z} \int_{-\infty}^{\infty}\int_{-\infty}^{\infty} \psi(x,y) exp\left[\frac{i\pi}{\lambda z}\left((x-\xi)^2 + (y-\eta)^2\right)\right] dx\,dy \quad (15.1)$$

For our program, we will apply the Fresnel diffraction integral to the case of an ideal lens. As is well known, a physical property that characterizes an ideal lens is its capability of focusing a spatially unlimited plane wave. Therefore, at the plane of observation, the focused light distribution should consist of an ideal geometrical point. Analytically, the corresponding equation of this point at the plane of observation is represented as $\delta(\xi,\eta)$. Here the δ symbol represents a Dirac delta function.

In Equation (15.1), we use the following substitution:

$$\psi(x,y) = exp\left(-\frac{i\pi}{\lambda f}(x^2 + y^2)\right) \quad (15.2)$$

In Equation (15.2), $\psi(x,y)$ represents the transmittance function of the ideal lens. In the exponential function with an imaginary argument, the quadratic expression is referred to as the phase of the lens. We will now see that this quadratic negative phase results in a convergent wavefront.

Substituting Equation (15.2) into Equation (15.1) gives the following equation:

$$\psi_F(\xi,\eta) = \frac{exp\left(i\dfrac{2\pi f}{\lambda}\right)}{i\lambda f} \int_{-\infty}^{\infty}\int_{-\infty}^{\infty} exp\left(-\frac{i\pi}{\lambda f}(x^2+y^2)\right)$$
$$exp\left(\frac{i\pi}{\lambda f}\left((x-\xi)^2 + (y-\eta)^2\right)\right) dx\,dy \quad (15.3)$$

In Equation (15.3), we substituted z with f, the lens focal length.

By expanding the binomial terms in the second exponential in the integral of Equation (15.3) and canceling same terms, we get:

$$\psi_F(\xi,\eta) = \frac{exp\left(i\frac{2\pi f}{\lambda}\right)}{i\lambda f} exp\left(\frac{i\pi}{\lambda f}\left(\xi^2 + \eta^2\right)\right)$$

$$\int_{-\infty}^{\infty}\int_{-\infty}^{\infty} exp\left(-\frac{i2\pi}{\lambda f}(x\xi + y\eta)\right) dx\, dy \tag{15.4}$$

In Equation (15.4), we recognize that the integral corresponds to one of the representations found in the mathematical tables for a two-dimensional Dirac delta function; that is:

$$\int_{-\infty}^{\infty}\int_{-\infty}^{\infty} exp\left(-\frac{i2\pi}{\lambda f}(x\xi + y\eta)\right) dx\, dy = \delta\left(\frac{\xi}{\lambda f}, \frac{\eta}{\lambda f}\right) \tag{15.5}$$

Substituting Equation (15.5) into Equation (15.4) gives the following equation:

$$\psi_F(\xi,\eta) = \frac{exp\left(i\frac{2\pi f}{\lambda}\right)}{i\lambda f} exp\left(\frac{i\pi}{\lambda f}\left(\xi^2 + \eta^2\right)\right)\delta(\xi,\eta) \tag{15.6}$$

We now apply the $f(\xi,\eta)\delta\left(\frac{\xi}{\lambda f}, \frac{\eta}{\lambda f}\right) = f(0,0)(\lambda f)^2 \delta(\xi,\eta)$ property

for $\lambda > 0$ and $f > 0$, which allows us to simplify Equation (15.6) as follows:

$$\psi_F(\xi,\eta) = -i\lambda f exp\left(i\frac{2\pi f}{\lambda}\right)\delta(\xi,\eta) \tag{15.7}$$

Equation (15.7) demonstrates that when an ideal lens is illuminated by a plane wave that propagates parallel to the optical axes, the lens concentrates (or focuses) the light precisely at the center of the observation plane. The focusing spot consists of an ideal geometrical point, provided that the plane of observation is placed precisely at a lens focal distance from the initial plane.

15.2 Departure from the Ideal Lens

As properties of real lenses deviate from ideal ones, we must devise a more realistic approach. Let's add a linear term to the ideal lens phase of Equation (15.2), as follows:

$$\psi\left(x,y\right)=exp\left(-\frac{i\pi}{\lambda f}\left(x^2+y^2+ax\right)\right) \qquad (15.8)$$

In Equation (15.8), the parameter a represents a constant term. Substituting Equation (15.8) into Equation (15.1) and calculating the integral gives the following:

$$\psi_F\left(\xi,\eta\right)=-i\lambda f\,exp\left(i\frac{2\pi f}{\lambda}\right)exp\left(i\frac{\pi a^2}{\lambda f}\right)\delta\left(\xi-a\right)\delta\left(\eta\right) \qquad (15.9)$$

Equation (15.9) shows that the focused spot has been shifted from the origin in the x-direction, due to the linear term introduced in Equation (15.8). We conclude that the lens has tilted the wavefront with respect to the optical axes. An analog analysis applies to the y-direction.

This approach can be made more general by replacing the phase of the lens by a transmittance function, as follows:

$$\psi\left(x,y\right)=exp\left(i\phi\left(x,y\right)\right) \qquad (15.10)$$

Now, based on the experience gain in our example, we will assume that the phase function in Equation (15.10) depends on the combination of three independent variables:

$$\phi\left(x,y\right)=\phi\left(x^2+y^2,a^2,ax\right) \qquad (15.11)$$

Equation (15.11) can now be expanded in a similar manner to a Taylor series:

$$\phi\left(x^2 + y^2, a^2, ax\right) = A_{0,0,0} + A_{1,0,0}\left(x^2 + y^2\right) + A_{0,1,0}a^2 + A_{0,0,1}ax +$$
$$A_{2,0,0}\left(x^2 + y^2\right)^2 + A_{0,2,0}\left(a^2\right)^2 + A_{0,0,2}\left(ax\right)^2 + \quad\quad (15.12)$$
$$A_{1,1,0}\left(x^2 + y^2\right)a^2 + A_{1,0,1}\left(x^2 + y^2\right)(ax) + A_{0,1,1}\left(a^2\right)(ax) + \cdots$$

In Equation (15.12), each coefficient in the series has three sub-indexes. Each sub-index corresponds to the power of its corresponding expansion term. The first sub-index corresponds to the power of the term $(x^2 + y^2)$. The second sub-index corresponds to the power of a^2. Finally, the third sub-index corresponds to the power of ax. For example, $A_{1,0,1}$ is the coefficient of the term of the products of $(x^2 + y^2)^1$ by $(a^2)0$ by $(ax)^1$.

15.3 The Wave Aberration Function in Cylindrical Coordinates

Equation (15.12) is one of the possible expansions of an aberrated wavefront. An algebraic sum of these terms can represent a real lens. Due to circular symmetry in the lens-manufacturing process, the expansion may fit better for analytical lens modeling if the expansion is expressed in cylindrical coordinates. Then, we express x and y as follows:

$$x = \rho cos(\theta); y = \rho sin(\theta) \quad\quad (15.13)$$

In Equation (15.13) the variables ρ and θ are, as usual, the radial and polar coordinates, respectively.

Substituting Equation (15.13) into Equation (15.12) gives the following:

$$
\begin{aligned}
\phi\left(\rho^2, a^2, a\rho\cos(\theta)\right) = {} & A_{0,0,0} + A_{1,0,0}\left(\rho^2\right) + A_{0,1,0}a^2 + A_{0,0,1}a\rho\cos(\theta) + \\
& A_{2,0,0}\left(\rho^2\right)^2 + A_{0,2,0}\left(a^2\right)^2 + A_{0,0,2}\left(a\rho\cos(\theta)\right)^2 + \\
& A_{1,1,0}\left(\rho^2\right)a^2 + A_{1,0,1}\left(\rho^2\right)\left(a\rho\cos(\theta)\right) + \\
& A_{0,1,1}\left(a^2\right)\left(a\rho\cos(\theta)\right) + \cdots
\end{aligned}
\tag{15.14}
$$

Note that there are other possible expressions for the coefficients. Table 15-1 gives a brief listing of common names for the aberration terms in Equation (15.14).

Table 15-1. *Definition of Some Aberration Terms*

Coefficient	Term	Typical Name
$A_{1,0,0}$	ρ^2	Focus
$A_{0,1,0}$	a^2	Piston
$A_{0,0,1}$	$a\rho\cos(\theta)$	Tilt
$A_{2,0,0}$	$(\rho^2)^2$	Spherical
$A_{0,2,0}$	$(a^2)^2$	Piston
$A_{0,0,2}$	$(a\rho\cos(\theta))^2$	Astigmatism
$A_{1,1,0}$	$\rho^2 a^2$	Field curvature
$A_{1,0,1}$	$\rho^2(a\rho\cos(\theta))$	Coma
$A_{0,1,1}$	$a^2(a\rho\cos(\theta))$	Distortion

In the following section, we describe the program that will stereoscopically plot the aberration terms in cylindrical coordinates.

15.4 Stereoscopic Plot of Wave Aberration Terms in Cylindrical Coordinates

As in previous chapters, we need two points of projection to create two images slightly shifted horizontally. The following code sets the coordinates of the projecting points. As in our previous examples, D is the distance between the plane of projection and the screen.

```
D=800;
VX1=100; VY1=200; VZ1=0;
VX2=130; VY2=200; VZ2=0;
```

We will place the plot of the aberration terms at the middle between the plane of projection and the screen, using the percentage variable P with a value of 0.5.

Next, we set the number of pixels for the plot and create the mesh, as shown in Listing 15-1.

Listing 15-1. Creating the Mesh

```
import numpy as np
N=40;  # Number of pixels to represent the function
y=np.zeros( (N+1,N+1) );
# Creating Mesh array
x1=np.zeros( (N+1,N+1) ); z1=np.zeros( (N+1,N+1) );
```

As in previous chapters, the vertical heights are represented by the y-coordinate; x represents the horizontal coordinate and z represents the depth.

Now we create the radial. and polar coordinates using the code in Listing 15-2.

Listing 15-2. Creating and Filling the Radial and Polar Coordinates

```
Pi=np.pi;
Rho=np.zeros(N+1); Theta=np.zeros(N+1);
for n in range(0,N+1):
    Rho[n]=n/N;
    Theta[n]=n/N*2*Pi;
```

The size of both arrays is N+1. The radial array, Rho, has N+1 entries, with entries ranging from 0 to 1. The polar array, Theta, stores values from 0 to 2π.

To control the sizes of the width and depth of the plots, we will define a scaling factor, L.

```
L=70; # Horizontal and depth scale factor.
```

Now, we set D equal to 800, which is the distance between the plane of projection and the screen. We also set the percentage value P to 0.5.

```
D=800;
P=0.5; #Place the function at z=D/2
```

Now we can create the mesh in the x-z plane with the code shown in Listing 15-3.

Listing 15-3. Creating the Mesh in the x-z Plane

```
ZGO=P*D;
for n in range (0,N+1):
    for m in range(0,N+1):#Filling Mesh
        x1[n][m]=L*Rho[n]*np.cos(Theta[m]);
        z1[n][m]=L*Rho[n]*np.sin(Theta[m])+ZGO;
```

We will also define a vertical scaling amplitude for y, as follows:

```
Amplitude=100; # Vertical scale factor.
```

Now we can fill the vertical array with data of one of the aberration terms. In the example in Listing 15-4, we use the term that corresponds to spherical aberration.

Listing 15-4. Filling the Vertical Array

```
for n in range(0,N+1): #Filling function pixels
    for m in range(0,N+1):
        # Spherical aberration
        y[n][m]=Amplitude * Rho[n]**4;
```

In this code, the spherical aberration term is independent of Theta. For an aberration term depending on Theta, such as tilt for example, the code would be as follows:

```
for n in range(0,N+1): # Filling function pixels
    for m in range(0,N+1):
        # Tilt
        y[n][m]=Amplitude * Rho[n]*np.cos(Theta[m]);
```

The remaining functions of the program are the same as in previous chapters. The complete code for main.py and File.kv are shown in Listing 15-5 and Listing 15-6, respectively.

Listing 15-5. Code for the main.py File

```
from kivy.app import App
from kivy.uix.floatlayout import FloatLayout
from kivy.graphics import Line, Ellipse, Color
from kivy.clock import Clock
from kivy.core.image import Image as CoreImage
from PIL import Image, ImageDraw, ImageFont
import io
import os
```

```python
import numpy as np
from kivy.lang import Builder

Builder.load_file(
    os.path.join(os.path.dirname(os.path.abspath(
                        __file__)), 'File.kv')
                );
# Avoid Form1 of being resizable
from kivy.config import Config
Config.set("graphics","resizable", False);
Config.set('graphics', 'width',  '480');
Config.set('graphics', 'height', '680');

D=800;
VX1=100; VY1=200; VZ1=0;
VX2=130; VY2=200; VZ2=0;

P=0.5; # Place the function at z=D/2
N=40;  # Number of pixels to represent the function
y=np.zeros( (N+1,N+1) );
# Mesh
x1=np.zeros( (N+1,N+1) ); z1=np.zeros( (N+1,N+1) );
L=70;
Pi=np.pi;
XGO=0; ZGO=P*D; Amplitude=100;
Rho=np.zeros(N+1); Theta=np.zeros(N+1);
for n in range(0,N+1):
    Rho[n]=n/N;
    Theta[n]=n/N*2*Pi;

for n in range (0,N+1):
    for m in range(0,N+1):#Filling Mesh
        x1[n][m]=L*Rho[n]*np.cos(Theta[m]);
        z1[n][m]=L*Rho[n]*np.sin(Theta[m])+ZGO;
```

```python
for n in range(0,N+1): #Filling function pixels
    for m in range(0,N+1):
        y[n][m]=Amplitude * Rho[n]**4;

PointList=np.zeros( (N+1,2) );
def GraphFunction(VX,VY,VZ,Which):
    global x1,y, z1, N;
    # MaxY=np.max(y)

    if (Which==0):
        r,g,b = 200, 0, 0; #red Image
        Draw=Draw1
    else:
        r,g,b= 0, 200, 200; #cyan image
        Draw=Draw2
    for n in range (0,N+1): #Horizontal Lines
        for m in range (0,N+1):
            Factor=(D-VZ)/(D-z1[n][m]-VZ);
            xA=XC+Factor*(x1[n][m]-VX)+VX;
            yA=YC-Factor*(y[n][m]-VY)-VY;
            PointList[m]=xA,yA;
        List=tuple( map(tuple,PointList) );
        Draw.line( List, fill=(r,g,b), width=2 );

    for n in range (0,N+1): #Vertical Lines
        for m in range (0,N+1):
            Factor=(D-VZ)/(D-z1[m][n]-VZ);
            xA=XC+Factor*(x1[m][n]-VX)+VX;
            yA=YC-Factor*(y[m][n]-VY)-VY;
            PointList[m]=xA,yA;
        List=tuple( map(tuple,PointList) );
        Draw.line( List, fill=(r,g,b), width=2 );
```

```
        Font = ImageFont.truetype('Gargi.ttf', 40);
        Draw1.text( (10,10), "3D", fill =
                        (255,0,0,1), font=Font);
        Draw2.text( (30,10), "3D", fill =
                        (0,255,255,1), font=Font);
def ShowScene(B):
    Array1=np.array(PilImage1);
    Array2=np.array(PilImage2);
    Array3=Array1 | Array2;

    PilImage3=Image.fromarray(Array3);

    Memory=io.BytesIO();
    PilImage3.save(Memory, format="png");
    Memory.seek(0);
    ImagePNG=CoreImage(Memory, ext="png");

    B.ids.Screen1.texture=ImagePNG.texture;
    ImagePNG.remove_from_cache()
    Memory.close();
    PilImage3.close();
    Array1=None;
    Array2=None;
    Array3=None;

def ClearObjects():
    Draw1.rectangle( (0, 0, W-10, H-10), fill=
                        (60, 70, 30, 1) );
    Draw2.rectangle( (0, 0, W-10, H-10), fill=
                        (60, 70, 30, 1) );

def RotateFunction(B, Sense):
    global XGO, ZGO
```

```
if Sense==-1:
    Teta=np.pi/180*(-4.0);
else:
    Teta=np.pi/180*(4.0);
Cos_Teta=np.cos(Teta)
Sin_Teta=np.sin(Teta);

X0=XG0;  Y0=0;  Z0=ZG0 # Center of rotation

for n in range(0,N+1):
    for m in range(0,N+1):
        if (B.ids.Button3.state=="down" or
                B.ids.Button4.state=="down"):
            yP=(y[n][m]-Y0)*Cos_Teta \
                + (x1[n][m]-X0)*Sin_Teta + Y0;
            xP=-(y[n][m]-Y0)*Sin_Teta \
                +(x1[n][m]-X0)*Cos_Teta + X0;
            y[n][m]=yP;
            x1[n][m]=xP;

        if (B.ids.Button5.state=="down" or
                B.ids.Button6.state=="down"):
            yP=(y[n][m]-Y0)*Cos_Teta \
                + (z1[n][m]-Z0)*Sin_Teta + Y0;
            zP=-(y[n][m]-Y0)*Sin_Teta \
                +(z1[n][m]-Z0)*Cos_Teta + Z0;
            y[n][m]=yP;
            z1[n][m]=zP;

        if (B.ids.Button7.state=="down" or
                B.ids.Button8.state=="down"):
            xP=(x1[n][m]-X0)*Cos_Teta \
                + (z1[n][m]-Z0)*Sin_Teta + X0;
```

```
            zP=-(x1[n][m]-X0)*Sin_Teta \
                +(z1[n][m]-Z0)*Cos_Teta + Z0;
            x1[n][m]=xP;
            z1[n][m]=zP;
class Form1(FloatLayout):
    def __init__(Handle, **kwargs):
        super(Form1, Handle).__init__(**kwargs);
        Event1=Clock.schedule_once(Handle.Initialize);

    def Initialize(B, *args):
        global W,H, XC,YC;
        global PilImage1,PilImage2, Draw1,Draw2;
        # P= Percentage of the D distance
        global P, Amplitude;
        W,H=B.ids.Screen1.size;
        XC=int (W/2)+P/(1-P)*VX1+30;
        YC=int(H/2)-P/(1-P)*VY1+110;
        PilImage1= Image.new('RGB', (W-10, H-10),
                             (60, 70, 30));
        Draw1 = ImageDraw.Draw(PilImage1);
        PilImage2= Image.new('RGB', (W-10, H-10),
                             (60, 70, 30));
        Draw2 = ImageDraw.Draw(PilImage2);
        Font = ImageFont.truetype('Gargi.ttf', 70)
        Draw1.text( (30,200), "3D Images", fill =
                             (255,0,0,1), font=Font);
        Draw2.text( (50,200), "3D Images", fill =
                             (0,255,255,1), font=Font);
        ShowScene(B);
```

```
def Button1_Click(B):
    global Draw1, Draw2;
    ClearObjects(); # Clearing Draw1 and Draw2
    GraphFunction(VX1,VY1,VZ1,0);
    GraphFunction(VX2,VY2,VZ2,1);
    ShowScene(B);

def Button2_Click(B):
    ClearObjects(); # Clearing Draw1 and Draw2
    Font = ImageFont.truetype('Gargi.ttf', 70)
    Draw1.text( (30,200), "3D Images", fill =
                        (255,0,0,1), font=Font);
    Draw2.text( (50,200), "3D Images", fill =
                        (0,255,255,1), font=Font);
    ShowScene(B);

def Button3_Click(B):
    RotateFunction(B,1);
    ClearObjects(); # Clearing Draw1 and Draw2
    GraphFunction(VX1,VY1,VZ1,0);
    GraphFunction(VX2,VY2,VZ2,1);
    ShowScene(B);

def Button4_Click(B):
    RotateFunction(B,-1),
    ClearObjects();
    GraphFunction(VX1,VY1,VZ1,0);
    GraphFunction(VX2,VY2,VZ2,1);
    ShowScene(B);

def Button5_Click(B):
    RotateFunction(B,-1),
    ClearObjects();
```

273

```
        GraphFunction(VX1,VY1,VZ1,0);
        GraphFunction(VX2,VY2,VZ2,1);
        ShowScene(B);

    def Button6_Click(B):
        RotateFunction(B,1),
        ClearObjects();
        GraphFunction(VX1,VY1,VZ1,0);
        GraphFunction(VX2,VY2,VZ2,1);
        ShowScene(B);

    def Button7_Click(B):
        RotateFunction(B,-1),
        ClearObjects();
        GraphFunction(VX1,VY1,VZ1,0);
        GraphFunction(VX2,VY2,VZ2,1);
        ShowScene(B);

    def Button8_Click(B):
        RotateFunction(B,1),
        ClearObjects();
        GraphFunction(VX1,VY1,VZ1,0);
        GraphFunction(VX2,VY2,VZ2,1);
        ShowScene(B);

# This is the Start Up code.
class StartUp (App):
    def build (BU):
        BU.title="Form1"
        return Form1();
if __name__ =="__main__":
    StartUp().run();
```

Listing 15-6. Code for the file.kv File

```
#:set W 440
#:set H 440
<Form1>:
    id : Form1
    Image:
        id: Screen1
        size_hint: None,None
        pos_hint: {"x":0.04, "y":0.34}
        size: W,H
        canvas.before:
            Color:
                rgba: 0.9, 0.9, 0, 1
            RoundedRectangle:
                pos:   self.pos
                size: self.size
    Button:
        id: Button1
        on_press: Form1.Button1_Click()
        text: "Button1"
        size_hint: None,None
        pos_hint: {"x": 0.2, "y":0.03}
        size: 100,30

    Button:
        id: Button2
        on_press: Form1.Button2_Click()
        text: "Button2"
        size_hint: None,None
        pos_hint: {"x": 0.63, "y":0.03}
        size: 100,30
```

```
Button:
    id: Button3
    on_press: Form1.Button3_Click()
    text: "Button3"
    size_hint: None,None
    pos_hint: {"x": 0.05, "y":0.12}
    size: 100,30
    always_release: True
Button:
    id: Button4
    on_press: Form1.Button4_Click()
    text: "Button4"
    size_hint: None,None
    pos_hint: {"x": 0.73, "y":0.12}
    size: 100,30

Button:
    id: Button5
    on_press: Form1.Button5_Click()
    text: "Button5"
    size_hint: None,None
    pos_hint: {"x": 0.05, "y":0.20}
    size: 100,30
Button:
    id: Button6
    on_press: Form1.Button6_Click()
    text: "Button6"
    size_hint: None,None
    pos_hint: {"x": 0.73, "y":0.20}
    size: 100,30
```

```
Button:
    id: Button7
    on_press: Form1.Button7_Click()
    text: "Button7"
    size_hint: None,None
    pos_hint: {"x": 0.05, "y":0.28}
    size: 100,30
Button:
    id: Button8
    on_press: Form1.Button8_Click()
    text: "Button8"
    size_hint: None,None
    pos_hint: {"x": 0.73, "y":0.28}
    size: 100,30
```

Figure 15-3 shows plots of five aberration terms obtained with the program, corresponding to the coefficients $A_{0,0,1}$, $A_{0,0,2}$, $A_{1,0,0}$, $A_{1,0,1}$, and $A_{2,0,0}$ of Equation (15.12).

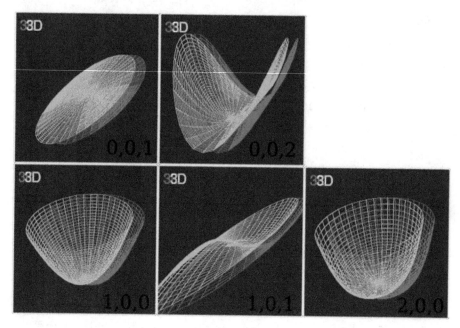

Figure 15-3. *Wavefront aberration terms corresponding to the coefficients* $A_{0,0,1}$, $A_{0,0,2}$, $A_{1,0,0}$, $A_{1,0,1}$, *and* $A_{2,0,0}$ *of Equation (15.12), plotted with the program*

15.5 Summary

In this chapter, we introduced elements for plotting stereoscopic 3D cylindrical functions. In particular, we presented working examples of Seidel aberrations. We provided a brief outline of the Fresnel diffraction integral and applied this integral to review the focusing properties of ideal lenses. We extended these concepts to lens aberrations, illustrating programming methods for plotting the aberration terms in stereoscopic views.

## CHAPTER 16

Stereoscopic Plotting of Three-Dimensional Conics

In this chapter, we describe basic principles for plotting stereoscopic three-dimensional conics. Figure 16-1 shows two screenshots of this program running on an Android cell phone showing plots of a hyperboloid at two different angles of rotation.

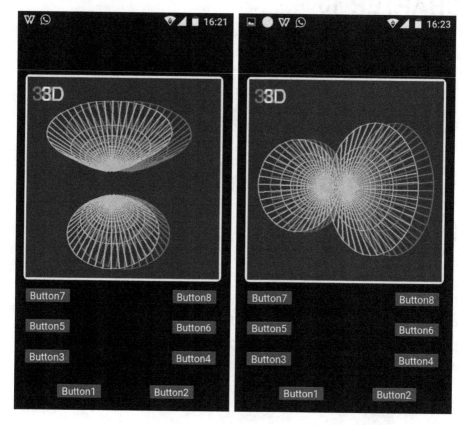

Figures 16-1. *The program running on an Android cell phone showing plots of a hyperboloid at two different angles of rotation*

The functionality of the buttons in the program is the same as in previous chapters.

In the following section, we describe the analytical approach.

16.1 Analytical Approach

Let's consider an ellipse on the coordinate plane x-y, as depicted in Figure 16-2.

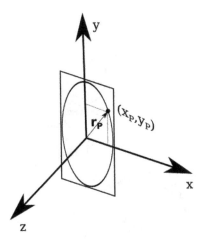

Figure 16-2. *Ellipse on a coordinate plane x-y*

The equation of the ellipse can be written as follows:

$$\frac{x^2}{a^2} + \frac{y^2}{b^2} = 1 \qquad (16.1)$$

In Equation (16.1), as usual, the constant parameters a and b represent the length of the horizontal and vertical semi-axes, respectively.

Let's consider a point with coordinates (x_P, y_P) on the plane x-y, at an arbitrary position on the ellipse and pointed by a vector r_p, as depicted in Figure 16-2.

The goal is to generate a three-dimensional ellipsoid by rotating the plane that contains the ellipse of Figure 16-2 around the y-axis, as depicted in Figure 16-3. The three-dimensional geometric plot, so generated, will be referred to as an *ellipsoid of rotation*. In this example, the ellipse rotates about one of its principal axes. Then, the plot so generated is known as an *ellipsoid of revolution*.

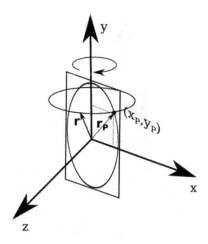

Figure 16-3. *Rotation of the ellipse in Figure 16-2*

In Figure 16-3, let $r = xi + yj + zk$ and $r_p = x_p i + y_p j$, where $i, j,$ and k are the Cartesian unit direction vectors. Note that the magnitude of r and r_p are equal. Therefore, we can write the following:

$$x^2 + y^2 + z^2 = x_p^2 + y_p^2 \tag{16.2}$$

Since the point (x_P, y_P) is a point of the ellipse, it satisfies Equation (16.1).

It can be observed from Figure 16-3 that $y = y_p$. Therefore, canceling equal terms in Equation (16.2) and using Equation (16.1) gives the following:

$$\frac{x^2}{a^2} + \frac{y^2}{b^2} + \frac{z^2}{a^2} = 1 \tag{16.3}$$

Equation (16.3) represents an ellipse of revolution.

If in Equation (16.3), we allow all the constants to be different, we obtain a more general expression, written as follows:

$$\frac{x^2}{a^2} + \frac{y^2}{b^2} + \frac{z^2}{c^2} = 1 \tag{16.4}$$

Equation (16.4) is the equation of a three-dimensional ellipsoid. In the following section, we describe our stereoscopic plotting approach of the ellipsoid.

16.2 Stereoscopic Ellipsoid Plotting

This approach consists of representing the ellipsoid in spherical coordinates. Before doing so, it is necessary to consider that in our geometrical situation, the vertical axis corresponds to y. The horizontal axis corresponds to x and z represents depth. Therefore, for programming purposes, we will rewrite Equation (16.4) as follows:

$$\frac{y^2}{a^2} + \frac{x^2}{b^2} + \frac{z^2}{c^2} = 1 \tag{16.5}$$

Accordingly, the spherical system will be represented as in Figure 16-4.

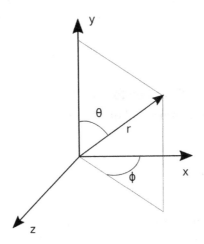

Figure 16-4. *Spherical coordinate system used in this program*

From Figure 16-4, the coordinates of the position vector can be written as follows:

$$x = r\sin(\theta)\cos(\phi) \tag{16.6}$$

$$y = r\cos(\theta) \tag{16.7}$$

$$z = r\sin(\theta)\sin(\phi) \tag{16.8}$$

Substituting Equations (16.6)-(16.8) into Equation (16.5) gives the following equation:

$$\left(\frac{r\cos(\theta)}{a}\right)^2 + \left(\frac{r\sin(\theta)\cos(\phi)}{b}\right)^2 + \left(\frac{r\sin(\theta)\sin(\phi)}{c}\right)^2 = 1 \tag{16.9}$$

From Equation (16.9), the radial distance r is expressed as follows:

$$r = \frac{1}{\sqrt{\left(\dfrac{\cos(\theta)}{a}\right)^2 + \left(\dfrac{\sin(\theta)\cos(\phi)}{b}\right)^2 + \left(\dfrac{\sin(\theta)\sin(\phi)}{c}\right)^2}} \tag{16.10}$$

Equation (16.10) will be used to generate our plot.

We will first set the number of pixels and the constant ellipse values a, b, and c, as follows:

a=100; b=90; c=60;

Next we set the variable D, which is the distance between the plane of projection and the screen, to 800. We also set coordinates of the left and right points of projection, as follows:

D=800;
VX1=100; VY1=100; VZ1=0;
VX2=140; VY2=100; VZ2=0;

We will use the percentage variable P with the value 0.5 to place the ellipsoid in the middle, between the screen and the plane of projection. We also set the number of pixels as follows:

```
D=600; #Distance from plane of projection to screen
P=0.5; #Place the function at z=D/2
N=40;  #Number of pixels to represent the function
ZGO=P*D; # z Offset to place the function
```

Next, we create and fill the arrays corresponding to r, Theta, and Phi, as shown in Listing 16-1.

Listing 16-1. Creating and Filling the r, Theta, and Phi Arrays

```
import numpy as np
Pi=np.pi;
Theta=np.zeros(N+1);
Phi=np.zeros(N+1);
r=np.zeros( (N+1,N+1) );

for n in range(0,N+1):
    Theta[n]=n/N*Pi;
    Phi[n]=n/N*2*Pi;

for n in range(0,N+1):
    for m in range(0,N+1):
        r[n][m]=1/np.sqrt( (np.sin(Theta[n])
                        *np.cos(Phi[m])/a)**2 +
                (np.sin(Theta[n])*np.sin(Phi[m])/b)**2
                        +(np.cos(Theta[n])/c)**2  );
```

In this code, Theta entries range from 0 to π, and Phi ranges from 0 to 2π. Both arrays have N+1 entries. The radial distance is represented by the two-dimensional array (N+1) x (N+1), r, and stores the values given by Equation (16.10).

The next step consists of creating and filling the mesh. The code is shown in Listing 16-2.

Listing 16-2. Creating Mesh Arrays

```
x1=np.zeros( (N+1,N+1) ); z1=np.zeros( (N+1,N+1) );
for n in range (0,N+1):
    for m in range(0,N+1):#Filling Mesh
        x1[n][m]=r[n][m]*np.sin(Theta[n])\
                                *np.cos(Phi[m]);
        z1[n][m]=r[n][m]*np.sin(Theta[n])\
                                *np.sin(Phi[m])+ZGO;
        y[n][m]=r[n][m]*np.cos(Theta[n]);
```

The two nested for loops are used to fill the mesh according to Equations (16.6)-(16.8).

The functions to plot and rotate the ellipsoid are similar to their corresponding ones described in previous chapters. Figure 16-5 shows a stereoscopic plot of an ellipsoid with $a=100$, $b=90$, and $c=60$, obtained with the program code.

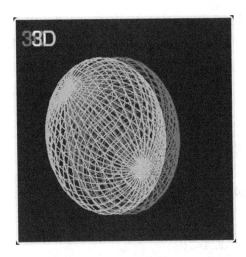

Figure 16-5. *Stereoscopic scene of an ellipsoid with a=100, b=90, and c=60, plotted with the code*

The complete code listings for main.py and File.kv are shown in Listings 16-3 and 16-4, respectively.

Listing 16-3. Code for the main.py (Ellipsoid) File

```
from kivy.app import App
from kivy.uix.floatlayout import FloatLayout
from kivy.graphics import Line, Ellipse, Color
from kivy.clock import Clock
from kivy.core.image import Image as CoreImage
from PIL import Image, ImageDraw, ImageFont
import io
import os
import numpy as np
from kivy.lang import Builder
```

```
Builder.load_file(
    os.path.join(os.path.dirname(os.path.abspath(
                        __file__)), 'File.kv')
            );
#Avoid Form1 of being resizable
from kivy.config import Config
Config.set("graphics","resizable", False);
Config.set('graphics', 'width',  '480');
Config.set('graphics', 'height', '680');

D=800;
VX1=100; VY1=100; VZ1=0;
VX2=140; VY2=100; VZ2=0;

P=0.5; #Place the function at z=D/2
N=40;  #Number of pixels to represent the function
y=np.zeros( (N+1,N+1) );
#creating Mesh arrays
x1=np.zeros( (N+1,N+1) ); z1=np.zeros( (N+1,N+1) );
L=130;  r0=L/5;
XG0=0; ZG0=P*D; Amplitude=150;

a=40; b=40; c=60;
Pi=np.pi;
Theta=np.zeros(N+1);
Phi=np.zeros(N+1);
r=np.zeros( (N+1,N+1) );

for n in range(0,N+1):
    Theta[n]=n/N*Pi;
    Phi[n]=n/N*2*Pi;
```

```python
for n in range(0,N+1):
    for m in range(0,N+1):
        r[n][m]=1/np.sqrt( (np.sin(Theta[n])
                        *np.cos(Phi[m])/a)**2 +
            (np.sin(Theta[n])*np.sin(Phi[m])/b)**2
                        +(np.cos(Theta[n])/c)**2  );

for n in range (0,N+1):
    for m in range(0,N+1):#Filling Mesh
        x1[n][m]=r[n][m]*np.sin(Theta[n])\
                            *np.cos(Phi[m]);
        z1[n][m]=r[n][m]*np.sin(Theta[n])\
                            *np.sin(Phi[m])+ZGO;
        y[n][m]=r[n][m]*np.cos(Theta[n]);
PointList=np.zeros( (N+1,2) );
def GraphFunction(VX,VY,VZ,Which):
    global x1,y, z1, N;
    #MaxY=np.max(y)

    if (Which==0):
        r,g,b = 200, 0, 0; #red Image
        Draw=Draw1
    else:
        r,g,b= 0, 200, 200; #cyan image
        Draw=Draw2
    for n in range (0,N+1): #Horizontal Lines
        for m in range (0,N+1):
            Factor=(D-VZ)/(D-z1[n][m]-VZ);
            xA=XC+Factor*(x1[n][m]-VX)+VX;
            yA=YC-Factor*(y[n][m]-VY)-VY;
            PointList[m]=xA,yA;
        List=tuple( map(tuple,PointList) );
        Draw.line( List, fill=(r,g,b), width=2 );
```

```
    for n in range (0,N+1): #Vertical Lines
        for m in range (0,N+1):
            Factor=(D-VZ)/(D-z1[m][n]-VZ);
            xA=XC+Factor*(x1[m][n]-VX)+VX;
            yA=YC-Factor*(y[m][n]-VY)-VY;
            PointList[m]=xA,yA;
        List=tuple( map(tuple,PointList) );
        Draw.line( List, fill=(r,g,b), width=2 );

        Font = ImageFont.truetype('Gargi.ttf', 40)
        Draw1.text( (10,10), "3D", fill =
                            (255,0,0,1), font=Font);
        Draw2.text( (30,10), "3D", fill =
                            (0,255,255,1), font=Font);

def ShowScene(B):
    Array1=np.array(PilImage1);
    Array2=np.array(PilImage2);
    Array3=Array1 | Array2;

    PilImage3=Image.fromarray(Array3);

    Memory=io.BytesIO();
    PilImage3.save(Memory, format="png");
    Memory.seek(0);
    ImagePNG=CoreImage(Memory, ext="png");

    B.ids.Screen1.texture=ImagePNG.texture;
    ImagePNG.remove_from_cache()
    Memory.close();
    PilImage3.close();
    Array1=None;
    Array2=None;
    Array3=None;
```

```python
def ClearObjects():
    Draw1.rectangle( (0, 0, W-10, H-10), fill =
                                (60, 70, 30, 1) );
    Draw2.rectangle( (0, 0, W-10, H-10), fill =
                                (60, 70, 30, 1) );

def RotateFunction(B, Sense):
    global XGO, ZGO
    if Sense==-1:
        Teta=np.pi/180*(-4.0);
    else:
        Teta=np.pi/180*(4.0);
    Cos_Teta=np.cos(Teta)
    Sin_Teta=np.sin(Teta);

    XO=XGO;  YO=0;   ZO=ZGO # Center of rotation

    for n in range(0,N+1):
        for m in range(0,N+1):
            if (B.ids.Button3.state=="down" or
                    B.ids.Button4.state=="down"):
                yP=(y[n][m]-YO)*Cos_Teta \
                    + (x1[n][m]-XO)*Sin_Teta + YO;
                xP=-(y[n][m]-YO)*Sin_Teta \
                        +(x1[n][m]-XO)*Cos_Teta + XO;
                y[n][m]=yP;
                x1[n][m]=xP;

            if (B.ids.Button5.state=="down" or
                    B.ids.Button6.state=="down"):
                yP=(y[n][m]-YO)*Cos_Teta \
                        + (z1[n][m]-ZO)*Sin_Teta + YO;
                zP=-(y[n][m]-YO)*Sin_Teta \
                        + (z1[n][m]-ZO)*Cos_Teta + ZO;
```

```
                    y[n][m]=yP;
                    z1[n][m]=zP;

            if (B.ids.Button7.state=="down" or
                    B.ids.Button8.state=="down"):
                xP=(x1[n][m]-X0)*Cos_Teta \
                    + (z1[n][m]-Z0)*Sin_Teta + X0;
                zP=-(x1[n][m]-X0)*Sin_Teta \
                    +(z1[n][m]-Z0)*Cos_Teta + Z0;
                x1[n][m]=xP;
                z1[n][m]=zP;

class Form1(FloatLayout):
    def __init__(Handle, **kwargs):
        super(Form1, Handle).__init__(**kwargs);
        Event1=Clock.schedule_once(Handle.Initialize);

    def Initialize(B, *args):
        global W,H, XC,YC;
        global PilImage1,PilImage2, Draw1,Draw2;
        # P= Percentage of the D distance
        global P, Amplitude;
        W,H=B.ids.Screen1.size;
        XC=int (W/2)+P/(1-P)*VX1+18;
        YC=int(H/2)-P/(1-P)*VY1+10;
        PilImage1= Image.new('RGB', (W-10, H-10),
                                    (60, 70, 30));
        Draw1 = ImageDraw.Draw(PilImage1);
        PilImage2= Image.new('RGB', (W-10, H-10),
                                    (60, 70, 30));
        Draw2 = ImageDraw.Draw(PilImage2);
        Font = ImageFont.truetype('Gargi.ttf', 70)
```

```python
    Draw1.text( (30,200), "3D Images", fill =
                        (255,0,0,1), font=Font);
    Draw2.text( (50,200), "3D Images", fill =
                        (0,255,255,1), font=Font);
    ShowScene(B);

def Button1_Click(B):
    global Draw1, Draw2;
    ClearObjects(); # Clearing Draw1 and Draw2
    GraphFunction(VX1,VY1,VZ1,0);
    GraphFunction(VX2,VY2,VZ2,1);
    ShowScene(B);

def Button2_Click(B):
    ClearObjects(); # Clearing Draw1 and Draw2
    Font = ImageFont.truetype('Gargi.ttf', 70)
    Draw1.text( (30,200), "3D Images", fill =
                        (255,0,0,1), font=Font);
    Draw2.text( (50,200), "3D Images", fill =
                        (0,255,255,1), font=Font);
    ShowScene(B);

def Button3_Click(B):
    RotateFunction(B,1);
    ClearObjects(); # Clearing Draw1 and Draw2
    GraphFunction(VX1,VY1,VZ1,0);
    GraphFunction(VX2,VY2,VZ2,1);
    ShowScene(B);

def Button4_Click(B):
    RotateFunction(B,-1),
    ClearObjects();
```

```
    GraphFunction(VX1,VY1,VZ1,0);
    GraphFunction(VX2,VY2,VZ2,1);
    ShowScene(B);

def Button5_Click(B):
    RotateFunction(B,-1),
    ClearObjects();
    GraphFunction(VX1,VY1,VZ1,0);
    GraphFunction(VX2,VY2,VZ2,1);
    ShowScene(B);

def Button6_Click(B):
    RotateFunction(B,1),
    ClearObjects();
    GraphFunction(VX1,VY1,VZ1,0);
    GraphFunction(VX2,VY2,VZ2,1);
    ShowScene(B);

def Button7_Click(B):
    RotateFunction(B,-1),
    ClearObjects();
    GraphFunction(VX1,VY1,VZ1,0);
    GraphFunction(VX2,VY2,VZ2,1);
    ShowScene(B);

def Button8_Click(B):
    RotateFunction(B,1),
    ClearObjects();
    GraphFunction(VX1,VY1,VZ1,0);
    GraphFunction(VX2,VY2,VZ2,1);
    ShowScene(B);
```

```
# This is the Start Up code.
class StartUp (App):
    def build (BU):
        BU.title="Form1"
        return Form1();
if __name__ =="__main__":
    StartUp().run();
```

Listing 16-4. Code for the file.kv File

```
#:set W 440
#:set H 440
<Form1>:
    id : Form1
    Image:
        id: Screen1
        size_hint: None,None
        pos_hint: {"x":0.04, "y":0.34}
        size: W,H
        canvas.before:
            Color:
                rgba: 0.9, 0.9, 0, 1
            RoundedRectangle:
                pos:  self.pos
                size: self.size
    Button:
        id: Button1
        on_press: Form1.Button1_Click()
        text: "Button1"
        size_hint: None,None
        pos_hint: {"x": 0.2, "y":0.03}
        size: 100,30
```

```
Button:
    id: Button2
    on_press: Form1.Button2_Click()
    text: "Button2"
    size_hint: None,None
    pos_hint: {"x": 0.63, "y":0.03}
    size: 100,30

Button:
    id: Button3
    on_press: Form1.Button3_Click()
    text: "Button3"
    size_hint: None,None
    pos_hint: {"x": 0.05, "y":0.12}
    size: 100,30
    always_release: True
Button:
    id: Button4
    on_press: Form1.Button4_Click()
    text: "Button4"
    size_hint: None,None
    pos_hint: {"x": 0.73, "y":0.12}
    size: 100,30

Button:
    id: Button5
    on_press: Form1.Button5_Click()
    text: "Button5"
    size_hint: None,None
    pos_hint: {"x": 0.05, "y":0.20}
    size: 100,30
```

```
Button:
    id: Button6
    on_press: Form1.Button6_Click()
    text: "Button6"
    size_hint: None,None
    pos_hint: {"x": 0.73, "y":0.20}
    size: 100,30

Button:
    id: Button7
    on_press: Form1.Button7_Click()
    text: "Button7"
    size_hint: None,None
    pos_hint: {"x": 0.05, "y":0.28}
    size: 100,30
Button:
    id: Button8
    on_press: Form1.Button8_Click()
    text: "Button8"
    size_hint: None,None
    pos_hint: {"x": 0.73, "y":0.28}
    size: 100,30
```

16.3 Hyperboloid

As in the case of the ellipsoid, we will first consider the equation of a
hyperbola on the x-y plane.

For programming purposes and without loss of generality, we focus on
a vertical hyperbola, as depicted in Figure 16-6.

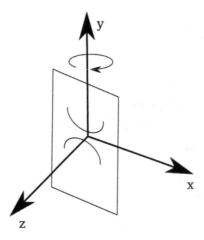

Figure 16-6. *Vertical hyperbola on the plane x-y*

The equation for the vertical hyperbola can be written as follows:

$$\frac{x^2}{a^2} - \frac{y^2}{b^2} = 1 \tag{16.11}$$

We now allow the plane of the hyperbola to rotate in a similar manner as we did with the ellipse. Then, using Equation (16.11) and Equation (16.2), we obtain the equation of a vertical circular hyperboloid as follows:

$$\frac{x^2}{a^2} - \frac{y^2}{b^2} - \frac{z^2}{b^2} = 1 \tag{16.12}$$

By allowing the constant terms that correspond to x, y, and z to be different between them in Equation (16.12), we'll create a more general vertical hyperboloid equation. Using our geometrical situation, the equation is as follows:

$$\frac{y^2}{a^2} - \frac{x^2}{b^2} - \frac{z^2}{c^2} = 1 \tag{16.13}$$

To plot the hyperboloid given by Equation (16.13), we use spherical coordinates in a similar way as we did with the ellipsoid in Section 16.2. Then, substituting Equations (16.6)-(16.8) into Equation (16.13) gives the following:

$$\left(\frac{r\cos(\theta)}{a}\right)^2 - \left(\frac{r\sin(\theta)\cos(\phi)}{b}\right)^2 - \left(\frac{r\sin(\theta)\sin(\phi)}{c}\right)^2 = 1 \qquad (16.14)$$

Using Equation (16.14) gives the following:

$$r = \frac{1}{\sqrt{\left(\frac{\cos(\theta)}{a}\right)^2 - \left(\frac{\sin(\theta)\cos(\phi)}{b}\right)^2 - \left(\frac{\sin(\theta)\sin(\phi)}{c}\right)^2}} \qquad (16.15)$$

The argument within the square root in Equation (16.15) can be zero or negative for some values. Therefore, the radial distance can result in an undefined or a complex number. This characteristic is a natural consequence of the hyperboloid shape, as it consists of two separated surfaces. Therefore, to avoid plotting at these values, we will proceed as follows.

We will vary the angle ϕ between 0 and 2π. However, the values that θ can take must be split into two intervals, one for plotting the upper surface and the other for the bottom surface. The first interval is between 0 and some value $\theta_0 < \theta_{Max}$ and the second one is between π and $\pi + \theta_0$. Here, θ_{Max} is the maximum allowed value that θ can take to avoid undefined or complex values in Equation (16.15). It is possible to exactly calculate θ_{Max}; however, for illustrative purposes, it will be sufficient to propose and test some values.

Because the θ variable requires two angular intervals, it will be convenient to use two independent arrays, which we call ThetaA and ThetaB. For the variable ϕ, only one array is required, called Phi. The code for creating and filling the arrays is shown in Listing 16-5.

Listing 16-5. Filling Two Independent Arrays for the Hyperboloid

```python
import numpy as np
N=40; Pi=np.pi;
Theta0=Pi/180*(40);
Phi=np.zeros(N+1);
ThetaA=np.zeros(N+1); rA=np.zeros( (N+1,N+1) );
ThetaB=np.zeros(N+1); rB=np.zeros( (N+1,N+1) );

for n in range(0,N+1):
    ThetaA[n]=n/N*Theta0; #from 0 to Theta0
    ThetaB[n]=n/N*Theta0 +Pi; #from Pi to(Pi+Theta0)

Phi0=Pi/180*360
for n in range(0,N+1):
    Phi[n]=(n-N/2)/N*Phi0;
```

In this code, θ_0, represented in the code by Theta0, was set to 40 degrees. We set this value arbitrarily as a first trial. The multiplying factor $\pi/180$ converts entries from degrees to radians. For simplicity, we tested different values for θ_0, taking care of attaining only real values for the radial distance as given by Equation (16.15). The ThetaA, ThetaB, and Phi arrays all have sizes N+1.

Next, since we will plot the upper and bottom surfaces independently, we need to create two mesh sets, as shown in Listing 16-6.

Listing 16-6. Creating Two Mesh Sets

```python
y1A=np.zeros( (N+1,N+1) );
y1B=np.zeros( (N+1,N+1) );
x1A=np.zeros( (N+1,N+1) );
x1B=np.zeros( (N+1,N+1) );
z1A=np.zeros( (N+1,N+1) ); #Mesh
z1B=np.zeros( (N+1,N+1) ); #Mesh
```

For the two surfaces, we need two arrays for the radial distance. Each array will be filled with values given by Equation (16.14). The corresponding code is shown in Listing 16-7.

Listing 16-7. Creating Two Arrays for the Radial Distances

```
rA=np.zeros( (N+1,N+1) );  rB=np.zeros( (N+1,N+1) );
for n in range(0,N+1):
    for m in range(0,N+1):
        rA[n][m]=1/np.sqrt( (np.cos(ThetaA[n])/a)**2
            -(np.sin(ThetaA[n])*np.sin(Phi[m])/b)**2
        -(np.sin(ThetaA[n])*np.cos(Phi[m])/c)**2  );
        rB[n][m]=1/np.sqrt( (np.cos(ThetaB[n])/a)**2
            -(np.sin(ThetaB[n])*np.sin(Phi[m])/b)**2
        -(np.sin(ThetaB[n])*np.cos(Phi[m])/c)**2  );
```

We can fill both mesh values using Equations (16.6)-(16.8), as shown in Listing 16-8.

Listing 16-8. Filling the Two Mesh Values

```
L=5;
for n in range (0,N+1):
    for m in range(0,N+1):#Filling MeshA
        x1A[n][m]=L*rA[n][m]*np.sin(ThetaA[n])*\
                                np.cos(Phi[m]);
        z1A[n][m]=L*rA[n][m]*np.sin(ThetaA[n])*\
                                np.sin(Phi[m])+ZGO;
        y1A[n][m]=L*rA[n][m]*np.cos(ThetaA[n]);

for n in range (0,N+1):
    for m in range(0,N+1):#Filling MeshB
        x1B[n][m]=L*rB[n][m]*np.sin(ThetaB[n])\
                                *np.cos(Phi[m]);
```

```
z1B[n][m]=L*rB[n][m]*np.sin(ThetaB[n])\
                        *np.sin(Phi[m])+ZGO;
y1B[n][m]=L*rB[n][m]*np.cos(ThetaB[n]);
```

In this code listing, L is a scaling factor that allows us to change the dimensions of the plot.

The GraphFunction(VX,VY,VZ,Which) and RotateFunction(B, Sense) functions are similar to the ones described in previous chapters. There is a slight difference, however. Instead of using one array for plotting only one surface, these functions use two arrays for plotting the upper and bottom surfaces.

The code for main.py that corresponds to the hyperboloid is shown in Listing 16-9.

Listing 16-9. main.py (for the Hyperboloid)

```
from kivy.app import App
from kivy.uix.floatlayout import FloatLayout
from kivy.graphics import Line, Ellipse, Color
from kivy.clock import Clock
from kivy.core.image import Image as CoreImage
from PIL import Image, ImageDraw, ImageFont
import io
import os
import numpy as np
from kivy.lang import Builder

Builder.load_file(
    os.path.join(os.path.dirname(os.path.abspath(
                        __file__)), 'File.kv')
            );
#Avoid Form1 of being resizable
from kivy.config import Config
```

```python
Config.set("graphics","resizable", False);
Config.set('graphics', 'width',  '480');
Config.set('graphics', 'height', '680');

D=600;
VX1=-15; VY1=0; VZ1=0;
VX2=15; VY2=0; VZ2=0;

P=0.0; #Place the function at z=D/2
N=40;  #Number of pixels to represent the function

y1A=np.zeros( (N+1,N+1) );
y1B=np.zeros( (N+1,N+1) );
x1A=np.zeros( (N+1,N+1) );
x1B=np.zeros( (N+1,N+1) );
z1A=np.zeros( (N+1,N+1) ); #Mesh
z1B=np.zeros( (N+1,N+1) ); #Mesh

XG0=0; ZG0=P*D;
a=10; b=9; c=9;
Pi=np.pi;
Theta0=Pi/180*(40);
Phi=np.zeros(N+1);
ThetaA=np.zeros(N+1); rA=np.zeros( (N+1,N+1) );
ThetaB=np.zeros(N+1); rB=np.zeros( (N+1,N+1) );

for n in range(0,N+1):
    ThetaA[n]=n/N*Theta0; #from 0 to Theta0
    ThetaB[n]=n/N*Theta0 +Pi; #from Pi to(Pi+Theta0)

Phi0=Pi/180*360
for n in range(0,N+1):
    Phi[n]=(n-N/2)/N*Phi0;
```

```
for n in range(0,N+1):
    for m in range(0,N+1):
        rA[n][m]=1/np.sqrt( (np.cos(ThetaA[n])/a)**2
            -(np.sin(ThetaA[n])*np.sin(Phi[m])/b)**2
            -(np.sin(ThetaA[n])*np.cos(Phi[m])/c)**2  );
        rB[n][m]=1/np.sqrt( (np.cos(ThetaB[n])/a)**2
            -(np.sin(ThetaB[n])*np.sin(Phi[m])/b)**2
            -(np.sin(ThetaB[n])*np.cos(Phi[m])/c)**2  );

L=5;
for n in range (0,N+1):
    for m in range(0,N+1):#Filling MeshA
        x1A[n][m]=L*rA[n][m]*np.sin(ThetaA[n])*\
                                np.cos(Phi[m]);
        z1A[n][m]=L*rA[n][m]*np.sin(ThetaA[n])*\
                                np.sin(Phi[m])+ZGO;
        y1A[n][m]=L*rA[n][m]*np.cos(ThetaA[n]);

for n in range (0,N+1):
    for m in range(0,N+1):#Filling MeshB
        x1B[n][m]=L*rB[n][m]*np.sin(ThetaB[n])\
                                *np.cos(Phi[m]);
        z1B[n][m]=L*rB[n][m]*np.sin(ThetaB[n])\
                                *np.sin(Phi[m])+ZGO;
        y1B[n][m]=L*rB[n][m]*np.cos(ThetaB[n]);

PointList=np.zeros( (N+1,2) );
def GraphFunction(VX,VY,VZ,Which):

    if (Which==0):
        r,g,b = 200, 0, 0; #red Image
        Draw=Draw1
```

```
else:
    r,g,b= 0, 200, 200; #cyan image
    Draw=Draw2
#Drawing surface A
for n in range (0,N+1): #Horizontal Lines A
    for m in range (0,N+1):
        Factor=(D-VZ)/(D-z1A[n][m]-VZ);
        xA=XC+Factor*(x1A[n][m]-VX)+VX;
        yA=YC-Factor*(y1A[n][m]-VY)-VY;
        PointList[m]=xA,yA;
    List=tuple( map(tuple,PointList) );
    Draw.line( List, fill=(r,g,b), width=2 );

for n in range (0,N+1): #Vertical Lines A
    for m in range (0,N+1):
        Factor=(D-VZ)/(D-z1A[m][n]-VZ);
        xA=XC+Factor*(x1A[m][n]-VX)+VX;
        yA=YC-Factor*(y1A[m][n]-VY)-VY;
        PointList[m]=xA,yA;
    List=tuple( map(tuple,PointList) );
    Draw.line( List, fill=(r,g,b), width=2 );

#Drawing surface B
for n in range (0,N+1): #Horizontal Lines B
    for m in range (0,N+1):
        Factor=(D-VZ)/(D-z1B[n][m]-VZ);
        xA=XC+Factor*(x1B[n][m]-VX)+VX;
        yA=YC-Factor*(y1B[n][m]-VY)-VY;
        PointList[m]=xA,yA;
    List=tuple( map(tuple,PointList) );
    Draw.line( List, fill=(r,g,b), width=2 );
```

```
    for n in range (0,N+1): #Vertical Lines B
        for m in range (0,N+1):
            Factor=(D-VZ)/(D-z1B[m][n]-VZ);
            xA=XC+Factor*(x1B[m][n]-VX)+VX;
            yA=YC-Factor*(y1B[m][n]-VY)-VY;
            PointList[m]=xA,yA;
        List=tuple( map(tuple,PointList) );
        Draw.line( List, fill=(r,g,b), width=2 );
        Font = ImageFont.truetype('Gargi.ttf', 40);
        Draw1.text( (10,10), "3D", fill =
                        (255,0,0,1),font=Font);
        Draw2.text( (30,10), "3D", fill =
                        (0,255,255,1), font=Font);

def ShowScene(B):
    Array1=np.array(PilImage1);
    Array2=np.array(PilImage2);
    Array3=Array1 | Array2;

    PilImage3=Image.fromarray(Array3);

    Memory=io.BytesIO();
    PilImage3.save(Memory, format="png");
    Memory.seek(0);
    ImagePNG=CoreImage(Memory, ext="png");

    B.ids.Screen1.texture=ImagePNG.texture;
    ImagePNG.remove_from_cache()
    Memory.close();
    PilImage3.close();
    Array1=None;
    Array2=None;
    Array3=None;
```

```
def ClearObjects():
    Draw1.rectangle( (0, 0, W-10, H-10), fill=
                               (60, 70, 30, 1) );
    Draw2.rectangle( (0, 0, W-10, H-10), fill=
                               (60, 70, 30, 1) );

def RotateFunction(B, Sense):
    global XGO, ZGO
    if Sense==-1:
        Teta=np.pi/180*(-4.0);
    else:
        Teta=np.pi/180*(4.0);
    Cos_Teta=np.cos(Teta)
    Sin_Teta=np.sin(Teta);

    XO=XGO;  YO=0;  ZO=ZGO # Center of rotation

    for n in range(0,N+1):
        for m in range(0,N+1):
            if (B.ids.Button3.state=="down" or
                    B.ids.Button4.state=="down"):
                yP=(y1A[n][m]-YO)*Cos_Teta \
                    + (x1A[n][m]-XO)*Sin_Teta + YO;
                xP=-(y1A[n][m]-YO)*Sin_Teta\
                    +(x1A[n][m]-XO)*Cos_Teta + XO;
                y1A[n][m]=yP;
                x1A[n][m]=xP;

                yP=(y1B[n][m]-YO)*Cos_Teta \
                    + (x1B[n][m]-XO)*Sin_Teta + YO;
                xP=-(y1B[n][m]-YO)*Sin_Teta \
                    +(x1B[n][m]-XO)*Cos_Teta + XO;
                y1B[n][m]=yP;
                x1B[n][m]=xP;
```

```
    if (B.ids.Button5.state=="down" or
            B.ids.Button6.state=="down"):
    yP=(y1A[n][m]-Y0)*Cos_Teta\
        + (z1A[n][m]-Z0)*Sin_Teta + Y0;
    zP=-(y1A[n][m]-Y0)*Sin_Teta\
        +(z1A[n][m]-Z0)*Cos_Teta + Z0;
    y1A[n][m]=yP;
    z1A[n][m]=zP;

    yP=(y1B[n][m]-Y0)*Cos_Teta \
        + (z1B[n][m]-Z0)*Sin_Teta + Y0;
    zP=-(y1B[n][m]-Y0)*Sin_Teta \
        +(z1B[n][m]-Z0)*Cos_Teta + Z0;
    y1B[n][m]=yP;
    z1B[n][m]=zP;

    if (B.ids.Button7.state=="down" or
            B.ids.Button8.state=="down"):
    xP=(x1A[n][m]-X0)*Cos_Teta \
        + (z1A[n][m]-Z0)*Sin_Teta + X0;
    zP=-(x1A[n][m]-X0)*Sin_Teta \
        +(z1A[n][m]-Z0)*Cos_Teta + Z0;
    x1A[n][m]=xP;
    z1A[n][m]=zP;

    xP=(x1B[n][m]-X0)*Cos_Teta \
        + (z1B[n][m]-Z0)*Sin_Teta + X0;
    zP=-(x1B[n][m]-X0)*Sin_Teta \
        +(z1B[n][m]-Z0)*Cos_Teta + Z0;
    x1B[n][m]=xP;
    z1B[n][m]=zP;
```

```python
class Form1(FloatLayout):
    def __init__(Handle, **kwargs):
        super(Form1, Handle).__init__(**kwargs);
        Event1=Clock.schedule_once(Handle.Initialize);

    def Initialize(B, *args):
        global W,H, XC,YC;
        global PilImage1,PilImage2, Draw1,Draw2;
        # P= Percentage of the D distance
        global P, Amplitude;
        W,H=B.ids.Screen1.size;
        XC=int (W/2)+P/(1-P)*VX1+0;
        YC=int(H/2)-P/(1-P)*VY1+10;
        PilImage1= Image.new('RGB', (W-10, H-10),
                                    (60, 70, 30));
        Draw1 = ImageDraw.Draw(PilImage1);
        PilImage2= Image.new('RGB', (W-10, H-10),
                                    (60, 70, 30));
        Draw2 = ImageDraw.Draw(PilImage2);
        Font = ImageFont.truetype('Gargi.ttf', 70)
        Draw1.text( (30,200), "3D Images", fill =
                            (255,0,0,1), font=Font);
        Draw2.text( (50,200), "3D Images", fill =
                            (0,255,255,1), font=Font);
        ShowScene(B);

    def Button1_Click(B):
        global Draw1, Draw2;
        ClearObjects(); # Clearing Draw1 and Draw2
        GraphFunction(VX1,VY1,VZ1,0);
        GraphFunction(VX2,VY2,VZ2,1);
        ShowScene(B);
```

```python
def Button2_Click(B):
    ClearObjects(); # Clearing Draw1 and Draw2
    Font = ImageFont.truetype('Gargi.ttf', 70)
    Draw1.text( (30,200), "3D Images", fill =
                        (255,0,0,1), font=Font);
    Draw2.text( (50,200), "3D Images", fill =
                        (0,255,255,1), font=Font);
    ShowScene(B);

def Button3_Click(B):
    RotateFunction(B,1);
    ClearObjects(); # Clearing Draw1 and Draw2
    GraphFunction(VX1,VY1,VZ1,0);
    GraphFunction(VX2,VY2,VZ2,1);
    ShowScene(B);

def Button4_Click(B):
    RotateFunction(B,-1),
    ClearObjects();
    GraphFunction(VX1,VY1,VZ1,0);
    GraphFunction(VX2,VY2,VZ2,1);
    ShowScene(B);

def Button5_Click(B):
    RotateFunction(B,-1),
    ClearObjects();
    GraphFunction(VX1,VY1,VZ1,0);
    GraphFunction(VX2,VY2,VZ2,1);
    ShowScene(B);

def Button6_Click(B):
    RotateFunction(B,1),
    ClearObjects();
```

```
        GraphFunction(VX1,VY1,VZ1,0);
        GraphFunction(VX2,VY2,VZ2,1);
        ShowScene(B);

    def Button7_Click(B):
        RotateFunction(B,-1),
        ClearObjects();
        GraphFunction(VX1,VY1,VZ1,0);
        GraphFunction(VX2,VY2,VZ2,1);
        ShowScene(B);

    def Button8_Click(B):
        RotateFunction(B,1),
        ClearObjects();
        GraphFunction(VX1,VY1,VZ1,0);
        GraphFunction(VX2,VY2,VZ2,1);
        ShowScene(B);

# This is the Start Up code.
class StartUp (App):
    def build (BU):
        BU.title="Form1"
        return Form1();
if __name__ =="__main__":
    StartUp().run();
```

16.4 Summary

In this chapter, we introduced elements for plotting stereoscopic three-dimensional conics. We presented an analytical approach to constructing them. We also utilized working examples to illustrate the programming process.

CHAPTER 17

Two-Dimensional Fourier Transform

In this chapter, we present elements for calculating and plotting discrete two-dimensional Fourier transforms. Figure 17-1 provides two screenshots from an Android cell phone. The one on the left shows a rectangular, two-dimensional spatial-function. The right screenshot shows the corresponding discrete Fourier transform obtained using this program.

© Moisés Cywiak, David Cywiak 2021
M. Cywiak and D. Cywiak, *Multi-Platform Graphics Programming with Kivy*,
https://doi.org/10.1007/978-1-4842-7113-1_17

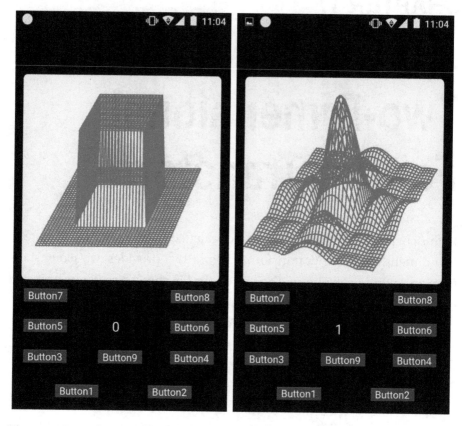

Figure 17-1. *Screenshots from an Android cell phone showing a two-dimensional spatial-function (left) and its corresponding Fourier transform obtained with this program (right)*

The functionality of Button1 to Button8 is the same as described in Chapter 5.

In this application, Button9 toggles the numerical indicator between 0 and 1. Accordingly, the screen shows the spatial function or its corresponding two-dimensional Fourier transform.

17.1 One-Dimensional Fourier Transform

Briefly speaking, the Fourier transform consists of an integral that transforms a function defined in an initial domain into another function in the frequency domain. The initial domain can be any n-dimensional space of interest.

The Fourier transform is frequently used in digital processing, probability, optics, quantum mechanics, economics, and many other fields. The transform can be one-, two-, three-, or n-dimensional.

Let's start by writing the following analytical expression for the one-dimensional Fourier transform:

$$F(u) = \int_{-\infty}^{\infty} f(x)\, exp(-i2\pi ux)\, dx \qquad (17.1)$$

In Equation (17.1), the function in the initial domain is $f(x)$, and the transformed function in the frequency domain is $F(u)$. The parameter i represents the imaginary unit. The initial domain is represented by the spatial x-coordinate and the frequency coordinate is represented by u.

To verify that u in Equation (17.1) represents frequency, let's consider that $f(x)$ is a sinusoidal function with period T and amplitude A:

$$f(x) = A cos\left(\frac{2\pi}{T} x\right) \qquad (17.2)$$

To calculate the Fourier transform of the function in the initial space given by Equation (17.2), we use Euler's identity to rewrite the equation as follows:

$$f(x) = \frac{A}{2}\left(exp\left(\frac{i2\pi}{T} x\right) + exp\left(\frac{-i2\pi}{T} x\right)\right) \qquad (17.3)$$

Substituting Equation (17.3) into Equation (17.1) gives us the following:

$$F(u) = \frac{A}{2}\int exp\left[-i2\pi\left(u - \frac{1}{T}\right)x\right]dx + \frac{A}{2}\int exp\left[-i2\pi\left(u + \frac{1}{T}\right)x\right]dx \quad (17.4)$$

The integrals in Equation (17.4) are precisely the definitions of the Dirac delta function. Therefore, Equation (17.4) gives the following:

$$F(u) = \frac{A}{2}\delta\left(u - \frac{1}{T}\right) + \frac{A}{2}\delta\left(u + \frac{1}{T}\right) \quad (17.5)$$

A physical interpretation of Equation (17.5) consists of visualizing $f(x)$ in Equation (17.2) as a vibrating string placed along the horizontal x-coordinate. The string vibrates vertically with a period equal to T, or equivalently with a frequency $\frac{1}{T}$. Then, Equation (17.5) indicates that the Fourier transform, $F(u)$, consists of two well defined points in the frequency domain located at $\frac{1}{T}$ and $\frac{-1}{T}$. We conclude, therefore, that when a string vibrates at a determined frequency, the Fourier transform consists of two points. The first one corresponds to the vibration frequency. The second, to the negative value of this frequency.

To proceed further with this interpretation of the Fourier transform, we now consider that the string in our previous example vibrates at two different frequencies, with amplitudes A_1 and A_2, as follows:

$$f(x) = A_1 cos\left(\frac{2\pi}{T_1}x\right) + A_2 cos\left(\frac{2\pi}{T_2}x\right) \quad (17.6)$$

As in the last example, using Euler's identity for each sinusoidal function allows us to calculate the Fourier transform of the expression given in Equation (17.6), as follows:

$$F(u) = \left[\frac{A_1}{2}\delta\left(u - \frac{1}{T_1}\right) + \frac{A_1}{2}\delta\left(u + \frac{1}{T_1}\right)\right] + \left[\frac{A_2}{2}\delta\left(u - \frac{1}{T_2}\right) + \frac{A_1}{2}\delta\left(u + \frac{1}{T_2}\right)\right] \quad (17.7)$$

From Equation (17.7), we notice that the Fourier transform consists of two well-defined points for each vibrating frequency. Each point corresponds to the positive or negative value of a frequency. Each point in the frequency space has an amplitude equal to half of its corresponding one.

Considering that the string vibrates at multiple frequencies, each frequency with a corresponding amplitude, the Fourier transform will give points at all the frequencies of vibration, including positives and negatives, along with their corresponding half amplitude values. Therefore, the Fourier transform provides the amplitude distribution of frequencies of a vibrating object and its spectral distribution.

In the following section, we introduce two functions frequently encountered in Fourier analysis.

17.2 The Rectangular and Sinc Functions

Two functions of special interest in Fourier studies are the $Rect(x, A)$ (rectangular) and the $sinc(x)$ functions.

The rectangular function is a rectangle of height 1 and width A. Analytically:

$$Rect(x, A) = \{1, if\ |x| \leq \frac{A}{2}\ 0,\ otherwise \tag{17.8}$$

Figure 17-2 depicts the rectangular function given by Equation (17.8).

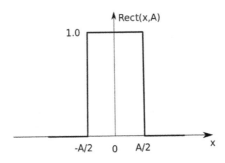

Figure 17-2. *The Rect(x, A) Function*

The Fourier transform of Equation (17.8) reads as follows:

$$F(u) = \int_{-\infty}^{\infty} Rect(x, A) exp(-i2\pi ux) dx \qquad (17.9)$$

To calculate the integral in Equation (17.9), we substitute Equation (17.8) into Equation (17.9):

$$F(u) = \int_{-A/2}^{A/2} exp(-i2\pi ux) dx \qquad (17.10)$$

Performing the integral of Equation (17.10) gives the following:

$$F(u) = A \frac{sin(\pi Au)}{\pi Au}; (u \neq 0) \qquad (17.11)$$

The frequency domain for $F(u)$, as expressed by Equation (17.11), is valid from $-\infty$ to ∞, except when u equals zero, where the expression becomes undefined. This drawback is overcome by assigning to the function the value corresponding to the limit when $u \to 0$. Therefore, $sinc(u)$ is defined as follows:

$$sinc(u) = \{ \frac{sin(\pi u)}{\pi u}, if\ u \neq 0\ 1, if\ u = 0 \qquad (17.12)$$

Equation (17.12), scaled by and multiplied by factor A, is plotted in Figure 17-3.

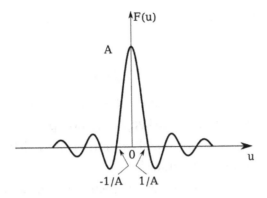

Figure 17-3. *Plot of Asinc(Au). Intercepts with the u-axis occur at* $u = \dfrac{\pm 1}{A}$

Although we want to focus on the two-dimensional Fourier transform, for illustrative purposes, we provide a brief code description for calculating the discrete one-dimensional Fourier transform in the next section.

17.3 Code for Calculating the Discrete One-Dimensional Fourier Transform

We need first to generate the spatial function. In the first working example, this function will be a two-dimensional rectangular function. We can obtain it as the product of two one-dimensional rectangles given by Equation (17.8). We will generate the one-dimensional Rect function using the code shown in Listing 17-1.

Listing 17-1. The Rect Function

```
import numpy as np
def Rect(x,a):
    if (np.abs(x)<=A/2):
        return 1;
    else:
        return 0;
```

Next, we set the number of pixels that will represent the discrete function.

```
N=200;
```

To better represent this function in the one-dimensional case, we can use a large number of pixels while keeping a short processing time. This is in contrast to the two-dimensional case, where a small N increment can result in very high processing times.

We now assign the values of the imaginary unit and π to the variables i and Pi, as follows.

```
i=1J;   Pi=np.pi;
```

Now, we will use two variables, L to set the x-range between ($-L/2$ to $L/2$), and A to define the width of the rectangular function, as follows:

```
L=1; A=L/2.4;
```

The width of the rectangle function was set to L/(2.4).

Next we create two one-dimensional arrays, each with size N+1, to store the values of the x-points and the values corresponding to the spatial function:

```
x=np.zeros(N+1);
f=np.zeros( N+1 );
```

Now we fill the arrays, as shown in Listing 17-2.

Listing 17-2. Setting Values for x and f

```
for n in range(0,N+1):
    x[n]=(n-N/2)/N*L
    f[n]=Rect(x[n],A);
```

In this for loop, we have assigned N+1 entries with values ranging from -L/2 to L/2 to the first array for storing the x-points. The N+1 values corresponding to the function are stored in the second array, f.

The following code creates the frequency array, as shown in Listing 17-3.

Listing 17-3. Setting Frequency Values

```
u=np.zeros(N+1);
B=10/A;
for n in range(0,N+1):
    u[n]=(n-N/2)/N*B;
```

In the for loop, the frequency (or spectral) array, u, stores N+1 equally spaced values ranging from -B/2 to B/2. The value 10/A assigned to the parameter B is set based in our experience when calculating the sinc function depicted in Figure 17-3.

Now we create an array to store the values of the Fourier transform as follows:

```
F=np.zeros( N+1, dtype=complex );
```

We have declared F as a one-dimensional array for storing N+1 complex numbers. This is necessary, as the calculations of the integral given by Equation (17.1) will give, in general, complex numbers.

At this point, u represents N+1 frequency points ranging from -B/2 to B/2. As a consequence, $F(u)$ will be also represented by a discrete array, F.

We can use a discrete summation on the elements of f to approximate the integral of the Fourier transform, as follows:

$$F[n] = \sum_{m=0}^{N} f[m] exp\left(-i2\pi u[n]x[m]\right) dx \qquad (17.13)$$

In Equation (17.13), dx is set to a positive value corresponding to the subtraction of two consecutive elements of the x-array as, for example, dx=x[1]-x[0].

We can calculate the discrete integral for each F[n] using the code shown in Listing 17-4.

Listing 17-4. Calculating the Discrete Integral

```
for n in range(0,N+1):
    S=0;
    for m in range(0,N+1):
        S=S+ f[m]*np.exp(-i*2*Pi*u[n]*x[m]);
    F[n]=S;
```

In this code, the inner for loop calculates the discrete integral corresponding to a particular F[n] entry, determined by the outer for loop. For each n iteration, the S parameter is set to 0, and it accumulates the value of the discrete integral. Once the inner for loop finishes, the F[n] parameter receives its corresponding value and the outer for loop continues. The process is repeated until all the F[n] values are filled.

Although this code for calculating the N+1 discrete integral works properly, it is not time-efficient. Fortunately, NumPy provides a time-efficient built-in function to perform the summation for each F[n]. When using NumPy, the summation looks as follows:

```
for n in range(0,N+1):
    F[n]=np.sum( f * np.exp(-i*2*Pi*u[n]*x) );
```

In this code, np.sum performs the appropriate summation by associating each element of the f array with its match in the x array. The arrays must be the same size.

By comparing the Fourier transforms obtained by these two examples, one can confirm that the examples give the same result.

The precision of the calculations depends on the discretization process and the accuracy of the computer's mathematical processor. Therefore, although we have demonstrated that the Fourier transform of a real-valued rectangular function should be a real-valued function, the resulting values of F[n] will be complex numbers. For practical purposes, the imaginary values are negligible compared to their real ones. However, we have to explicitly discard the imaginary parts of F[n] and keep only the real parts. This is done by plotting np.real(F[n]).

In the following section, we focus on the two-dimensional Fourier transform.

17.4 Two-Dimensional Fourier Transform

The two-dimensional Fourier transform is defined as follows:

$$F(u,v) = \int_{-\infty}^{\infty}\int_{-\infty}^{\infty} f(x,y)\, exp\left(-i2\pi\left(ux+vy\right)\right) dx\, dy \qquad (17.14)$$

In Equation (17.14), $f(x, y)$ represents a two-dimensional spatial function and $F(u, v)$ represents its corresponding Fourier transform. The u and v parameters are the corresponding frequencies for the x and y coordinates, respectively.

As a first example, we will consider a rectangular two-dimensional function, written as follows:

$$Rect(x,A,y,B) = Rect(x,A)\, Rect(x,B) \qquad (17.15)$$

The left plot of Figure 17-1 shows a screenshot of the program running on an Android cell phone with a plot of Equation (17.15).

The two-dimensional rectangular function in Equation (17.15) is separable in the x- and y-coordinates. However, as in general, not all the functions are separable. We will maintain our code as general as possible to permit calculations on non-separable $f(x, y)$ functions. Furthermore, as we describe in the following section, to improve the processing time, we will write the two-dimensional transform given by Equation (17.14) as follows:

$$F(u,v) = \int_{-\infty}^{\infty} exp(-i2\pi vy) \left(\int_{-\infty}^{\infty} f(x,y) exp(-i2\pi ux) dx \right) dy \qquad (17.16)$$

Equation (17.16) allows us to calculate the Fourier transform of the two-dimensional function by performing an integration on the x-coordinate first and then an integration over the y-coordinate.

In the following section, we describe this method.

17.5 Discrete Two-Dimensional Fourier Transform

To numerically calculate the Fourier transform, we need to represent the continuous spatial function by a discrete set of numbers stored in a two-dimensional array. Therefore, we must use a moderate number of pixels for this task. As with the two-dimensional case, increasing this number will greatly increase the processing time.

We will use 40x40 pixels to represent the spatial function as well as the function in the frequency space. The x- and z-coordinates will be stored in independent one-dimensional arrays with N+1 entries. Next, we will create the mesh with two-dimensional (N+1)x(N+1) arrays. The corresponding code for creating the spatial function and mesh is shown in Listing 17-5.

Listing 17-5. Setting Values for the Mesh and the Discrete Spatial
Function

```python
import numpy as np
N=40; #Number of pixels to represent the function
# Creating spatial coordinates
x=np.zeros(N+1);
z=np.zeros(N+1);
f=np.zeros( (N+1,N+1) );
# Creating the mesh
x1=np.zeros( (N+1,N+1) );
y1=np.zeros( (N+1,N+1) );
z1=np.zeros( (N+1,N+1) );
L=1;
for n in range (0,N+1):
    x[n]=(n-N/2)/N*L;
    z[n]=(n-N/2)/N*L;
dx=x[1]-x[0]; dz=z[1]-z[0];

for n in range(0,N+1):
    for m in range(0,N+1):
        f[n][m]=Rect(x[n],L/2)*Rect(z[m],L/2);
```

In this code, we created the one-dimensional arrays x and z with their
corresponding values. Using these arrays, we created the two-dimensional
discrete function, f. We also defined the dx and dz variables to be used
later in the integration.

We will also create corresponding arrays for the frequency parameters,
as shown in Listing 17-6.

Listing 17-6. Creating and Filling Frequency Parameters

```
B=10/L; # Bandwidth
u=np.zeros(N+1); v=np.zeros(N+1);
#F will store the discrete Fourier transform
F=np.zeros( (N+1,N+1), dtype=complex );
for n in range(0,N+1):
    u[n]=(n-N/2)/N*B;
    v[n]=u[n];
```

The goal is now to perform the discrete double integral that corresponds to Equation (17.16), written as follows:

$$F_{n,m} = \sum_{p=0}^{N} exp\left(-i2\pi u_n x_p\right)\sum_{q=0}^{N} f_{p,q} \, exp\left(-i2\pi v_m z_q\right) dx\,dz \qquad (17.17)$$

Equation (17.17), in terms of arrays, can be rewritten as follows:

$$F[n][m] = \sum_{p=0}^{N}\left[exp\left(-i2\pi u[n]x[p]\right)\sum_{q=0}^{N} f[p][q]exp\left(-i2\pi v[m]z[q]\right)\right]dx\,dz \qquad (17.18)$$

Note that the summation operations in Equation (17.18) are not independent from each other. The second summation is inside the first one.

The code corresponding to the summation over q that corresponds to a determined p value can be written as follows:

```
S=0;
for q in range(0,N+1):
      S=S+ f[p][q]*np.exp(-i*2*Pi*v[m]*z[q]);
```

In the for loop, we are storing the result of the summation in the variable S. The S variable is an accumulator. It starts with a value equal to 0, and at each for loop, it accumulates the corresponding value. The for loop is set from 0 to N+1 because Python finishes the for loop when q equals N. Therefore, the summation goes from 0 to N, as required by Equation (17.18).

Now, as Equation (17.18) has a double summation, we need two accumulators. The corresponding code is shown in Listing 17-7.

Listing 17-7. Discrete Two-Dimensional Integral Using Two Accumulators

```
for n in range(0,N+1):
    for m in range(0,N+1):
        S1=0;
        for p in range (0,N+1):
            S2=0;
            for q in range(0,N+1):
                if (f[p][q]==0):
                    continue;
                S2=S2+ f[p][q]*np.exp(-i*2*Pi*v[m]*z[q]);
            if (S2==0):
                continue;
            S1=S1+S2*np.exp(-i*2*Pi*u[n]*x[p]);
        F[n][m]=S1;
F=F*dx*dz;
```

In this code, we included two if statements to avoid calculations when f[p][q] or S2 equals 0. These statements, which may seem irrelevant, reduced the processing time from 30 to 10 seconds in our dual-core computer running at 3.0GHz, for N=40.

The previous code can be improved by using the built-in numpy.sum function, as shown in Listing 17-8.

Listing 17-8. Method Using One-NumPy-Sum and One Accumulator

```
for n in range(0,N+1):
    for m in range(0,N+1):
        S=0;
        for q in range(0,N+1):
            S=S+np.sum( f[q]*
                np.exp(-i*2*Pi*u[n]*x) )
                    *np.exp(-i*2*Pi*v[m]*z[q] );
        F[n][m]=S;
F=F*dx*dz;
```

In this code, we only need one accumulator, as NumPy will sum f[q] and x as one-dimensional arrays, performing the corresponding inner summation of Equation (17.18). We still have to calculate the outer summation with the for loop over the variable q.

The processing time using this code in our dual-core computer took about three seconds. Compared to ten seconds with the previous code, this represents approximately one-third of the processing time. The summation of arrays made by NumPy, therefore, are highly efficient.

To use two NumPy summations and avoid using accumulators for calculating the double summation expressed by Equation (17.18), we devised the code shown in Listing 17-9.

Listing 17-9. Method Using Double NumPy Summation by Introducing an Additional Array

```
C=np.zeros( (N+1,N+1), dtype=complex );
for n in range(0,N+1):
    for m in range(0,N+1):
        for q in range(0,N+1):
```

```
    C[n][q]=np.sum( f[q]
               *np.exp(- i*2*Pi*u[n]*x) );
    F[n][m]=np.sum( C[n]*np.exp(-i*2*Pi*v[m]*z) );
F=F*dx*dz;
```

In this code, we used the C array to store $(N+1) \times (N+1)$ complex values. With this approach, there is no need for accumulators, so we can use two NumPy summations to perform the required calculations. The processing time is one second.

This method is the most general, as it does not need separate functions in the integrals.

It is further possible to use double-NumPy summation without using the additional array, taking advantage of the exponential functions in the Fourier transform integral, as they are separable. This time we have to use an extra option of the built-in summation, specifying which axis of the double summation will be used. The code is shown in Listing 17-10.

Listing 17-10. Method with Double NumPy Sum Avoiding the Use of an Additional Array

```
for n in range(0,N+1):
    for m in range(0,N+1):
        F[n][m]= np.sum(  np.sum( f*np.exp(
                -i*2*Pi*v[m]*z),axis=1 )
                *np.exp(-i*2*Pi*u[n]*x), axis=0  );
F=F*dx*dz;
I=np.abs(F);
```

In this code, integration over z is performed first, and then integration over x. The processing time is now less than one second.

In the following listings, we provide the code listings corresponding to the `main.py` and `File.kv` files. We included two spatial functions—a two-dimensional rectangle expressed as the product of two rectangular functions given by Equation (17.8) and a circular function. The circular function has a vertical height equal of 1 inside a circle of radius R, and 0 outside it. Analytically, the circular function can be expressed as follows:

$$Circ(x,,y,R) = \{1 \, if \, \sqrt{x2 + y^{2}} \le R \, 0 \, otherwise \qquad (17.19)$$

The code for main.py and File.kv are shown in Listings 17-11 and 17-12, respectively.

Listing 17-11. Code for the main.py File

```
from kivy.app import App
from kivy.uix.floatlayout import FloatLayout
from kivy.graphics import Line, Ellipse, Color
from kivy.clock import Clock
import os
import numpy as np

from kivy.lang import Builder
Builder.load_file(
    os.path.join(os.path.dirname(os.path.abspath(
                        __file__)), 'File.kv')
            );

#Avoid Form1 of being resizable
from kivy.config import Config
Config.set("graphics","resizable", False)
Config.set('graphics', 'width', '480');
Config.set('graphics', 'height', '680');
#Here, we define two functions. We will use
#one of them in the calculations.
def Rect(s,a):
    if np.abs(s)<=a/2:
        return 1;
```

```python
    else:
        return 0;
def Circ(s,t,a):
    if np.sqrt(s**2 +t**2)<=a:
        return 1;
    else:
        return 0;

OBJECT=0;
D=4000;
VX=600; VY=1200; VZ=0;
P=0.5
ZGO=P*D;
N=40; #Number of pixels to represent the function
# Creating spatial coordinates
x=np.zeros(N+1);
z=np.zeros(N+1);
f=np.zeros( (N+1,N+1) );
# Creating the mesh
x1=np.zeros( (N+1,N+1) );
y1=np.zeros( (N+1,N+1) );
z1=np.zeros( (N+1,N+1) );
L=1;
for n in range (0,N+1):
    x[n]=(n-N/2)/N*L;
    z[n]=(n-N/2)/N*L;
dx=x[1]-x[0]; dz=z[1]-z[0];

for n in range(0,N+1):
    for m in range(0,N+1):
        #Here we need to uncomment the
        #function we want to use:
```

```
        #Option (1) 2D Rect function:
        #f[n][m]=Rect(x[n],L/2)*Rect(z[m],L/2);
        #Option (2) 2D Circ function:
        f[n][m]=Circ(x[n],z[m],L/4);

Scale_x=140; Scale_y=100; Scale_z=140;
# Filling the mesh
for n in range (0,N+1):
    for m in range(0,N+1):
        x1[n][m]=Scale_x * x[n];
        z1[n][m]=Scale_z * z[m]+ZG0;
        y1[n][m]=Scale_y*f[n][m];
i=1J; # Defining imaginary unit
Pi=np.pi;
# Creating and filling frequency parameters
B=10/L;
u=np.zeros(N+1); v=np.zeros(N+1);
# F will store the discrete Fourier transform
F=np.zeros( (N+1,N+1), dtype=complex );
# C is used to calculate the discrete integral
C=np.zeros( (N+1,N+1), dtype=complex );
u1=np.zeros( (N+1,N+1) );
v1=np.zeros( (N+1,N+1) );
I1=np.zeros( (N+1,N+1) );
for n in range(0,N+1):
    u[n]=(n-N/2)/N*B;
    v[n]=u[n];
for n in range(0,N+1):
    for m in range(0,N+1):
        for q in range(0,N+1):
            C[n][q]=np.sum( f[q]
                    *np.exp(-i*2*Pi*u[n]*x) );
```

```
F[n][m]=np.sum( C[n]
                *np.exp(-i*2*Pi*v[m]*z) )*dx*dz;
# We will plot the absolute value of the
# discrete integral
I=np.abs(F);
# Creating the mesh for plotting
Scale_u1=15; Scale_v1=15; Scale_I1=480;
for n in range(0,N+1):
    for m in range(0,N+1):
        u1[n][m]=Scale_u1 * u[n];
        v1[n][m]=Scale_v1 * v[m]+ZGO;
        I1[n][m]=Scale_I1*I[n][m];

# Array to store list of points
PointList=np.zeros( (N+1,2) );
def GraphFunction(xM, yM, zM,  B):
    global N, D, VX, VY, VZ;
    x1p=xM; y1p=yM; z1p=zM;
    B.ids.Screen1.canvas.clear(); # Clear the screen
     # Choose color to draw
    B.ids.Screen1.canvas.add( Color(1,0,0) );
    # Drawing horizontal lines
    for n in range (0,N+1):
        for m in range (0,N+1):
            Factor=(D-VZ)/(D-z1p[n][m]-VZ);
            xA=XC+Factor*(x1p[n][m]-VX) \
                        +VX+(P/(1-P))*VX;
            yA=YC+Factor*(y1p[n][m]-VY)\
                        +VY+(P/(1-P))*VY;
            PointList[m]=xA,yA;
        B.ids.Screen1.canvas.add( Line(points=
                    PointList.tolist(), width=1.3));
```

```
    # Drawing vertical lines
    for n in range (0,N+1):
        for m in range (0,N+1, 1):
            Factor=(D-VZ)/(D-z1p[m][n]-VZ);
            xA=XC+Factor*(x1p[m][n]-VX)+VX \
                                    +(P/(1-P))*VX;
            yA=YC+Factor*(y1p[m][n]-VY)+VY \
                                    +(P/(1-P))*VY;
            PointList[m]=xA,yA;
        B.ids.Screen1.canvas.add( Line(points=
                PointList.tolist(), width=1.3));

def RotateFunction(xM,yM,zM, B, Sense):
    global D, N;
    x1p=xM; y1p=yM; z1p=zM;
    if Sense==-1:
        Teta=np.pi/180*(-4.0);
    else:
        Teta=np.pi/180*(4.0);
    Cos_Teta=np.cos(Teta)
    Sin_Teta=np.sin(Teta);

    X0=0;  Y0=0;  Z0=ZG0 # Center of rotation

    for n in range(0,N+1):
        for m in range(0,N+1):
            if (B.ids.Button3.state=="down" or
                    B.ids.Button4.state=="down"):
                yP=(y1p[n][m]-Y0)*Cos_Teta  \
                    + (x1p[n][m]-X0)*Sin_Teta + Y0;
                xP=-(y1p[n][m]-Y0)*Sin_Teta \
                    +(x1p[n][m]-X0)*Cos_Teta + X0;
```

```
            y1p[n][m]=yP;
            x1p[n][m]=xP;

        if (B.ids.Button5.state=="down" or
                B.ids.Button6.state=="down"):
            yP=(y1p[n][m]-Y0)*Cos_Teta \
                + (z1p[n][m]-Z0)*Sin_Teta + Y0;
            zP=-(y1p[n][m]-Y0)*Sin_Teta \
                +(z1p[n][m]-Z0)*Cos_Teta + Z0;
            y1p[n][m]=yP;
            z1p[n][m]=zP;

        if (B.ids.Button7.state=="down" or
                B.ids.Button8.state=="down"):
            xP=(x1p[n][m]-X0)*Cos_Teta \
                + (z1p[n][m]-Z0)*Sin_Teta + X0;
            zP=-(x1p[n][m]-X0)*Sin_Teta \
                +(z1p[n][m]-Z0)*Cos_Teta + Z0;
            x1p[n][m]=xP;
            z1p[n][m]=zP;

class Form1(FloatLayout):
    def __init__(Handle, **kwargs):
        super(Form1, Handle).__init__(**kwargs);
        Event1=Clock.schedule_once(Handle.Initialize);

    def Initialize(B, *args):
        global W,H, XC,YC;
        W,H=B.ids.Screen1.size;
        XI,YI=B.ids.Screen1.pos
        XC=XI+int (W/2);
        YC=YI+int(H/2)-60;
```

```
def Button1_Click(B):
    if (OBJECT==0):
        GraphFunction(x1,y1,z1,B);
    else:
        GraphFunction(u1,I1,v1, B);

def Button2_Click(B):
    B.ids.Screen1.canvas.clear();

def Button3_Click(B):
    if (OBJECT==0):
        RotateFunction(x1,y1,z1,B,1);
        GraphFunction(x1,y1,z1, B);
    else:
        RotateFunction(u1,I1,v1,B,1);
        GraphFunction(u1, I1,v1, B);

def Button4_Click(B):
    if (OBJECT==0):
        RotateFunction(x1,y1,z1, B,-1),
        GraphFunction(x1,y1,z1, B);
    else:
        RotateFunction(u1,I1,v1,B,-1);
        GraphFunction(u1,I1, v1,B,);

def Button5_Click(B):
    if (OBJECT==0):
        RotateFunction(x1,y1,z1,B,-1),
        GraphFunction(x1,y1,z1,B);
    else:
        RotateFunction(u1,I1,v1,B,-1);
        GraphFunction(u1,I1,v1,B);
```

```
def Button6_Click(B):
    if (OBJECT==0):
        RotateFunction(x1,y1,z1,B,1),
        GraphFunction(x1,y1,z1,B);
    else:
        RotateFunction(u1,I1,v1,B,1);
        GraphFunction(u1,I1,v1,B);

def Button7_Click(B):
    if (OBJECT==0):
        RotateFunction(x1,y1,z1,B,-1),
        GraphFunction(x1,y1,z1,B);
    else:
        RotateFunction(u1,I1,v1,B,-1);
        GraphFunction(u1,I1,v1,B);

def Button8_Click(B):
    if (OBJECT==0):
        RotateFunction(x1,y1,z1,B,1),
        GraphFunction(x1,y1,z1,B);
    else:
        RotateFunction(u1,I1,v1,B,1);
        GraphFunction(u1,I1,v1, B);

def Button9_Click(B):
    global OBJECT
    OBJECT=(OBJECT+1)%2;
    B.ids.Label1.text=str(OBJECT);
    B.ids.Screen1.canvas.clear();
    if (OBJECT==0):
        GraphFunction(x1,y1,z1,B);
    else:
        GraphFunction(u1,I1,v1,B);
```

```
# This is the Start Up code.
class StartUp (App):
    def build (BU):
        BU.title="Form1"
        return Form1();
if __name__ =="__main__":
    StartUp().run();
```

Listing 17-12. Code for the file.kv File

```
#:set W 440
#:set H 440
<Form1>:
    id : Form1
    StencilView:
        id: Screen1
        size_hint: None,None
        pos_hint: {"x":0.04, "y":0.34}
        size: W,H
        canvas.before:
            Color:
                rgba: 0.9, 0.9, 0, 1
            RoundedRectangle:
                pos:  self.pos
                size: self.size
    Button:
        id: Button1
        on_press: Form1.Button1_Click()
        text: "Button1"
        size_hint: None,None
        pos_hint: {"x": 0.2, "y":0.03}
        size: 100,30
```

```
Button:
    id: Button2
    on_press: Form1.Button2_Click()
    text: "Button2"
    size_hint: None,None
    pos_hint: {"x": 0.63, "y":0.03}
    size: 100,30

Button:
    id: Button3
    on_press: Form1.Button3_Click()
    text: "Button3"
    size_hint: None,None
    pos_hint: {"x": 0.05, "y":0.12}
    size: 100,30
    always_release: True
Button:
    id: Button4
    on_press: Form1.Button4_Click()
    text: "Button4"
    size_hint: None,None
    pos_hint: {"x": 0.73, "y":0.12}
    size: 100,30

Button:
    id: Button5
    on_press: Form1.Button5_Click()
    text: "Button5"
    size_hint: None,None
    pos_hint: {"x": 0.05, "y":0.20}
    size: 100,30
```

```
Button:
    id: Button6
    on_press: Form1.Button6_Click()
    text: "Button6"
    size_hint: None,None
    pos_hint: {"x": 0.73, "y":0.20}
    size: 100,30

Button:
    id: Button7
    on_press: Form1.Button7_Click()
    text: "Button7"
    size_hint: None,None
    pos_hint: {"x": 0.05, "y":0.28}
    size: 100,30
Button:
    id: Button8
    on_press: Form1.Button8_Click()
    text: "Button8"
    size_hint: None,None
    pos_hint: {"x": 0.73, "y":0.28}
    size: 100,30

Button:
    id: Button9
    on_press: Form1.Button9_Click()
    text: "Button9"
    size_hint: None,None
    pos_hint: {"x": 0.4, "y":0.12}
    size: 100,30
```

```
Label:
    id: Label1
    text: "0"
    font_size: 30
    color: 1,1,0,1
    size_hint: None,None
    pos_hint: {"x": 0.38, "y":0.20}
    size: 100,30
```

17.6 The Fourier Transform of the Circular Function

Figure 17-4 shows plots of the circular function and its corresponding absolute value of the discrete Fourier transform obtained with the code in this chapter.

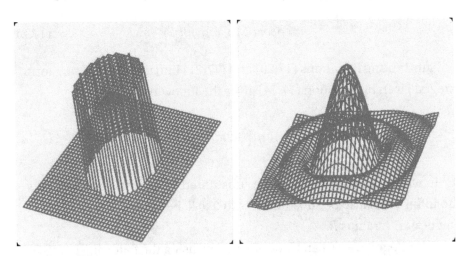

Figure 17-4. *Plots of the circular function and its corresponding absolute value of the discrete Fourier transform obtained with this chapter's code*

As with the rectangular function, the Fourier transform of the circular function has an exact analytical expression in terms of a Bessel function of the first kind. In the following section, we provide a brief demonstration of this aspect.

17.7 Fourier Transform of the Circular Function

The Fourier transform of the circular function of the previous section can be expressed by an exact analytical equation. We will begin by expressing the Fourier transform given by Equation (17.14) in cylindrical coordinates. For this purpose, we express the spatial coordinates as follows:

$$x = rcos(\theta); y = rsin(\theta) \tag{17.20}$$

Similarly, we express the frequency coordinates as follows:

$$u = \rho cos(\phi); v = \rho sin(\phi) \tag{17.21}$$

Substituting Equations (17.20) and (17.21) into the Fourier transform integral given by Equation (17.14) gives the following:

$$F(\rho,\phi) = \int_0^\infty \int_0^{2\pi} f(r) exp(-i2\pi\rho rcos(\theta - \phi)) r\, dr\, d\theta \tag{17.22}$$

In writing Equation (17.22), we substituted $f(x, y)$ with $f(r)$. The limits 0 to infinity will also be substituted with 0 to R, because of the circular function with radius R.

The integral over θ can be performed by using the following relation:

$$\int_0^{2\pi} exp((-ixcos(\theta - \phi)))\, d\theta = 2\pi J_0(x) \tag{17.23}$$

In Equation (17.23), J_0 is the Bessel function of the first kind, order zero. Substituting Equation (17.23) into Equation (17.22) gives the following:

$$F(\rho,\phi) = F(\rho) = 2\pi \int_0^R J_0(2\pi\rho r)\, r\, dr \qquad (17.24)$$

As indicated by Equation (17.24), the Fourier transform becomes a function only of ρ, because the integral in Equation (17.23) eliminates the ϕ dependence.

Using the change of variable, $s = 2\pi\rho r$, in Equation (17.24) gives the following:

$$F(\rho) = \frac{2\pi}{(2\pi\rho)^2} \int_0^{2\pi\rho R} J_0(s)\, s\, ds \qquad (17.25)$$

The integral in Equation (17.25) can be calculated by using the following identity:

$$\int_0^x J_0(s)\, ds = sJ_1(s)\big|_0^x = xJ_1(x) \qquad (17.26)$$

In Equation (17.26), $J_1(x)$ is the Bessel function of the first kind, order one.

By using Equation (17.26) in Equation (17.25), we obtain the following:

$$F(\rho) = 2\pi R^2 \frac{J_1(2\pi R\rho)}{2\pi R\rho} \qquad (17.27)$$

Based on Equation (17.27), we define the Bessel-sinc function, referred to as *Bsinc*:

$$Bsinc(\rho) = \{\frac{J_1(2\pi\rho)}{2\pi\rho}, if\, \rho \neq 0\ 0.5, \ if\, \rho = 0 \qquad (17.28)$$

In Equation (17.28), we assigned the value of 0.5 to the function at $\rho = 0$ according to the following limit:

$$\frac{J_1(2\pi\rho)}{2\pi\rho} = 0.5 \qquad (17.29)$$

Using the definition given by Equation (17.28) in Equation (17.27) results in:

$$F(\rho) = 2\pi R^2 Bsinc(R\rho) \qquad (17.30)$$

In Equation (17.30), $\rho = \sqrt{(u^2 + v^2)}$, therefore:

$$F(u,v) = 2\pi R^2 Bsinc\left(R\sqrt{(u^2 + v^2)}\right) \qquad (17.31)$$

Equation (17.31) is the appropriate expression to compare with the discrete Fourier transform obtained with this program. The code shown in Listing 17-13 uses SymPy to generate $F(u, v)$.

Listing 17-13. Generating the Discrete Function $F(u, v)$

```
import sympy as sp
def Bsinc(s):
    if (s!=0):
        return ( sp.besselj(1,s) )/s;
    else:
        return 0.5;

FP=np.zeros( (N+1,N+1), dtype=complex );
IP1=np.zeros( (N+1,N+1) );
R=L/4;
for n in range(0,N+1):
    for m in range(0,N+1):
```

```
      rho=np.sqrt( u[n]**2 +v[m]**2 )
      FP[n][m]=(2*Pi* R**2 )*Bsinc( 2*Pi*R*rho );
IP=np.abs(FP);
for n in range(0,N+1):
    for m in range(0,N+1):
        IP1[n][m]=Scale_I1*IP[n][m];
```

Now we can plot the function using the following:

```
GraphFunction(u1,IP1,v1,B);
```

Figure 17-5 shows a plot of the absolute values corresponding to the discrete Fourier transform (left) and a plot of the analytical solution given by Equation (17.30) (right).

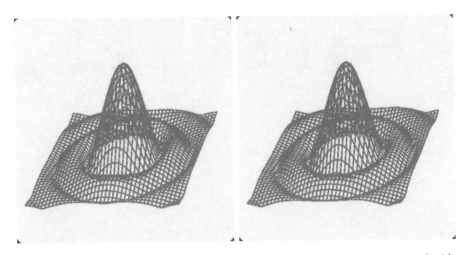

Figure 17-5. *Absolute values for the discrete Fourier transform (left) and of the analytical solution from Equation (17.30) (right)*

Comparing the plots in Figure 17-5 confirms that the calculations performed with the code corresponding to the discrete two-dimensional Fourier transform results in an accurate estimate of the two-dimensional analytical Fourier transform.

In the following chapter, we extend this method to plot stereoscopic two-dimensional Fourier transforms.

17.8 Summary

In this chapter, we presented elements for calculating and plotting discrete two-dimensional Fourier transforms. The chapter included brief analytical descriptions of the one- and two-dimensional Fourier transforms. We provided working examples for calculating the corresponding transforms. To enhance the flexibility of the calculations in the two-dimensional case, we introduced three methods for calculating the discrete double integrals, allowing us to compare their efficiency and applicability.

## CHAPTER 18

Stereoscopic Two-Dimensional Fourier Transform

In this chapter, we present elements for calculating and plotting stereoscopic two-dimensional Fourier transforms. Figure 18-1 provides two screenshots from an Android cell phone. On the left is a two-dimensional spatial function, and on the right is its corresponding Fourier transform obtained with the program.

© Moisés Cywiak, David Cywiak 2021   347
M. Cywiak and D. Cywiak, *Multi-Platform Graphics Programming with Kivy*,
https://doi.org/10.1007/978-1-4842-7113-1_18

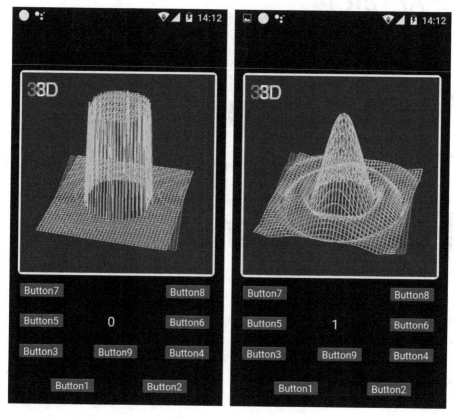

Figure 18-1. *Screenshots from an Android cell phone showing a two-dimensional spatial function (left) and its corresponding discrete Fourier transform obtained with the program (right)*

The buttons to rotate the plots work as described in the previous chapter.

18.1 Plotting the Functions

As in the previous chapter, we will place the plots in the middle between the plane of projection and the screen. We will use two points of projection to create the red and cyan images, as shown in Listing 18-1.

Listing 18-1. Defining Parameters for the Projections

```
OBJECT=0;
D=2000;
VX1=-60; VY1=600; VZ1=0;
VX2=60; VY2=600; VZ2=0;
P=0.5; #Place the function at z=D/2
N=40;   #Number of pixels to represent the function
```

By assigning 0 to the OBJECT parameter, we are shown the spatial plot. When this parameter is 1, we are making the plot active in the Fourier space.

The spatial and frequency axes, meshes, and functions are the same as described in the previous chapter.

Listings 18-2 and 18-3 provide the code for main.py and File.kv, respectively.

Listing 18-2. Code for the main.py File

```
from kivy.app import App
from kivy.uix.floatlayout import FloatLayout
from kivy.graphics import Line, Ellipse, Color
from kivy.clock import Clock
from kivy.core.image import Image as CoreImage
from PIL import Image, ImageDraw, ImageFont
import io
import os
import numpy as np
from kivy.lang import Builder

Builder.load_file(
    os.path.join(os.path.dirname(os.path.abspath(
                        __file__)), 'File.kv')
        );
```

```python
#Avoid Form1 of being resizable
from kivy.config import Config
Config.set("graphics","resizable", False);
Config.set('graphics', 'width',  '480');
Config.set('graphics', 'height', '680');

def Rect(s,a):
    if np.abs(s)<=a/2:
        return 1;
    else:
        return 0;
def Circ(s,t,a):
    if np.sqrt(s**2 +t**2)<=a:
        return 1;
    else:
        return 0;
OBJECT=0;

D=2000;
VX1=-60; VY1=600; VZ1=0;
VX2=60; VY2=600; VZ2=0;

P=0.5; #Place the function at z=D/2
N=40;  #Number of pixels to represent the function
#Spatial coordinates
x=np.zeros(N+1);
z=np.zeros(N+1);
f=np.zeros( (N+1,N+1) );
#Creating the mesh
x1=np.zeros( (N+1,N+1) );
y1=np.zeros( (N+1,N+1) );
z1=np.zeros( (N+1,N+1) );
L=1;
```

```
XGO=0; ZGO=P*D; Amplitude=130;

for n in range (0,N+1): #Filling the x-z axes
    x[n]=(n-N/2)/N*L;
    z[n]=(n-N/2)/N*L;
dx=x[1]-x[0]; dz=z[1]-z[0];
for n in range(0,N+1): #Filling function pixels
    for m in range(0,N+1):
        f[n][m]=Circ(x[n],z[m],L/4);

Scale_x=140; Scale_y=100; Scale_z=140;
#Filling Mesh
for n in range (0,N+1):
    for m in range(0,N+1):
        x1[n][m]=Scale_x* x[n];
        z1[n][m]=Scale_z*z[m]+ZGO;
        y1[n][m]=Scale_y*f[n][m];

#Defining frequency parameters
i=1J;
Pi=np.pi;
B=10/L;
u=np.zeros(N+1); v=np.zeros(N+1);
F=np.zeros( (N+1,N+1), dtype=complex );
C=np.zeros( (N+1,N+1), dtype=complex );
u1=np.zeros( (N+1,N+1) );
v1=np.zeros( (N+1,N+1) );
I1=np.zeros( (N+1,N+1) );
for n in range(0,N+1):
    u[n]=(n-N/2)/N*B;
    v[n]=u[n];
```

```
#Calculating the two-dimensional discrete integral
for n in range(0,N+1):
    for m in range(0,N+1):
        for q in range(0,N+1):
            C[n][q]=np.sum( f[q]*np.exp(
                                -i*2*Pi*u[n]*x) );
        F[n][m]=np.sum( C[n]*np.exp(
                                -i*2*Pi*v[m]*z) )*dx*dz;
I=np.abs(F);

#Creating mesh for plotting
Scale_u1=15; Scale_v1=15; Scale_I1=480;
for n in range(0,N+1):
    for m in range(0,N+1):
        u1[n][m]=Scale_u1 * u[n];
        v1[n][m]=Scale_v1 * v[m]+ZGO;
        I1[n][m]=Scale_I1*I[n][m];

PointList=np.zeros( (N+1,2) );
def GraphFunction(xM,yM,zM,Which):
    global VX1, VX2, VY1,VY2,VZ1,VZ2, N,D;
    x1p=xM; y1p=yM; z1p=zM;

    if (Which==0):
        r,g,b = 200, 0, 0; #red Image
        VX=VX1; VY=VY1; VZ=VZ1;
        Draw=Draw1
    else:
        r,g,b= 0, 200, 200; #cyan image
        VX=VX2; VY=VY2; VZ=VZ2;
        Draw=Draw2
```

```python
for n in range (0,N+1): #Horizontal Lines
    for m in range (0,N+1):
        Factor=(D-VZ)/(D-z1p[n][m]-VZ);
        xA=XC+Factor*(x1p[n][m]-VX)+VX \
                        + (P/(1-P))*VX;
        yA=YC-Factor*(y1p[n][m]-VY) \
                    -VY -(P/(1-P))*VY;
        PointList[m]=xA,yA;
    List=tuple( map(tuple,PointList) );
    Draw.line( List, fill=(r,g,b), width=2 );

for n in range (0,N+1): #Vertical Lines
    for m in range (0,N+1):
        Factor=(D-VZ)/(D-z1p[m][n]-VZ);
        xA=XC+Factor*(x1p[m][n]-VX)\
                    +VX + (P/(1-P))*VX;
        yA=YC-Factor*(y1p[m][n]-VY) \
                    -VY -(P/(1-P))*VY;
        PointList[m]=xA,yA;
    List=tuple( map(tuple,PointList) );
    Draw.line( List, fill=(r,g,b), width=2 );

    Font = ImageFont.truetype('Gargi.ttf', 40)
    Draw1.text( (10,10), "3D", fill =
                        (255,0,0,1), font=Font);
    Draw2.text( (30,10), "3D", fill =
                        (0,255,255,1), font=Font);

def ShowScene(B):
    Array1=np.array(PilImage1);
    Array2=np.array(PilImage2);
    Array3=Array1 | Array2;
```

```
PilImage3=Image.fromarray(Array3);

Memory=io.BytesIO();
PilImage3.save(Memory, format="png");
Memory.seek(0);
ImagePNG=CoreImage(Memory, ext="png");

B.ids.Screen1.texture=ImagePNG.texture;
ImagePNG.remove_from_cache()
Memory.close();
PilImage3.close();
Array1=None;
Array2=None;
Array3=None;

def ClearObjects():
    Draw1.rectangle( (0, 0, W-10, H-10), fill=
                                (60, 70, 30, 1) );
    Draw2.rectangle( (0, 0, W-10, H-10), fill=
                                (60, 70, 30, 1) );

def RotateFunction(xM,yM,zM,B, Sense):
    global D,N, XGO,ZGO;
    x1p=xM; y1p=yM; z1p=zM;
    if Sense==-1:
        Teta=np.pi/180*(-4.0);
    else:
        Teta=np.pi/180*(4.0);
    Cos_Teta=np.cos(Teta)
    Sin_Teta=np.sin(Teta);

    XO=XGO;  YO=0;  ZO=ZGO # Center of rotation
```

```
for n in range(0,N+1):
    for m in range(0,N+1):
        if (B.ids.Button3.state=="down" or
                B.ids.Button4.state=="down"):
            yP=(y1p[n][m]-YO)*Cos_Teta \
                + (x1p[n][m]-XO)*Sin_Teta + YO;
            xP=-(y1p[n][m]-YO)*Sin_Teta \
                +(x1p[n][m]-XO)*Cos_Teta + XO;
            y1p[n][m]=yP;
            x1p[n][m]=xP;

        if (B.ids.Button5.state=="down" or
                B.ids.Button6.state=="down"):
            yP=(y1p[n][m]-YO)*Cos_Teta \
                + (z1p[n][m]-ZO)*Sin_Teta + YO;
            zP=-(y1p[n][m]-YO)*Sin_Teta \
                +(z1p[n][m]-ZO)*Cos_Teta + ZO;
            y1p[n][m]=yP;
            z1p[n][m]=zP;

        if (B.ids.Button7.state=="down" or
                B.ids.Button8.state=="down"):
            xP=(x1p[n][m]-XO)*Cos_Teta \
                + (z1p[n][m]-ZO)*Sin_Teta + XO;
            zP=-(x1p[n][m]-XO)*Sin_Teta \
                +(z1p[n][m]-ZO)*Cos_Teta + ZO;
            x1p[n][m]=xP;
            z1p[n][m]=zP;

class Form1(FloatLayout):
    def __init__(Handle, **kwargs):
        super(Form1, Handle).__init__(**kwargs);
        Event1=Clock.schedule_once(
                        Handle.Initialize);
```

```
def Initialize(B, *args):
    global W,H, XC,YC, PilImage1,PilImage2, Draw1,Draw2;
    # P= Percentage of the D distance
    global P, Amplitude;
    W,H=B.ids.Screen1.size;
    XC=int (W/2)+0;
    YC=int(H/2)+70;
    PilImage1= Image.new('RGB', (W-10, H-10),
                                   (60, 70, 30));
    Draw1 = ImageDraw.Draw(PilImage1);
    PilImage2= Image.new('RGB', (W-10, H-10),
                                   (60, 70, 30));
    Draw2 = ImageDraw.Draw(PilImage2);
    Font = ImageFont.truetype('Gargi.ttf', 70);
    Draw1.text( (30,200), "3D Images", fill =
                          (255,0,0,1), font=Font);
    Draw2.text( (50,200), "3D Images", fill =
                          (0,255,255,1), font=Font);
    ShowScene(B);

def Button1_Click(B):
    global Draw1, Draw2;
    ClearObjects(); # Clearing Draw1 and Draw2
    if (OBJECT==0):
        GraphFunction(x1,y1,z1,0);
        GraphFunction(x1,y1,z1,1);
    if (OBJECT==1):
        GraphFunction(u1,I1,v1,0);
        GraphFunction(u1,I1,v1,1);
    ShowScene(B);
```

```
def Button2_Click(B):
    ClearObjects(); # Clearing Draw1 and Draw2
    Font = ImageFont.truetype('Gargi.ttf', 70);
    Draw1.text( (30,200), "3D Images", fill =
                          (255,0,0,1), font=Font);
    Draw2.text( (50,200), "3D Images", fill =
                          (0,255,255,1), font=Font);
    ShowScene(B);

def Button3_Click(B):
    ClearObjects(); # Clearing Draw1 and Draw2
    if (OBJECT==0):
        RotateFunction(x1,y1,z1,B,1);
        GraphFunction(x1,y1,z1,0);
        GraphFunction(x1,y1,z1,1);
    if (OBJECT==1):
        RotateFunction(u1,I1,v1,B,1);
        GraphFunction(u1,I1,v1,0);
        GraphFunction(u1,I1,v1,1);
    ShowScene(B);

def Button4_Click(B):
    ClearObjects();
    if (OBJECT==0):
        RotateFunction(x1,y1,z1,B,-1);
        GraphFunction(x1,y1,z1,0);
        GraphFunction(x1,y1,z1,1);
    if (OBJECT==1):
        RotateFunction(u1,I1,v1,B,-1);
        GraphFunction(u1,I1,v1,0);
        GraphFunction(u1,I1,v1,1);
    ShowScene(B);
```

```
def Button5_Click(B):
    ClearObjects();
    if (OBJECT==0):
        RotateFunction(x1,y1,z1,B,-1);
        GraphFunction(x1,y1,z1,0);
        GraphFunction(x1,y1,z1,1);
    if (OBJECT==1):
        RotateFunction(u1,I1,v1,B,-1);
        GraphFunction(u1,I1,v1,0);
        GraphFunction(u1,I1,v1,1);
    ShowScene(B);

def Button6_Click(B):
    ClearObjects();
    if (OBJECT==0):
        RotateFunction(x1,y1,z1,B,1);
        GraphFunction(x1,y1,z1,0);
        GraphFunction(x1,y1,z1,1);
    if (OBJECT==1):
        RotateFunction(u1,I1,v1,B,1);
        GraphFunction(u1,I1,v1,0);
        GraphFunction(u1,I1,v1,1);
    ShowScene(B);

def Button7_Click(B):
    ClearObjects();
    if (OBJECT==0):
        RotateFunction(x1,y1,z1,B,-1);
        GraphFunction(x1,y1,z1,0);
        GraphFunction(x1,y1,z1,1);
```

```
    if (OBJECT==1):
        RotateFunction(u1,I1,v1,B,-1);
        GraphFunction(u1,I1,v1,0);
        GraphFunction(u1,I1,v1,1);
    ShowScene(B);

def Button8_Click(B):
    ClearObjects();
    if (OBJECT==0):
        RotateFunction(x1,y1,z1,B,1),
        GraphFunction(x1,y1,z1,0);
        GraphFunction(x1,y1,z1,1);
    if (OBJECT==1):
        RotateFunction(u1,I1,v1,B,1),
        GraphFunction(u1,I1,v1,0);
        GraphFunction(u1,I1,v1,1);
    ShowScene(B);

def Button9_Click(B):
    global OBJECT
    OBJECT=(OBJECT+1)%2;
    B.ids.Label1.text=str(OBJECT);
    ClearObjects();
    if (OBJECT==0):
        GraphFunction(x1,y1,z1,0);
        GraphFunction(x1,y1,z1,1);
    if (OBJECT==1):
        GraphFunction(u1,I1,v1,0);
        GraphFunction(u1,I1,v1,1);
    ShowScene(B);
```

```
# This is the Start Up code.
class StartUp (App):
    def build (BU):
        BU.title="Form1"
        return Form1();
if __name__ =="__main__":
    StartUp().run();
```

Listing 18-3. Code for the File.kv File

```
#:set W 440
#:set H 440
<Form1>:
    id : Form1
    Image:
        id: Screen1
        size_hint: None,None
        pos_hint: {"x":0.04, "y":0.34}
        size: W,H
        canvas.before:
            Color:
                rgba: 0.9, 0.9, 0, 1
            RoundedRectangle:
                pos:  self.pos
                size: self.size
    Button:
        id: Button1
        on_press: Form1.Button1_Click()
        text: "Button1"
        size_hint: None,None
        pos_hint: {"x": 0.2, "y":0.03}
        size: 100,30
```

```
Button:
    id: Button2
    on_press: Form1.Button2_Click()
    text: "Button2"
    size_hint: None,None
    pos_hint: {"x": 0.63, "y":0.03}
    size: 100,30

Button:
    id: Button3
    on_press: Form1.Button3_Click()
    text: "Button3"
    size_hint: None,None
    pos_hint: {"x": 0.05, "y":0.12}
    size: 100,30
    always_release: True
Button:
    id: Button4
    on_press: Form1.Button4_Click()
    text: "Button4"
    size_hint: None,None
    pos_hint: {"x": 0.73, "y":0.12}
    size: 100,30

Button:
    id: Button5
    on_press: Form1.Button5_Click()
    text: "Button5"
    size_hint: None,None
    pos_hint: {"x": 0.05, "y":0.20}
    size: 100,30
```

```
Button:
    id: Button6
    on_press: Form1.Button6_Click()
    text: "Button6"
    size_hint: None,None
    pos_hint: {"x": 0.73, "y":0.20}
    size: 100,30

Button:
    id: Button7
    on_press: Form1.Button7_Click()
    text: "Button7"
    size_hint: None,None
    pos_hint: {"x": 0.05, "y":0.28}
    size: 100,30
Button:
    id: Button8
    on_press: Form1.Button8_Click()
    text: "Button8"
    size_hint: None,None
    pos_hint: {"x": 0.73, "y":0.28}
    size: 100,30

Button:
    id: Button9
    on_press: Form1.Button9_Click()
    text: "Button9"
    size_hint: None,None
    pos_hint: {"x": 0.4, "y":0.12}
    size: 100,30
```

```
Label:
    id: Label1
    text: "0"
    font_size: 30
    color: 1,1,0,1
    size_hint: None,None
    pos_hint: {"x": 0.38, "y":0.20}
    size: 100,30
```

18.2 Summary

In this chapter, we presented a working example for calculating and plotting stereoscopic two-dimensional Fourier transforms.

Index

A

Aberration terms, 264, 267, 277

Android cell phone, 13, 231, 279, 313, 314, 323, 347

B

Bessel-sinc function, 343

C

Cartesian coordinate plane, 9, 10

Cartesian coordinates, 193, 194, 233

Circular function, 330, 341, 342

Circular symmetry, 263

ClearObjects() function, 81

Cylindrical coordinates

    stereoscopic plot, 265, 266

    wave aberration, 263, 264

D

Dirac delta function, 260, 261, 316

Discrete integral, 322, 352

Discrete two-dimensional Fourier

    transform, 313, 324, 325, 345, 346

accumulators, 327, 328

    built-in summation, 329

    circular function, 330

    Discretization process, 323

    Double-NumPy summation, 329

E

Ellipsoid of revolution, 281

F

Factor0 parameter, 112

FillPolygon(B,P) function, 52

Fourier transform

    circular function, 341–344

    discrete, 345

    one-dimension, 315

    two-dimension, 323

Fresnel diffraction integral, 259–261

G

Gaussian function, 107–110, 112

GraphFunction(B) function, 147

Gravitational N-body

    buttons, 232

    dynamic equations, 236–238

© Moisés Cywiak, David Cywiak 2021
M. Cywiak and D. Cywiak, *Multi-Platform Graphics Programming with Kivy*,
https://doi.org/10.1007/978-1-4842-7113-1